The Prairie Peninsula

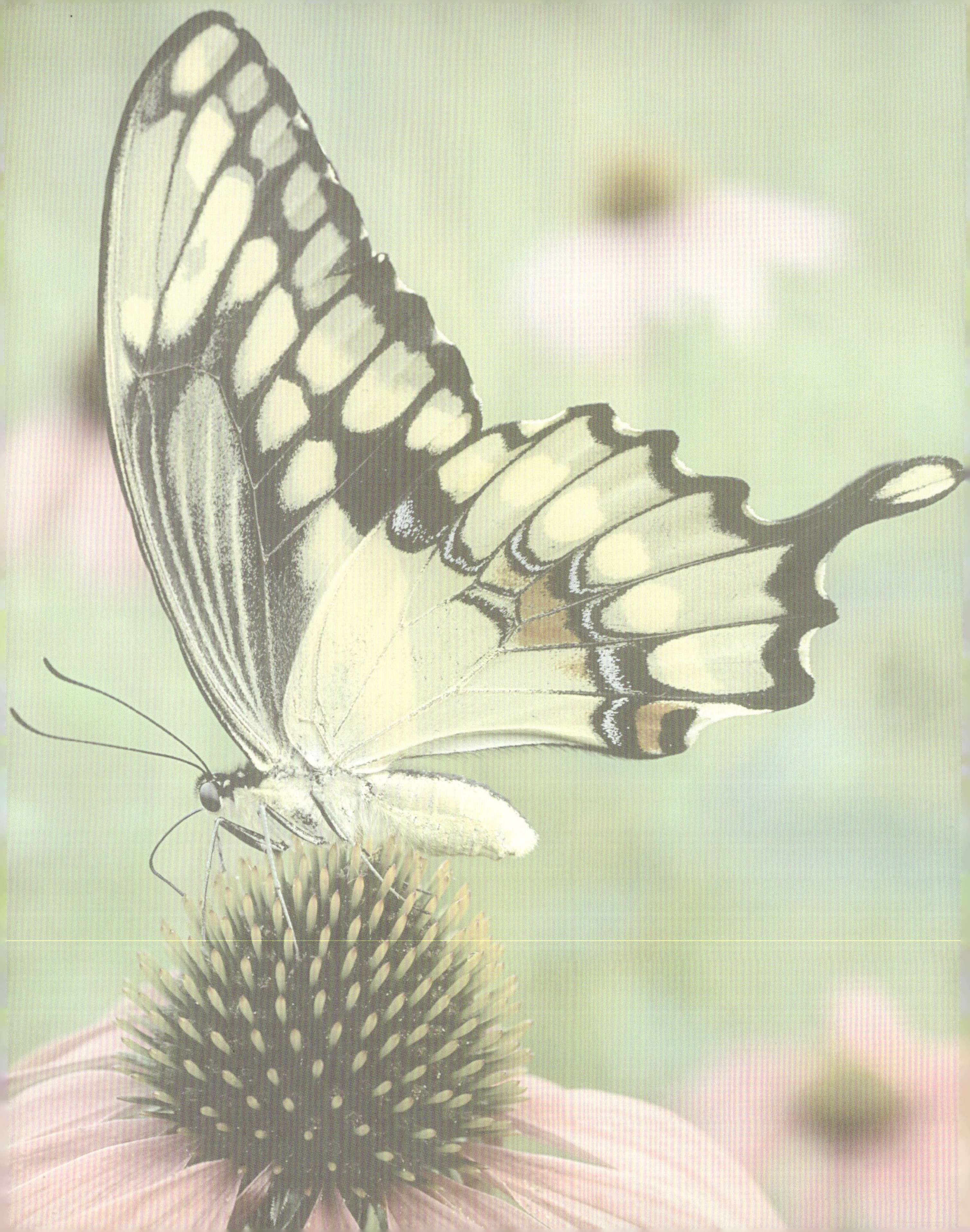

The Prairie Peninsula

GARY MESZAROS
GUY L. DENNY

THE KENT STATE UNIVERSITY PRESS
KENT, OHIO

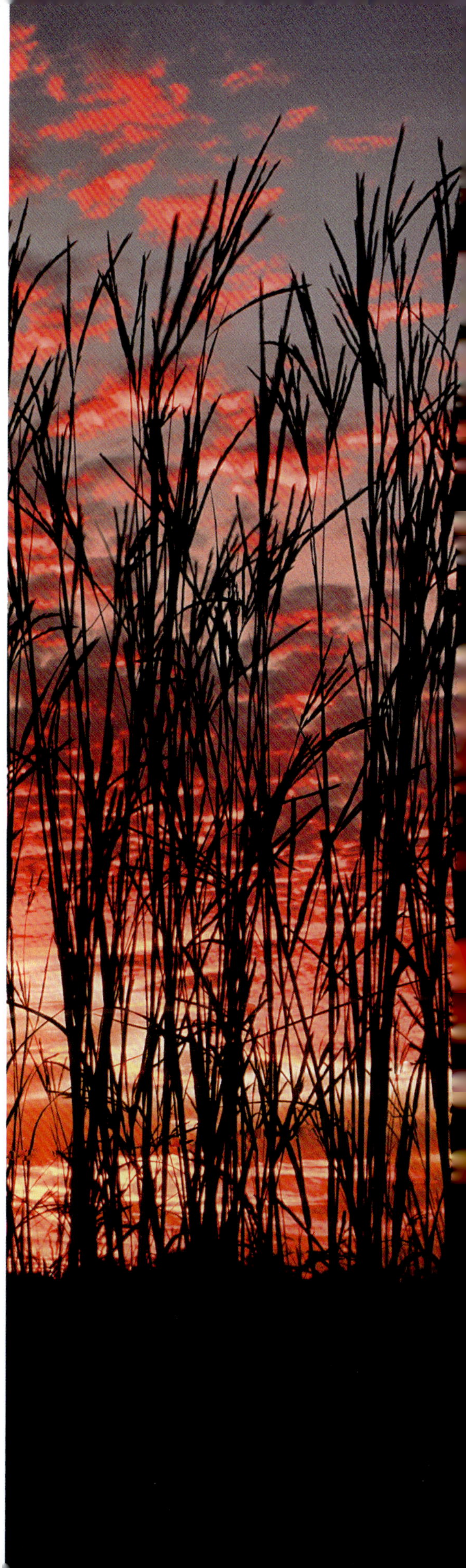

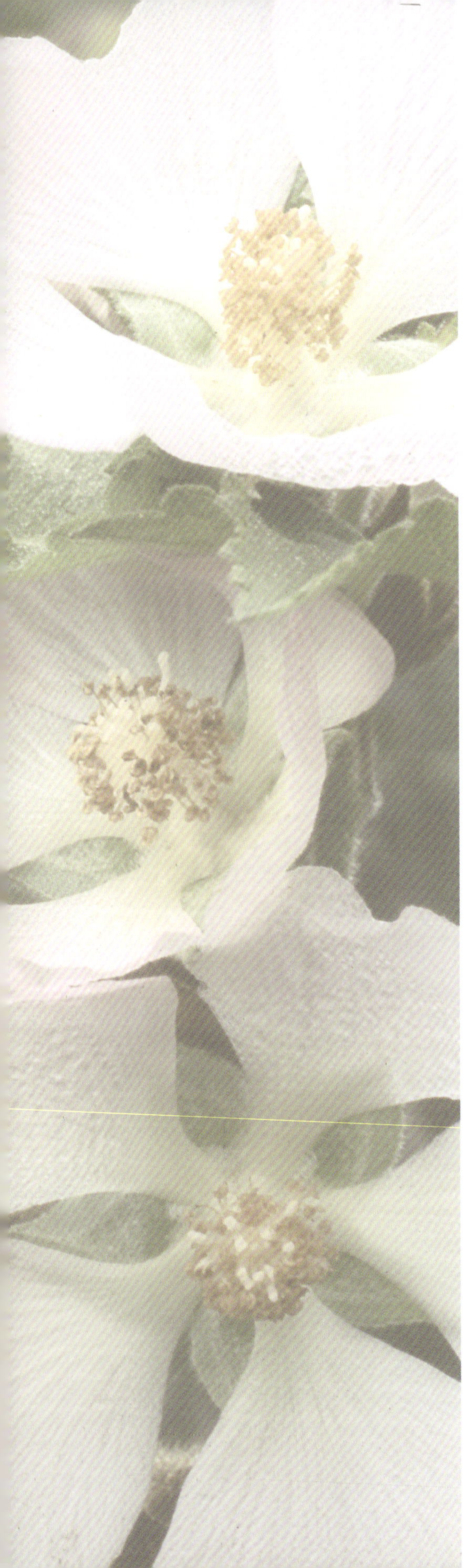

Library of Congress Catalog Card Number 2016054744
ISBN 978-1-60635-320-2
Manufactured in China

Library of Congress Cataloging-in-Publication Data

Names: Meszaros, Gary, author. | Denny, Guy, author.
Title: The prairie peninsula / Gary Meszaros, Guy L. Denny.
Description: Kent, Ohio : The Kent State University Press, 2017. |
Includes bibliographical references and index.
Identifiers: LCCN 2016054744 (print) | LCCN 2016055951 (ebook) |
ISBN 9781606353202 (pbk. : alk. paper) | ISBN 9781631012822 (ePub) |
ISBN 9781631012839 (ePDF)
Subjects: LCSH: Prairie ecology--Middle West.
Classification: LCC QH104.5.M47 M47 2017 (print) | LCC QH104.5.M47 (ebook) |
DDC 577.4/40977--dc23
LC record available at https://lccn.loc.gov/2016054744

21 20 19 18 17   5 4 3 2 1

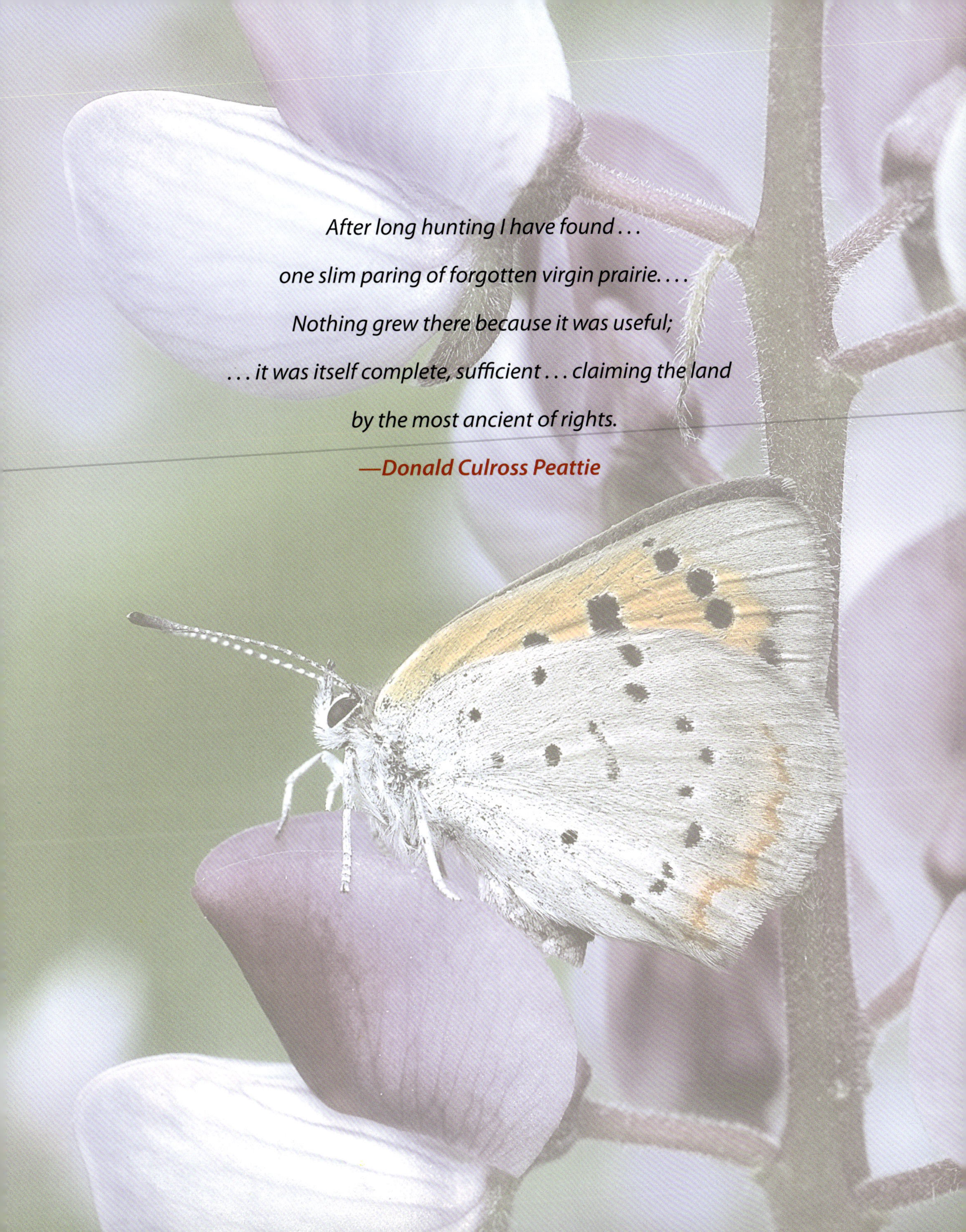

After long hunting I have found . . .

one slim paring of forgotten virgin prairie. . . .

Nothing grew there because it was useful;

. . . it was itself complete, sufficient . . . claiming the land

by the most ancient of rights.

—Donald Culross Peattie

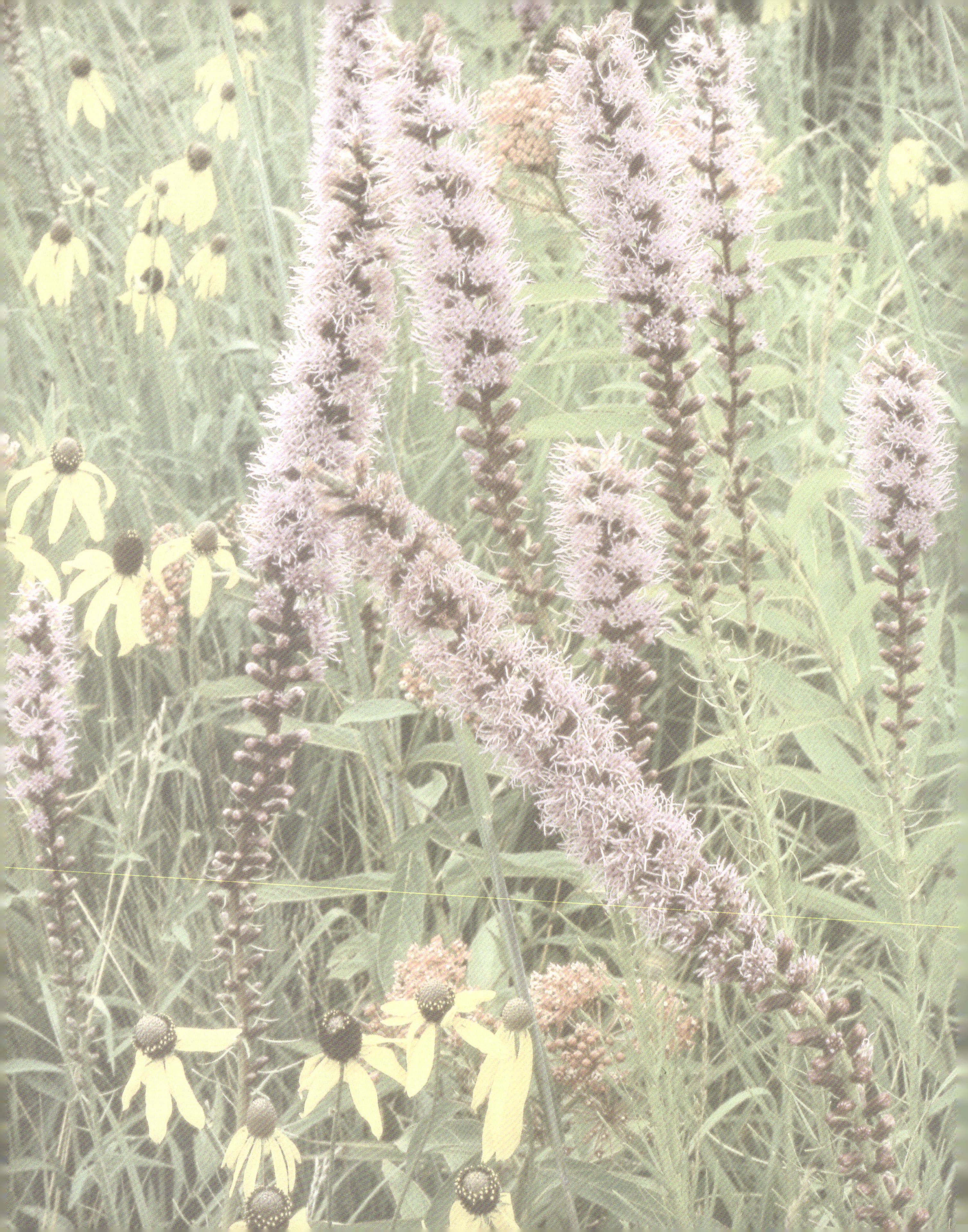

Contents

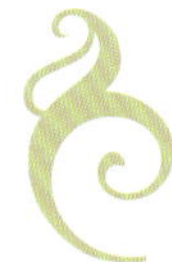

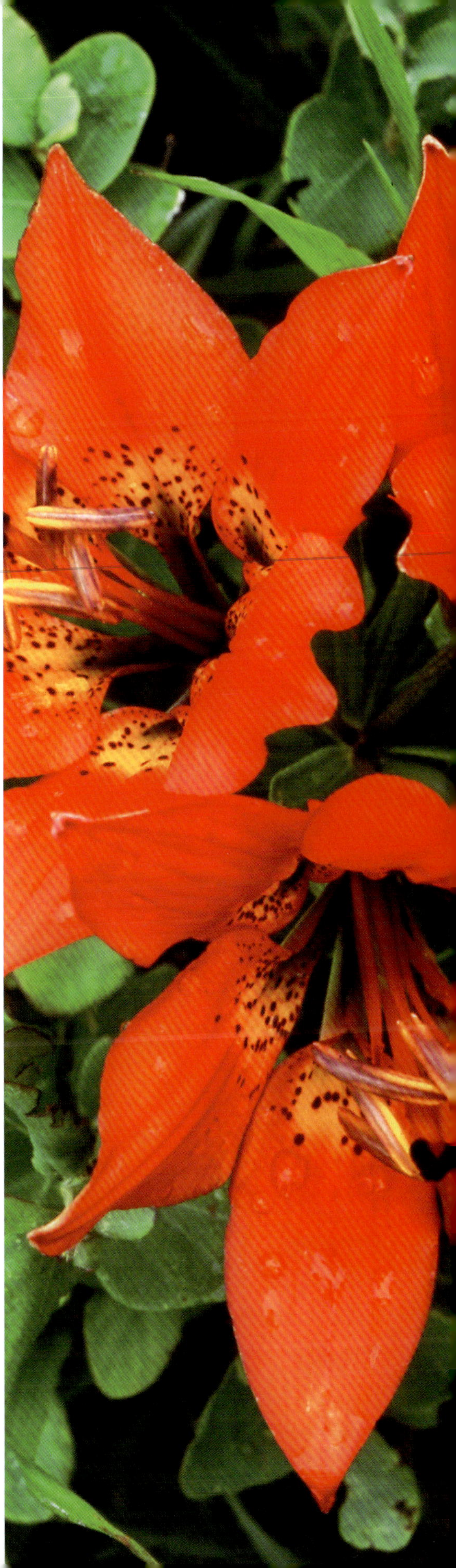

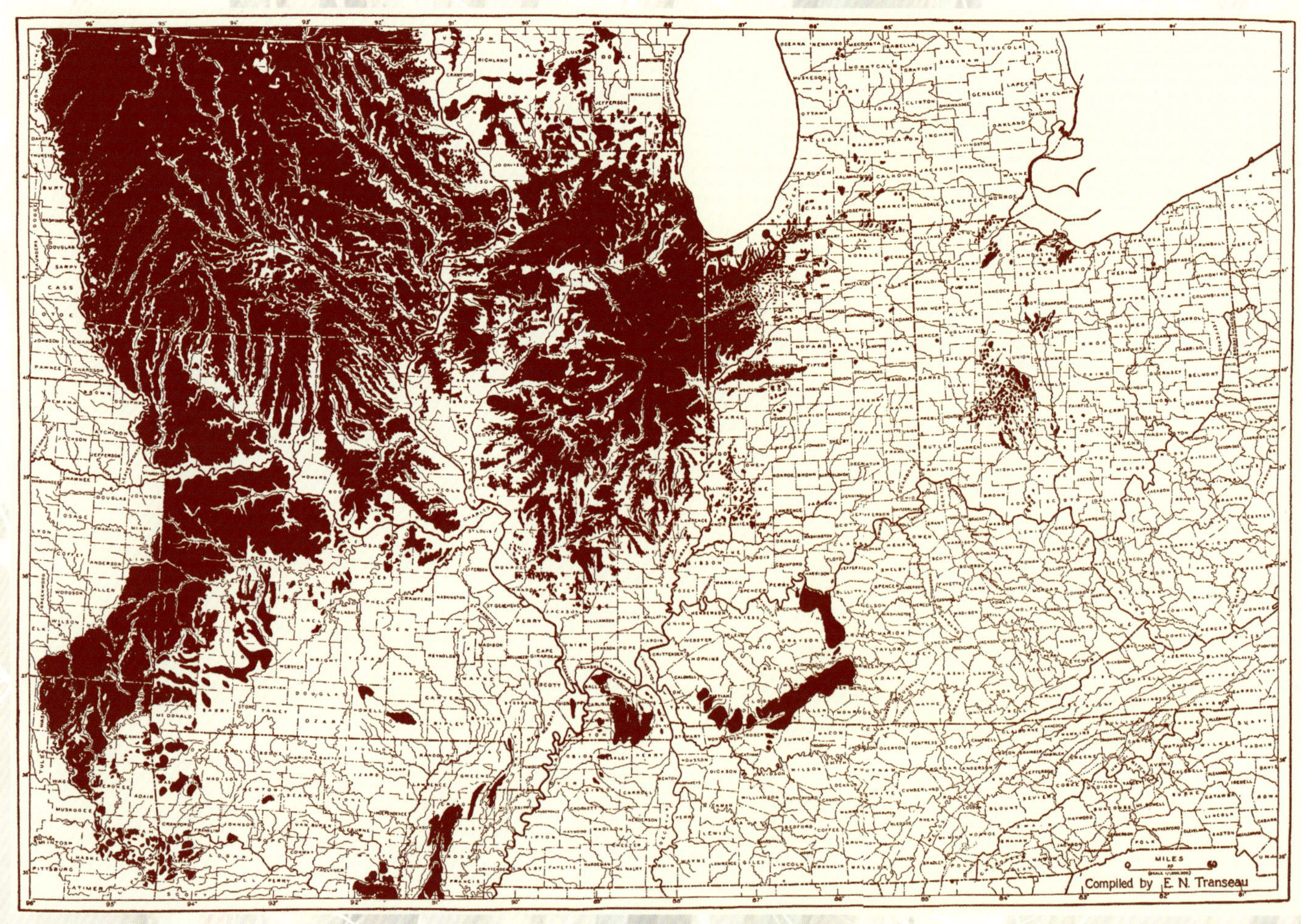

The Prairie Peninsula with outliers. Map by Edgar Nelson Transeau. (From Transeau, 1935. "The Prairie Peninsula," *Ecology* 16[3]. © 1935 by the Ecological Society of America. Reprinted with permission.)

Introduction

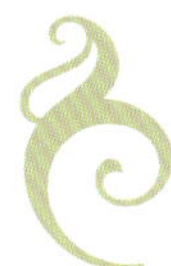

The prairie grassland biome covers the North American heartland, an eastward extension of which is the Prairie Peninsula. Composed primarily of tallgrass prairie, this biome lies between shortgrass prairies of the west and the eastern deciduous forest region. This book examines the many prairie types, floristic composition, and animals that are part of this ecosystem. Only fragments of the original tallgrass prairie remain, stretching from the eastern third of Kansas to the border of Pennsylvania. Through words and images, the authors tell the stories of surviving remnants and of efforts to save this part of our prairie heritage.

Early botanists were puzzled by the occurrence of isolated pockets of tallgrass prairie embedded within deciduous forest in the Midwest. Renowned Harvard botanist Asa Gray was the first to draw attention to this phenomenon, in an 1878 paper published in the *American Journal of Science* (Stuckey and Reese 1978). Henry Cowles of the University of Chicago studied plant ecology in prairie remnants from 1898 to 1934. Three of his students—Charles Adams, Edgar Transeau, and Paul Sears—played prominent roles in developing the "Prairie Peninsula" concept. Their research helped explain the presence of prairie outliers east of the tallgrass prairie biome. Henry Gleason of the New York Botanical Garden suggested that prairie outliers might be relicts of a dry period of postglacial warming (1923). Transeau first popularized the term "Prairie Peninsula" in his classic paper published in *Ecology* in 1935. He mapped it as a wedge-shaped peninsula spanning the midcontinent, from the Kansas border to a rounded apex in western Indiana. A few outliers reached as far east as southern Michigan, southern Ontario, and central Ohio (Stuckey and Reese 1978).

Even though the Prairie Peninsula is mainly composed of tallgrass prairie, close examination shows that many floristic variations depended on annual precipitation, type of substrate, topography, and rates of evaporation. To further support the hypothesis that postglacial climate was responsible for prairie being found so far east, Sears began analyzing pollen profiles (1948). Using radiocarbon dating of woody plant material, he determined the ages and types of vegetation present at various depths. His studies revealed that after the retreat of the Wisconsinan Glacier, a sequence of conifer to oak hardwood forest and finally grass pollen occurred during warming periods. A cycle of prolonged droughts probably occurred many times after each major glacial event. Evidence from radiocarbon dating suggested that the earth once again became warmer and drier around six thousand to four thousand years ago, during what scientists call the Hypsithermal Interval. This warming period greatly favored the eastward expansion of prairie grasslands. Not all trees disappeared; with deep taproots and largely fire-resistant bark, hardy species such as oaks and hickories persisted where soil retained moisture. Soon after the close of the Hypsithermal period, cooler and wetter conditions returned. As the forest expanded, environmental conditions limited suitable habitat favorable to prairie plants. The eastern edge of the Prairie Peninsula was once again forced back to the Indiana-Illinois border.

Our grasslands have certainly changed since historic times. It is hard to imagine that in just fifty years 150 million acres of tallgrass prairie disappeared under the steel plow. Today, only a few thousand acres of quality prairie remain within Prairie Peninsula. Regrettably, the loss of prairie continues. More and more native prairie lands formally set aside under the Conservation Reserve Program are being converted to row crops. After the land is farmed, one-third of its organic matter is lost. Even if the land is left to revert to prairie, most of its nutrients would have been destroyed or lost to erosion. The soil microorganisms that evolved over millennia and comprise the original prairie ecosystem are for the most part lost.

CHAPTER 1

A Heritage Lost

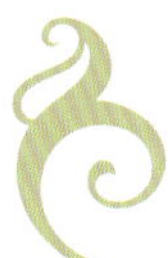

Early travelers journeying across the tallgrass prairie did not appreciate the impassable muddy roads, clouds of mosquitoes, stifling heat and humidity, and impenetrable stands of tall grasses. While passing the vast Castalia Prairie in Ohio in 1803, Maxfield Ludlow, an Englishman, pronounced "the whole area as not worth a farthing" (Sears 1967). Little did he realize that in just thirty years a new invention would change forever the face of the primeval prairie: in 1833, John Lane Sr. created the polished-steel self-scouring plow. John Deere, a fellow blacksmith, from Grand Detour, Illinois, improved upon the design and aggressively marketed his new invention.

Originally, tallgrass prairie had been subjected to open-range grazing. The steel plow allowed settlers to open the rich soil to agriculture. Using teams of oxen, they were now able to break tough prairie sod that did not foul the plowshare with wet root-filled soil. By 1852, the John Deere factories were selling more than ten thousand Grasshopper plows a year (Weaver 1954). At this point the western extension of the railroads allowed farmers to get their crops to eastern markets, further accelerating the prairies' demise, as the land was being quickly transformed into cornfields. Intensive efforts to drain and tile remaining wet areas made even more land available for agriculture. By the beginning of the twentieth century, the vast stretches of virgin prairie were gone.

Today, in our urban environment, with everything at our disposal, it is impossible for us to imagine how hard life was for early settlers. In summer there was little shelter from the searing heat. Hordes of biting mosquitoes, which sometimes carried malaria, were relentless. Many settlers died from malaria, or ague, as it was then called. Milk sickness took the lives of countless children and adults who consumed contaminated milk and butter. Pioneers did not realize that cows grazing on white snakeroot (*Ageratina altissima*) absorbed a toxic substance called tremetone that could be transferred to humans. Only in 1906, after thousands had died of milk sickness, did Edwin Moseley discover the relationship

At the westernmost edge of the tallgrass biome, little wood was available. Early settlers resorted to using prairie sod to build houses, called soddies. Dwellings varied from hillside dugouts to two-story structures. Cordgrass (*Spartina pectinata*) was the first choice as a building material, with big bluestem (*Andropogon gerardii*) a close second. It took an acre of sod to construct a house measuring only fourteen by sixteen feet with walls three feet thick. Wood was used to frame doors and sod-covered roofs, and sometimes salt was sprinkled onto the earthen floors to to harden them. Soddies were warm in winter and cool in summer. Settlers used buffalo chips and wads of cordgrass as fuel in hay-burning stoves, and as the railroads extended further west, they brought wood, glass, and hardware to the frontier.

Crossing the prairie in wagons, called prairie schooners, was an adventure. With few landmarks on the horizon, travelers could easily get lost in the waving sea of tall grasses. Axles and wheel spokes often broke or were buried in deep mud, making the journey laborious. Then there were hostile Indians, large prairie fires that sent flames thirty feet into the air, and stampeding buffalo herds.

The second half of the nineteenth century brought the mass slaughter of prairie wildlife. By 1900, like the prairie they roamed, the plains bison (*Bison bison*), gray wolf (*Canis lupus*), and eastern elk (*Cervus canadensis*) would become extirpated east of the Mississippi River.

Plains bison were an important part of the prairie ecosystem. They grazed large areas each year, hundreds of square miles, and returned the consumed plants to the soil as recycled nutrients and nitrogen-rich fertilizer. Eating mainly grasses and sedges, bison also influenced species diversity by providing living space for the many colorful plants and animals we see in prairies. Historically, millions of the animals could be found west of the Mississippi River. East of the Mississippi, bison were never as common. When encountered, herds were usually no more than a few hundred animals. In the east, where rainfall exceeded evaporation rates, Indians had burned large areas of prairie to maintain and improve hunting grounds and keep trees from reclaiming grasslands. Frequent fires, both man-made and natural, kept trees from overwhelming prairie openings. Eastern elk and white-tailed deer (*Odocoileus virginianus*) grazed along with bison in the prairie openings.

The early settlers quickly hunted to extinction the once-plentiful eastern elk. In the 1830s, bison had already disappeared from Indiana. By the turn of the twentieth century, only about three hundred of what had once been millions would survive in the United States and Canada.

There was no more plaintive sound than prairie chickens (*Tympanuchus cupido*) booming. The birds were common table fare for early settlers; in the 1850s, about 14 million were scattered across the prairie; the patchwork of farmlands and prairie created ideal habitats for the birds. Even in the early twentieth century, hunting seasons were in place in states as far east as Ohio. As late as 1912, about 1 million acres of prairie remained, with prairie chickens found in 92 of Illinois's 108 counties. As more Grand Prairie was turned into cropland, populations dropped to twenty-five thousand by 1933. The last strongholds in Lee and Iroquois counties disappeared in 1960. Due to the drastic decline of the birds, the Prairie Chicken Foundation was formed in Illinois in 1959. Today, thanks to the work of a number of organizations spearheaded by The Nature Conservancy, small breeding populations have been reintroduced into Marion County, Illinois.

Nature lovers would give much to see waves of billowing grass covered with numerous wildflowers and herds of grazing buffalo. This romantic notion, though, falls short of prairie pioneers' reality. Settlers had to survive in an environment that brought daily peril and much toil. Crops had to be harvested, fruits and vegetables preserved and stored. Where firewood was scarce, buffalo chips were gathered and stockpiled for the long winter; clean drinking water was hauled long distances, and livestock was protected from wolves and other predators. A settler may have occasionally looked up at a meadow full of flowers, but few had time to enjoy its splendor.

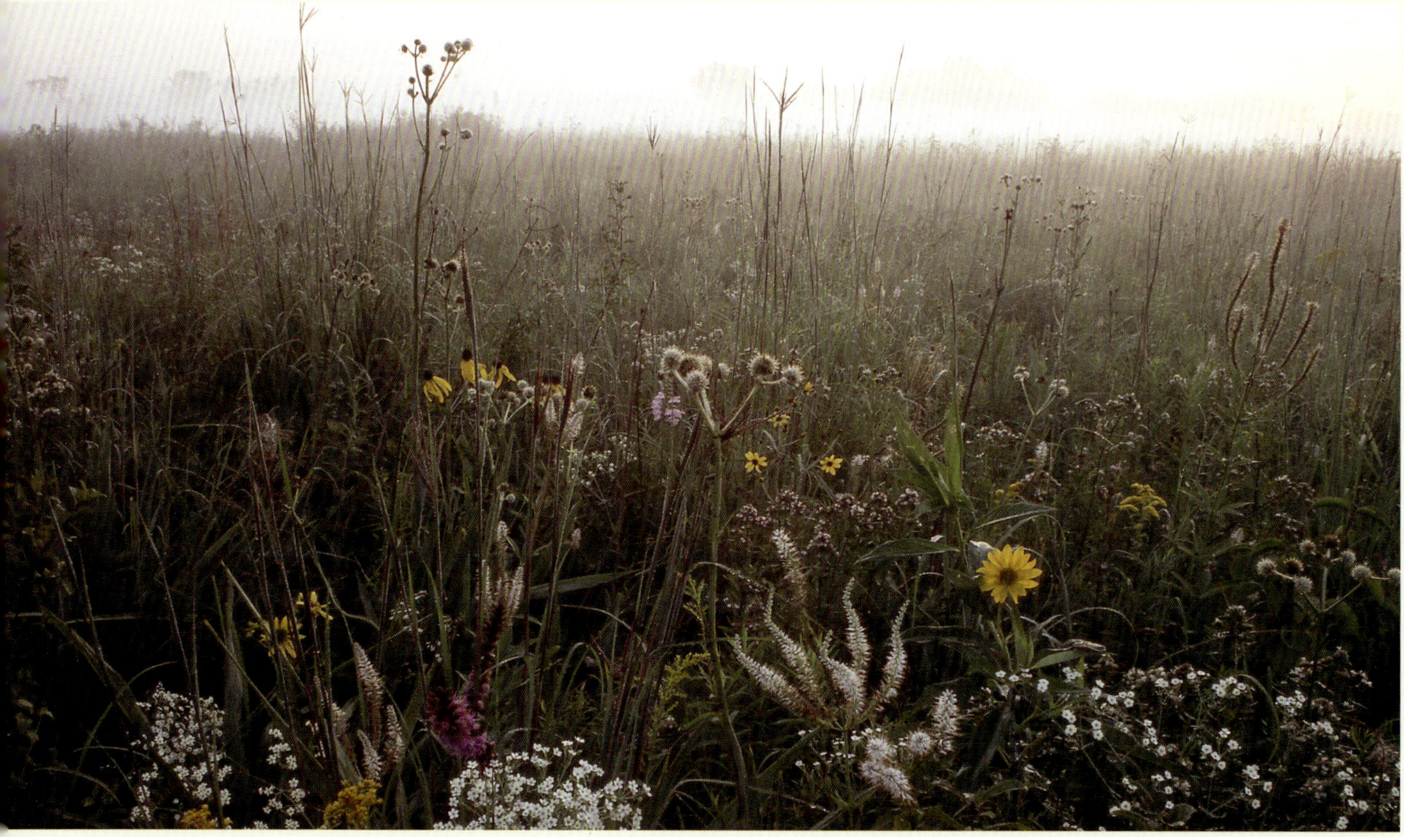

A misty morning sun rises over a rare black soil remnant in Illinois. Today, less than 1 percent of the original Prairie Peninsula survives.

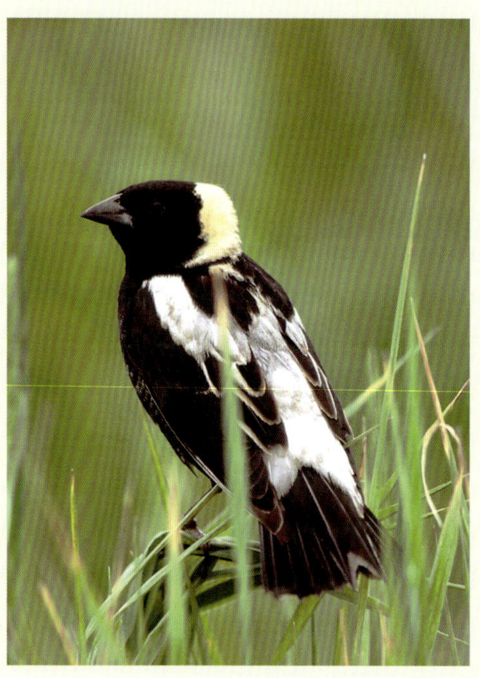

Bobolinks (*Dolichonyx oryzivorus*) breed in wet meadows. A species of special concern in Ohio and Illinois, these formally dressed blackbirds have lost much of their original habitat.

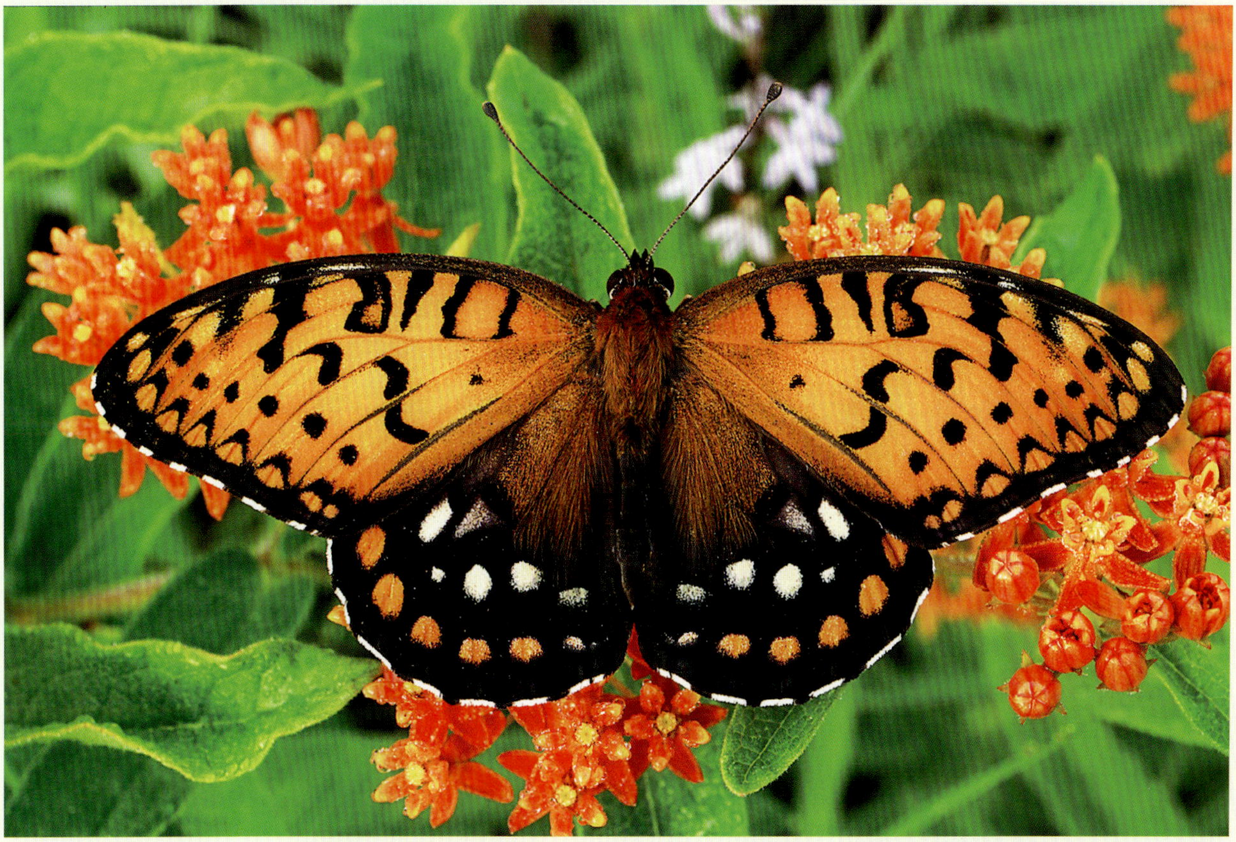

Regal fritillary butterflies (*Speyeria idalia*) went into major decline in the 1980s. Currently, populations east of the Mississippi are largely restricted to a few prairie remnants.

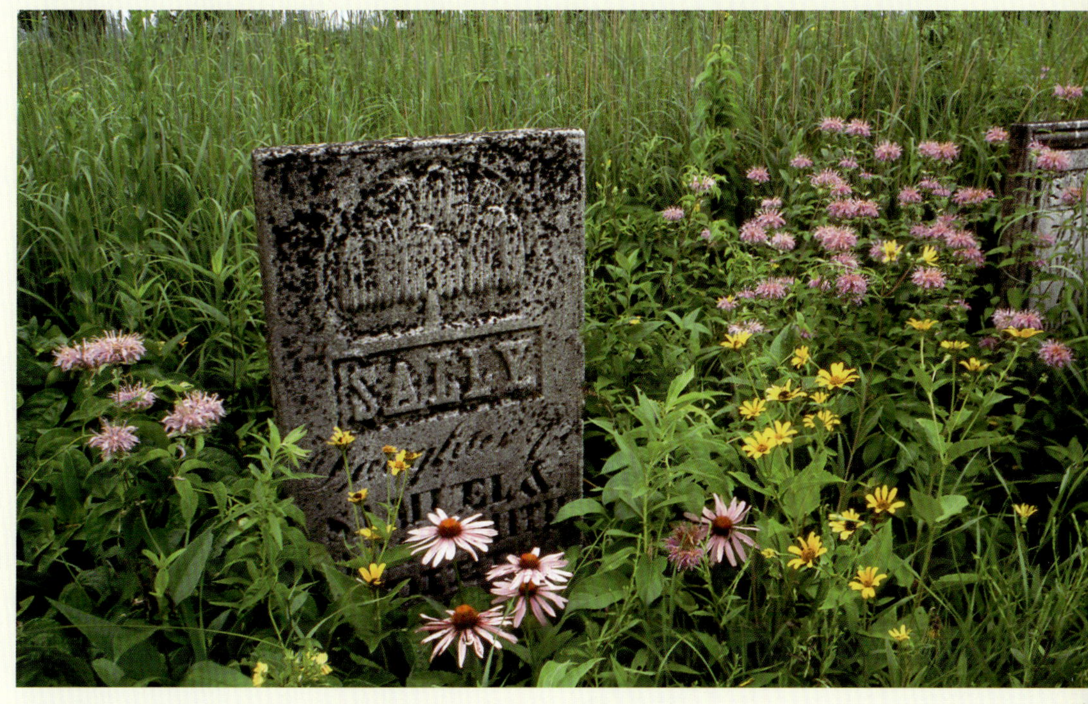

Some of the best black soil remnants can be found in old settler cemeteries. Here, flowers adorn gravestones at Smith Cemetery in Madison County, Ohio. Prairie cemeteries are time capsules of pioneer history.

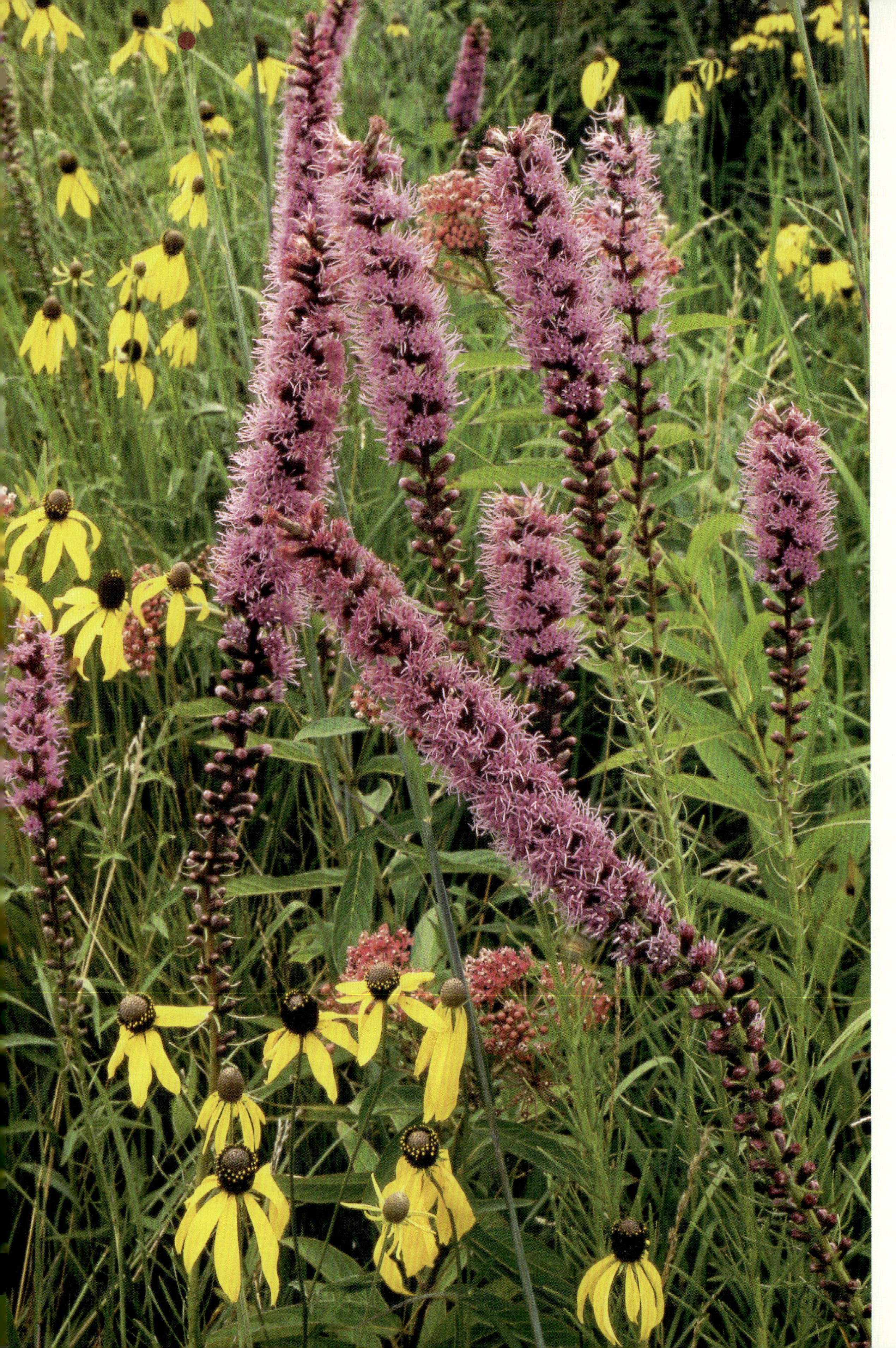

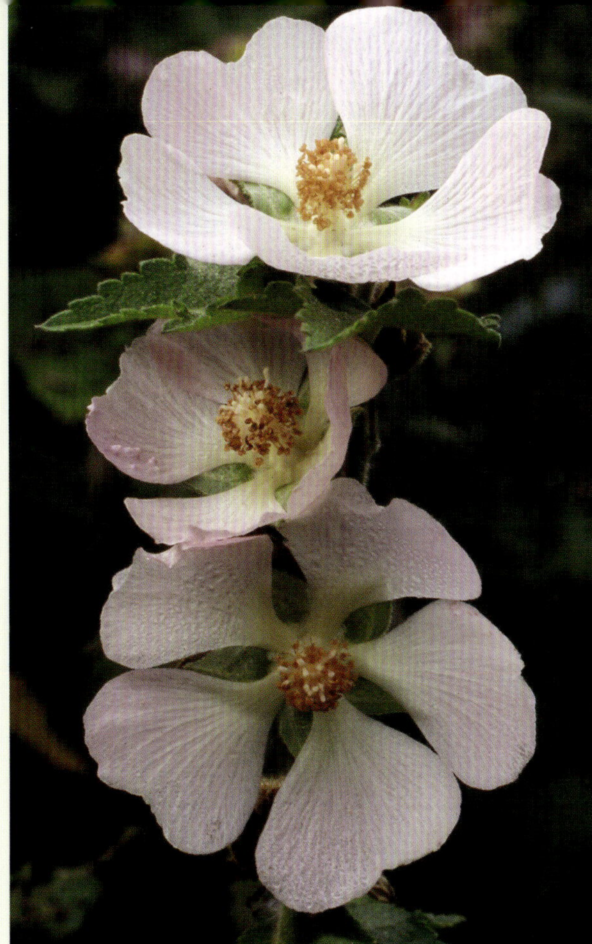

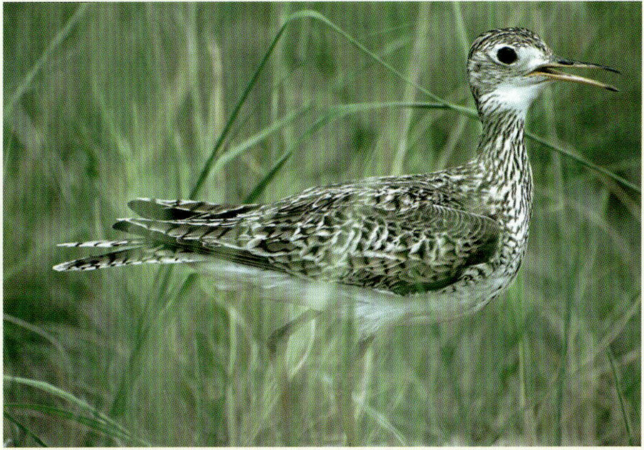

Rare breeders east of the Mississippi, upland sandpipers (*Bartramia longicauda*) can be found in grassy meadows.

The federally endangered Kankakee mallow's (*Iliamna remota*) original range was restricted to one county in Illinois's Kankakee Sands region.

Loggerhead shrikes (*Lanius ludovicianus*) have all but vanished from the Prairie Peninsula. Modern farming practices have destroyed almost all remaining edge habitat.

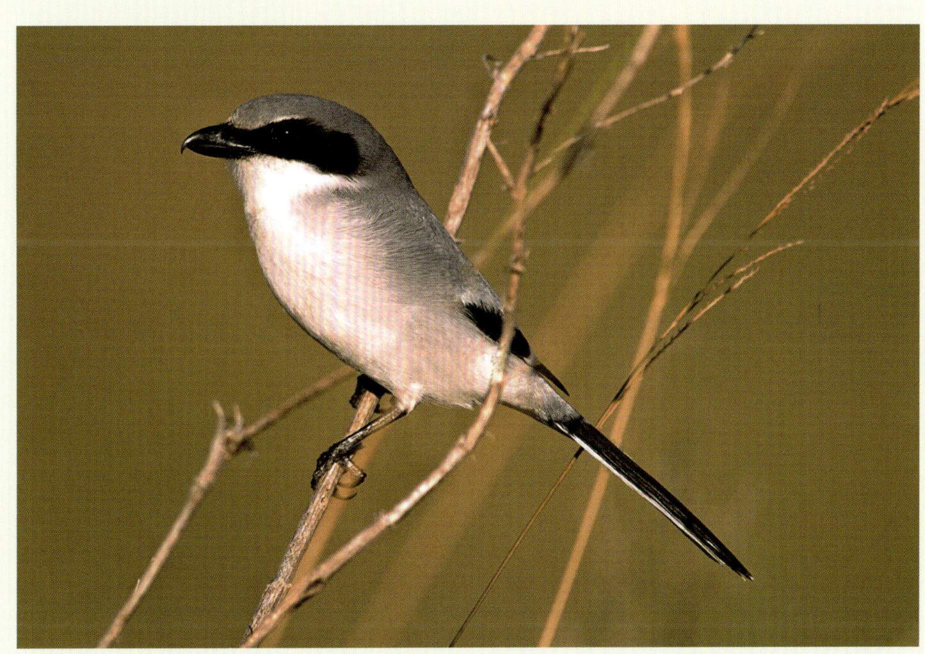

Opposite: Wands of marsh blazing stars (*Liatris spicata*) and gray-headed coneflowers (*Rathibida pinnata*) bloom in a railroad right-of-way. Narrow strips of original prairie can occasionally be found along old railroad lines.

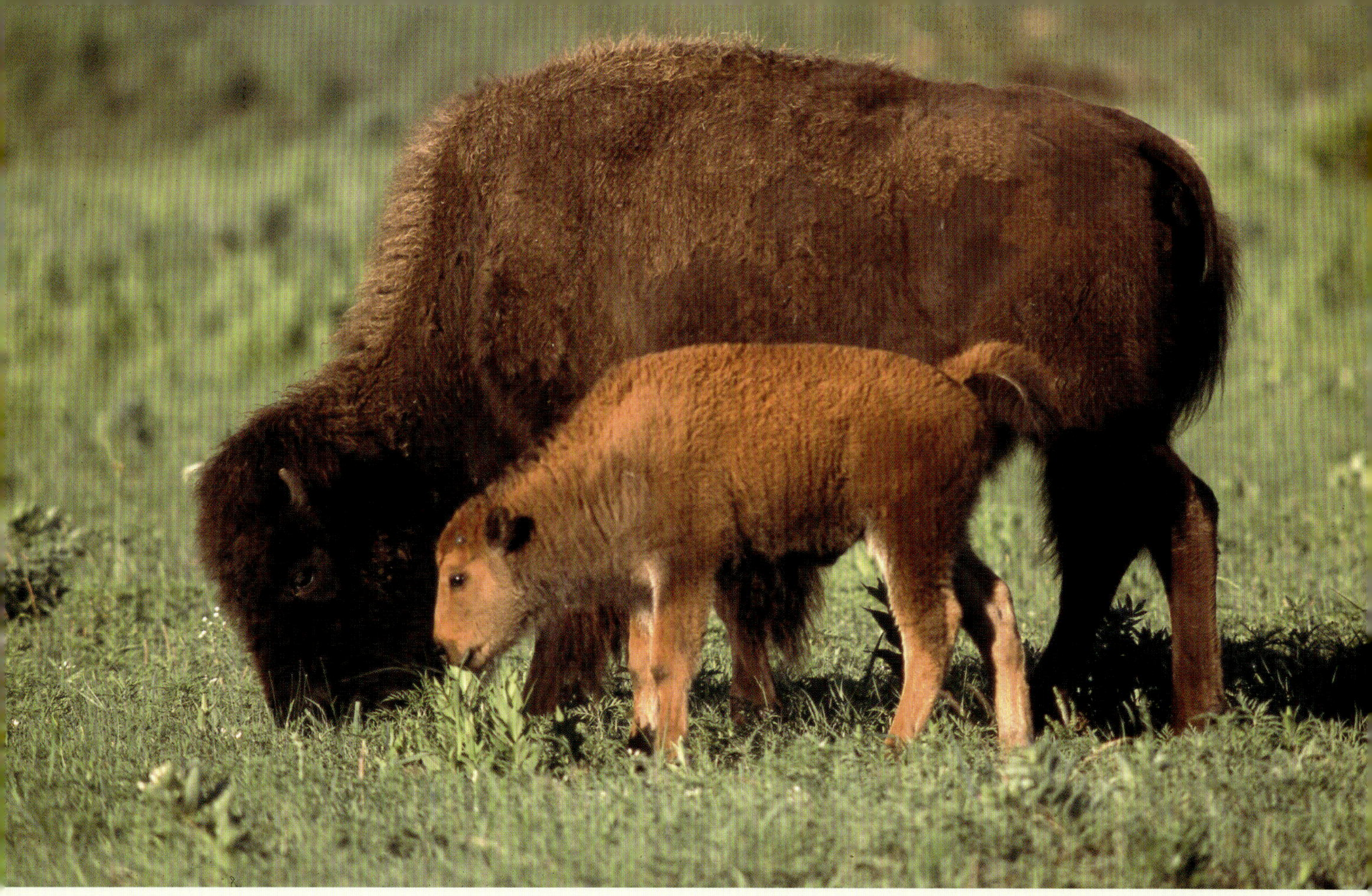

Plains bison originally could be found all the way to the Atlantic seaboard. By the turn of the twentieth century, only about three hundred of what had once been countless millions survived in the United States and Canada.

Small herds of plains bison (*Bison bison*), like this bull, roamed the Prairie Peninsula. By the middle of the nineteenth century, they were extirpated in Illinois. Today, small numbers are being reintroduced into a few large prairie restorations.

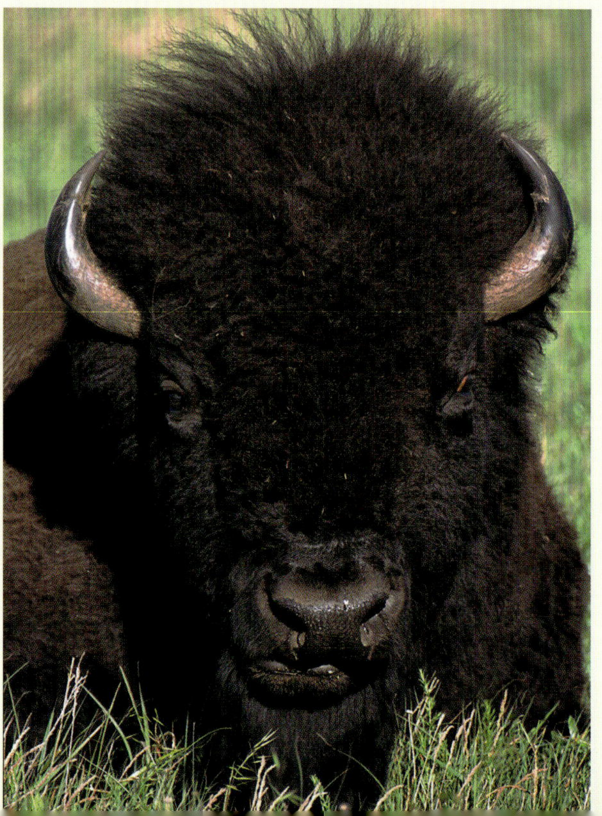

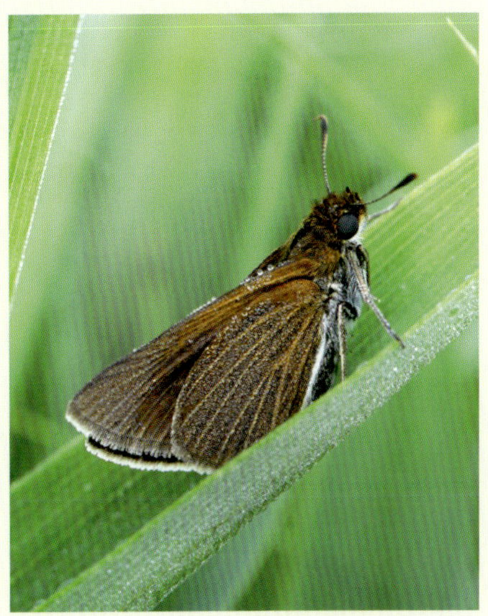

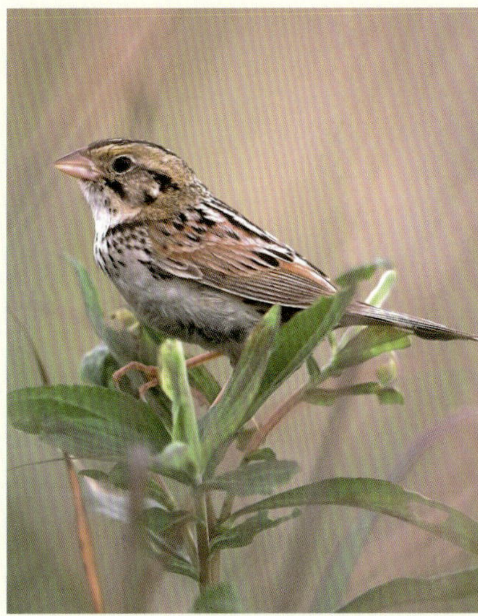

Rare Ottoe skippers (*Hesperia ottoe*) are prairie obligates, or prairie-dependent species. Small populations occur in original prairie.

Endangered throughout most of its range, the Henslow's sparrow (*Ammodramus henslowii*) is a specialist, breeding only in low grassy meadows. Its call is an unimpressive "tsilick."

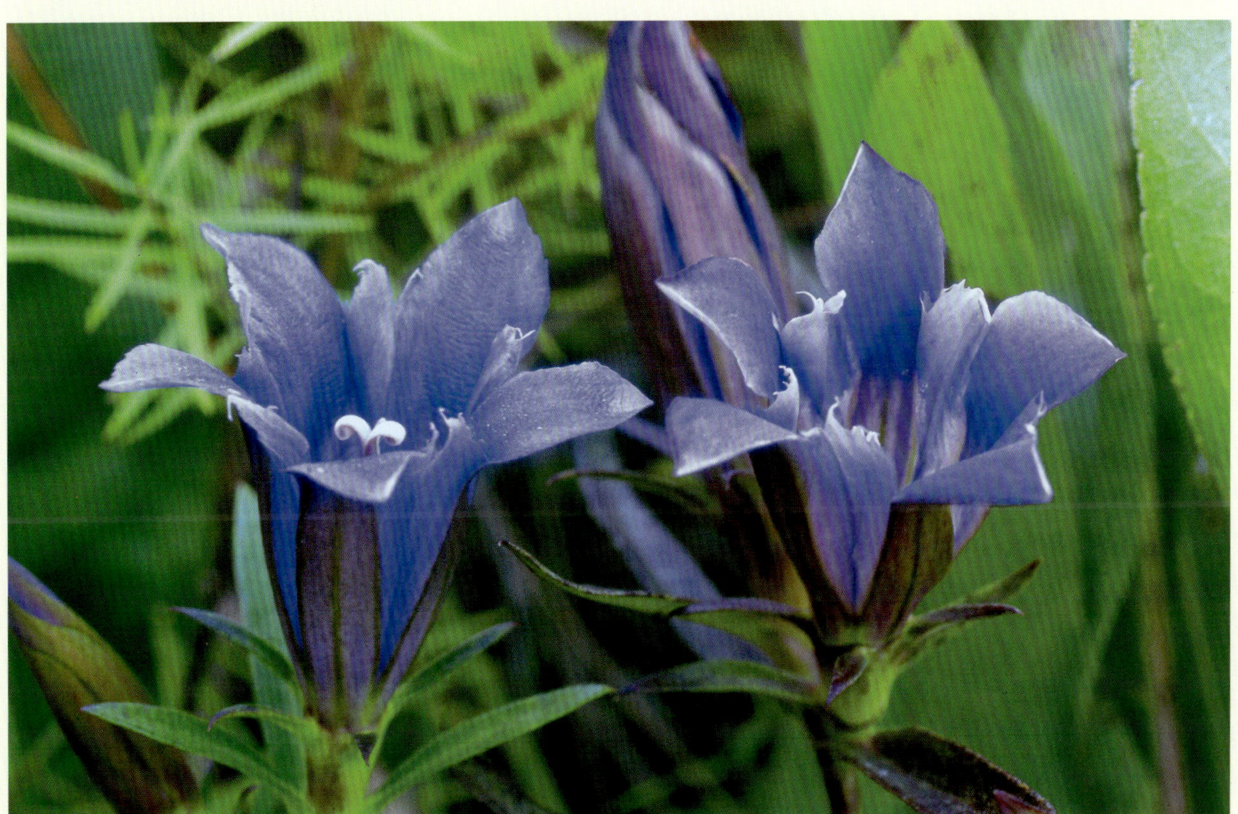

Spectacular blooms of downy, or prairie, gentians (*Gentiana puberulenta*) flower in Loda Cemetery prairie in Iroquois County, Illinois; its presence indicates undisturbed conditions.

About 5 million prairie chickens (*Tympanuchus cupido*) originally inhabited Illinois's Grand Prairie, where small populations have been reintroduced into Marion County. (*Photo by Dave Menke, U.S. Fish and Wildlife Service*)

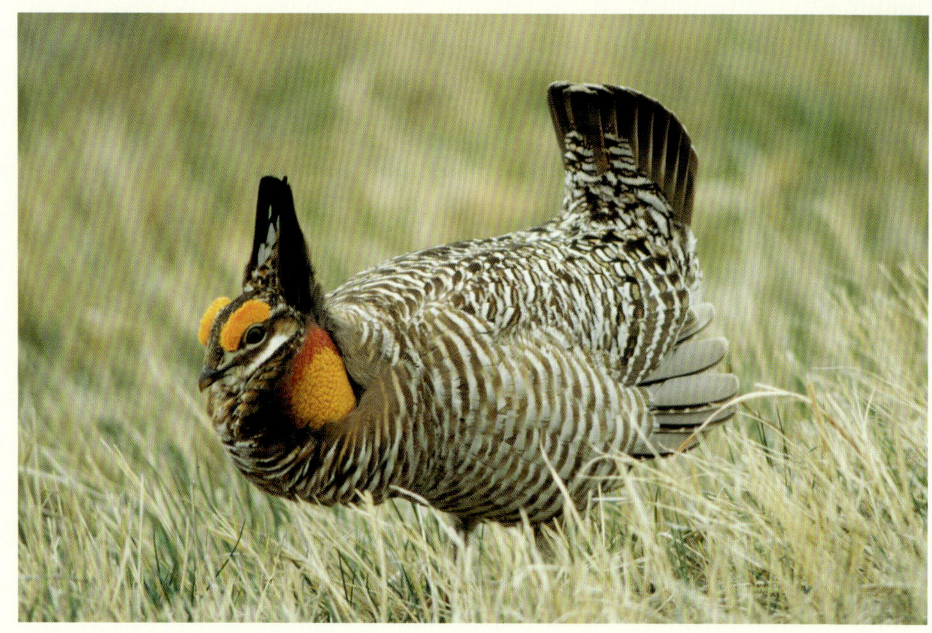

Below: Sullivant's, or prairie, milkweed (*Asclepias sullivantii*) is one of eleven milkweed species found growing in tallgrass prairie. Milkweed is an important source of nectar for pollinating insects; here, it blooms at the James Woodworth Prairie in Illinois.

Opposite: Tall stalks of big bluestem (*Andropogon gerardii*) stand out against an Illinois sunrise.

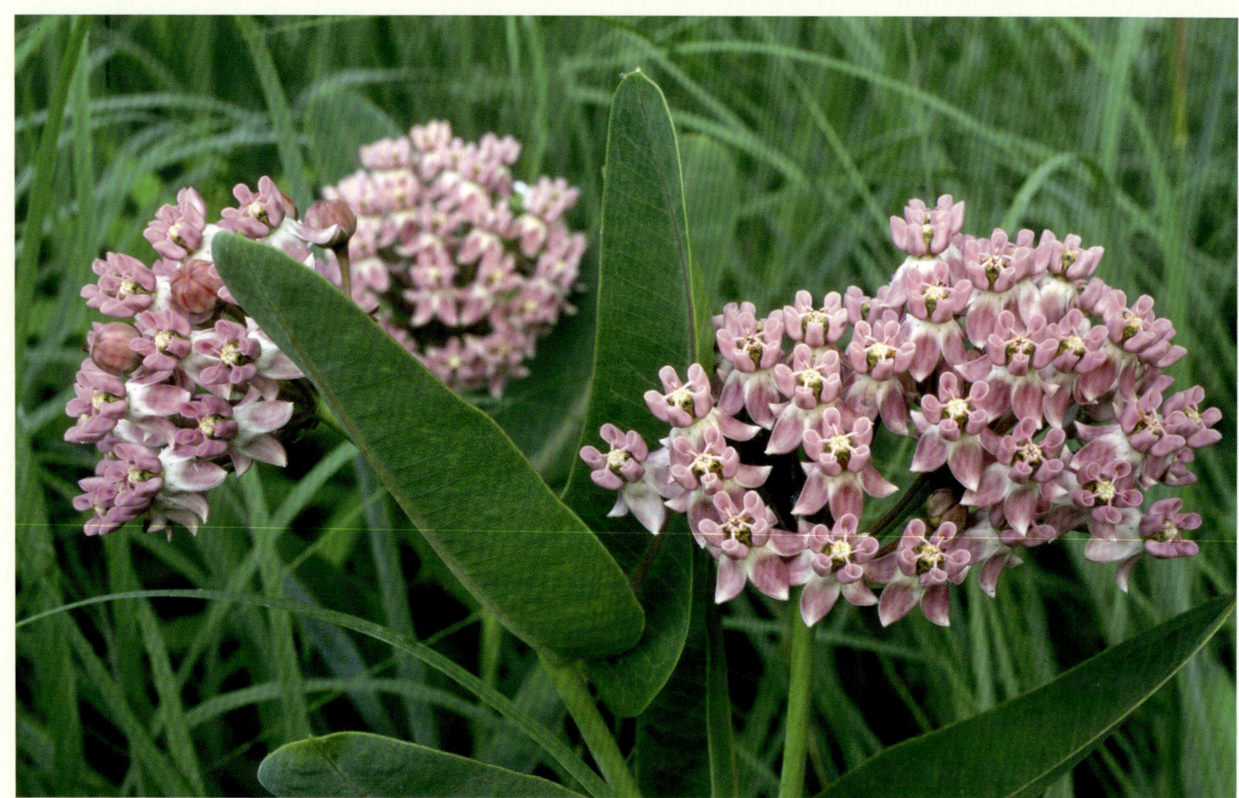

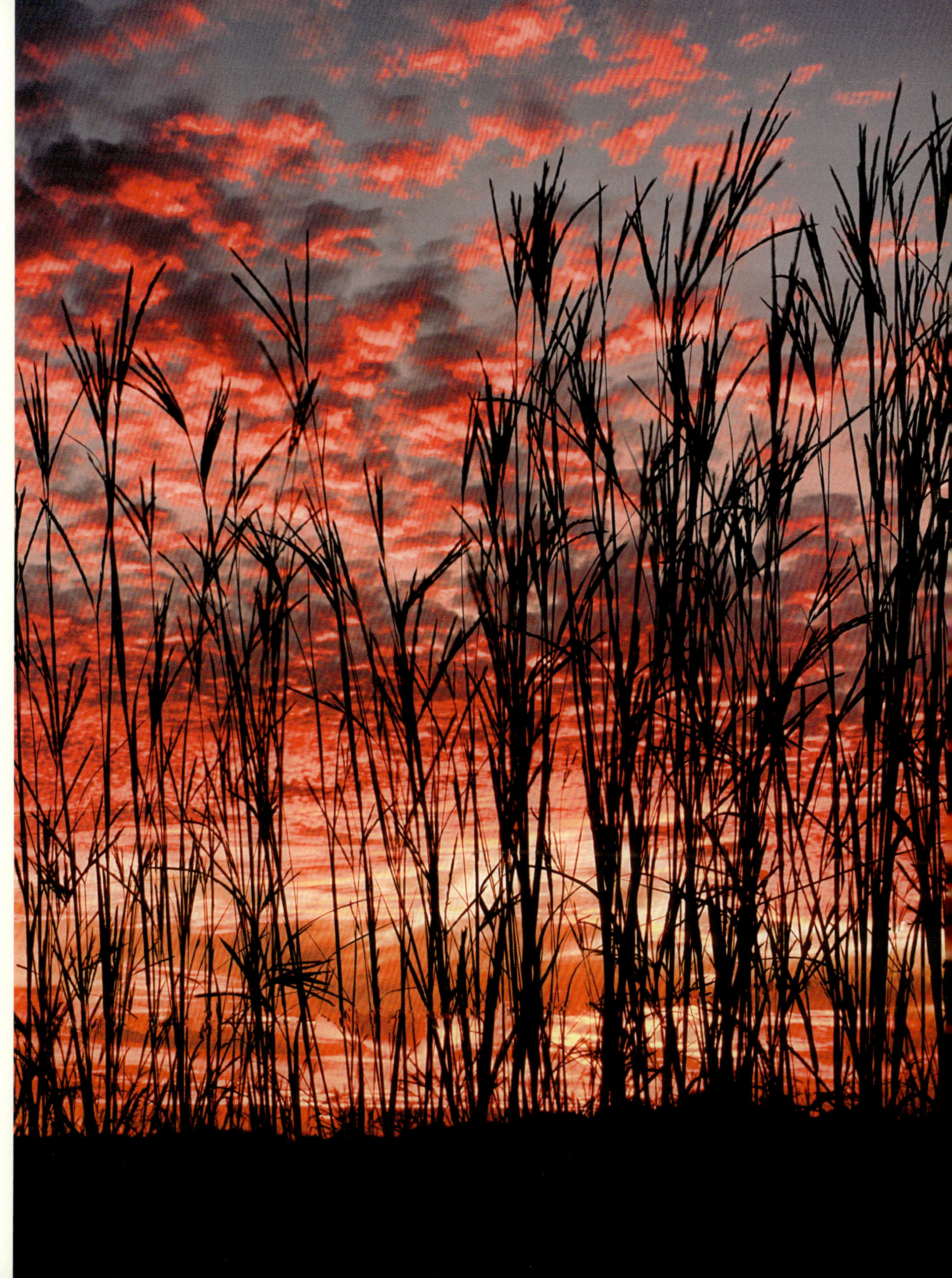

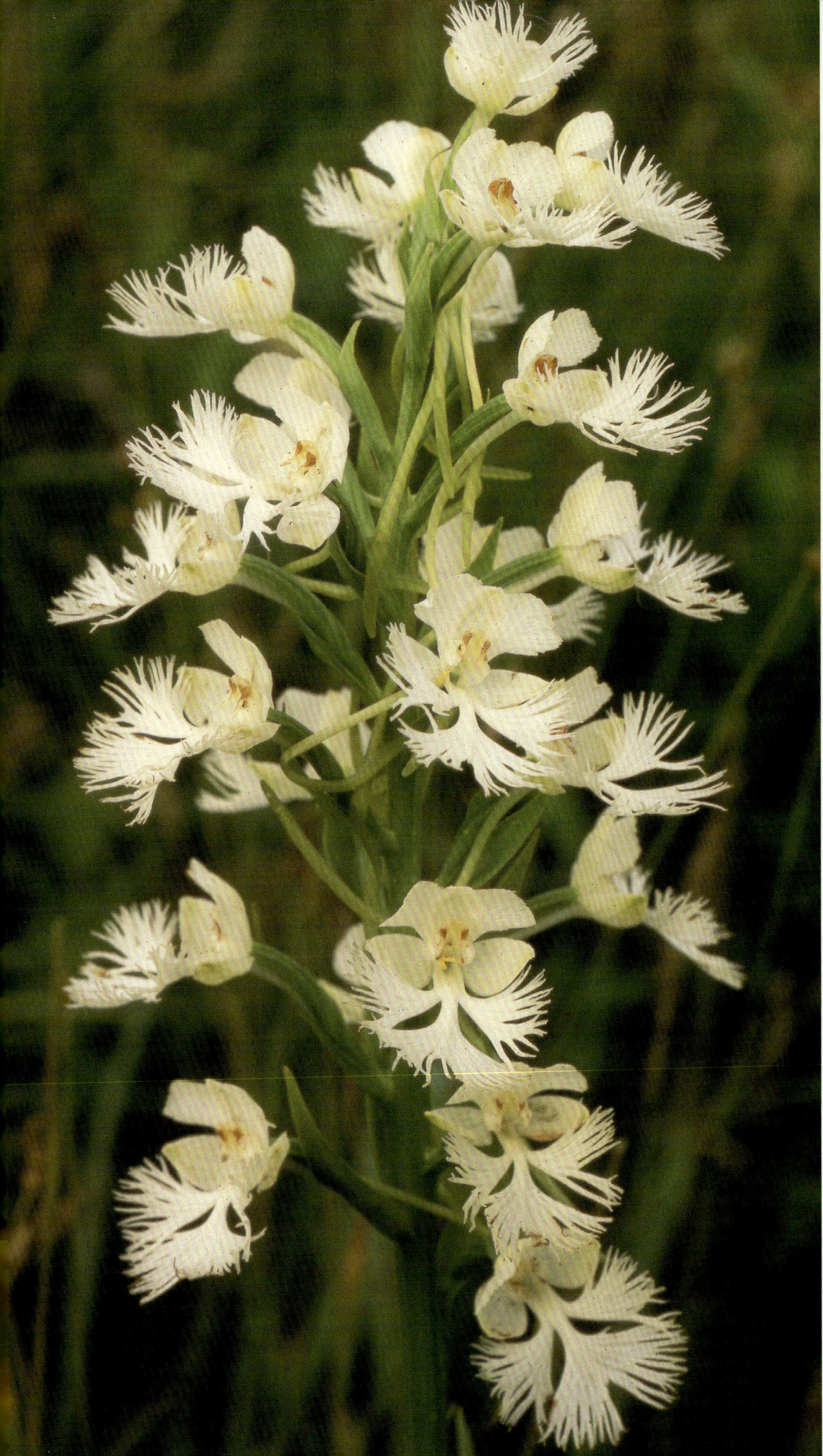

Opposite: Common eastern plains garter snakes (*Thamnophis radix*) range as far east as western Indiana. A disjunct population survives in central Ohio.

Federally threatened eastern prairie white-fringed orchids (*Platanthera leucophaea*) are occasionally found growing in wet meadows.

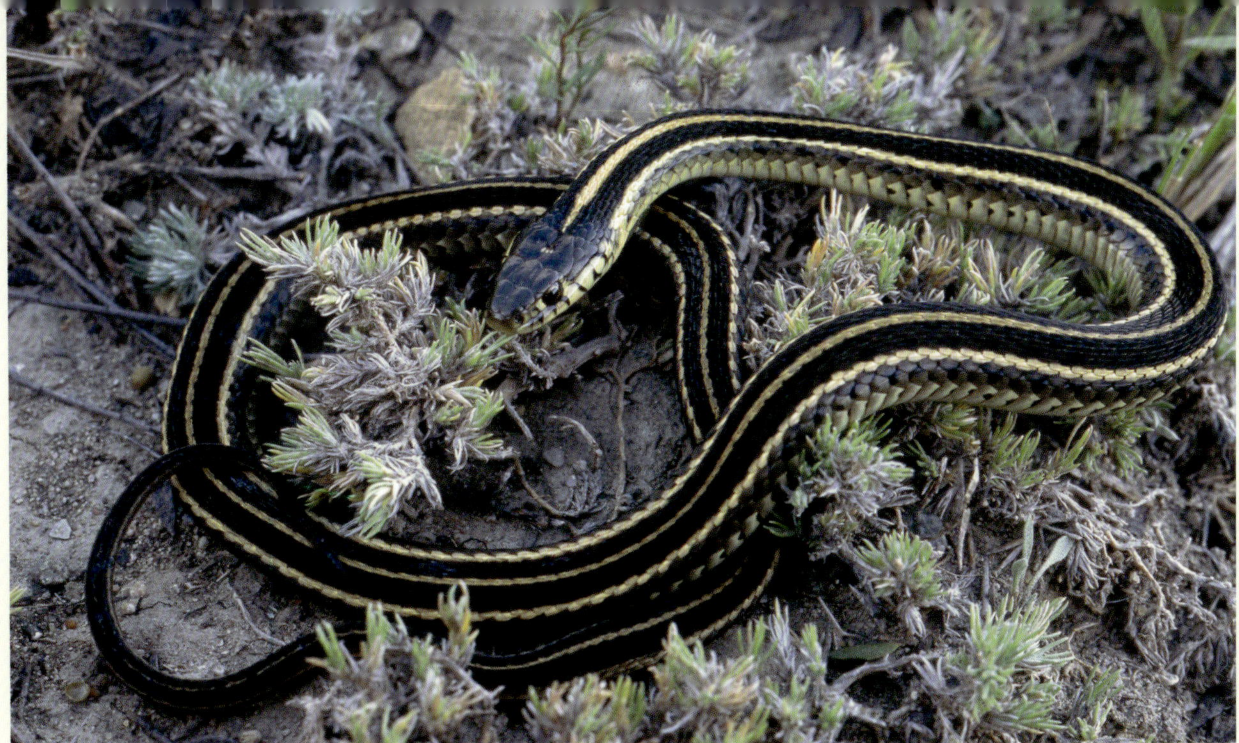

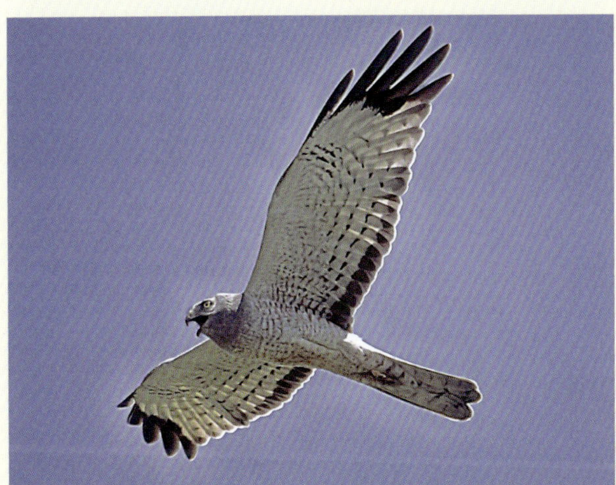

Northern harriers (*Cicrus cyaneus*) can be seen hunting over grasslands in search of mice, voles, and ground squirrels. They are rare breeders in the Prairie Peninsula.

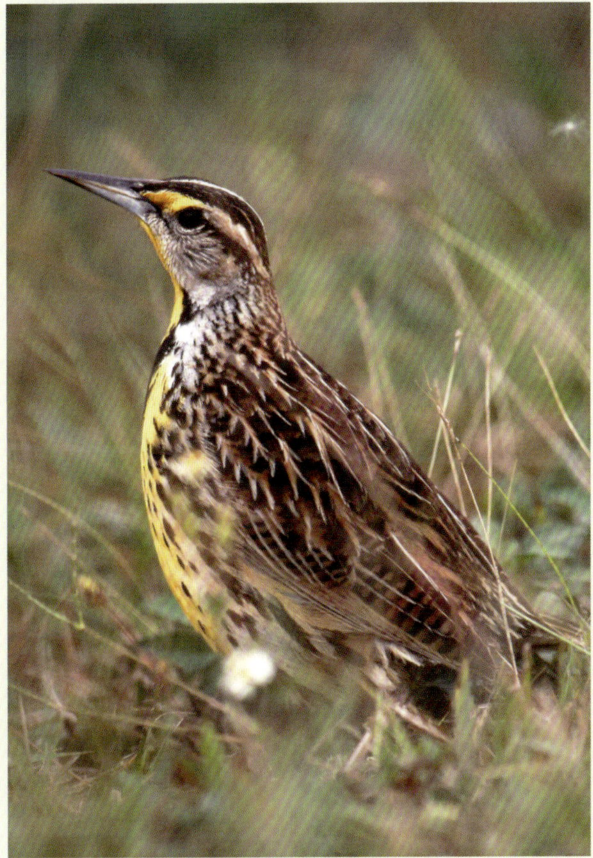

The lazy whistle of the eastern meadowlark (*Sturnella magna*), which sings from a favorite perch or hidden in grass, is a common sound in summer grasslands.

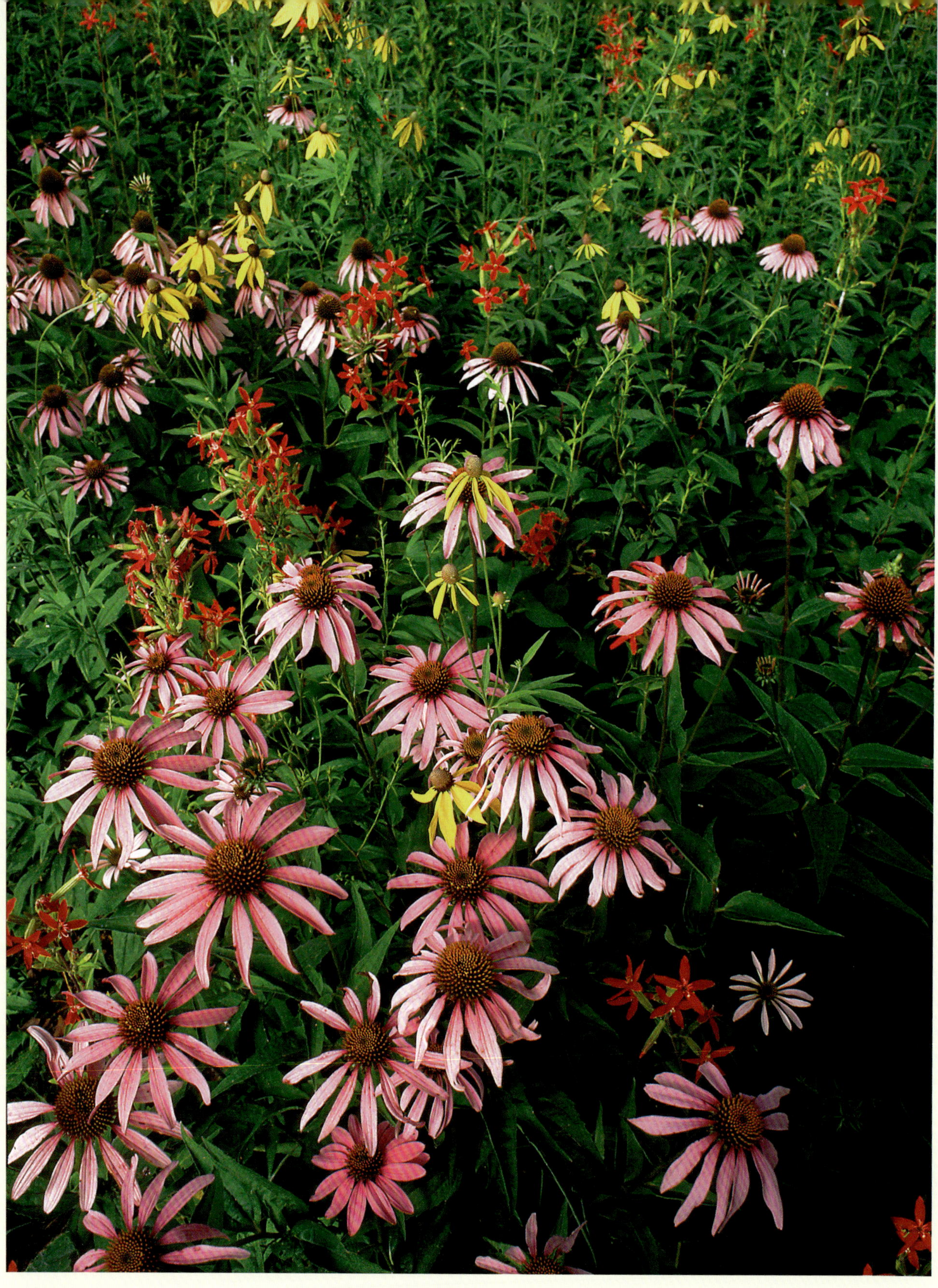

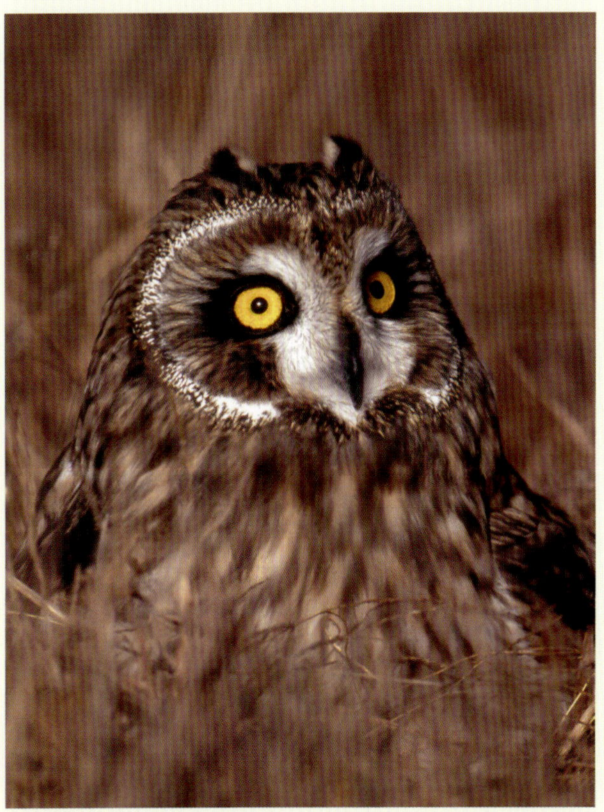

Short-eared owls (*Asio flammeus*), which rest during the day, appear in late evening. Excellent mousers, they control small rodent populations.

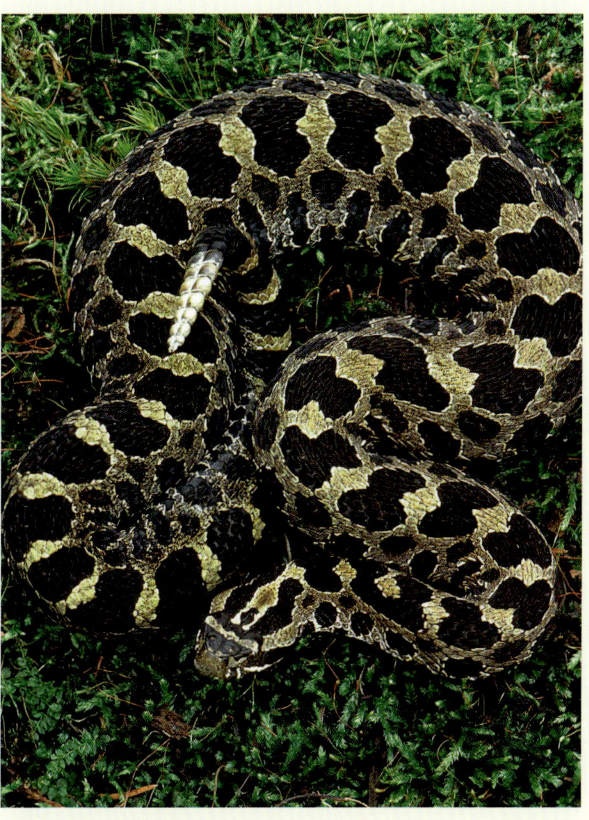

With the loss of wet prairie meadows, Eastern Massasauga rattlesnakes (*Sistrurus catenatus*) are now endangered throughout most of their range.

Opposite: A profusion of wildflowers blankets Bigelow cemetery in Ohio. Many showy plants were likely brought in from the surrounding prairie and transplanted as grave decorations.

CHAPTER 2

Prairie Ecosystems

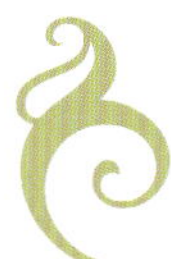

From the Kansas border to central Ohio, fourteen natural divisions of tallgrass prairie can be found. Though there is some overlap of floristic components, these divisions are based on topography, glacial history, soil type, and bedrock.

Lake Plain Sand Prairies, Mesic Sand Prairies, and Oak Savannas

Some of the largest prairie remnants can be found along the south shore of Lake Michigan and the western end of Lake Erie. Because so much remains of these habitats, sand prairies and oak savannas have undergone intensive study. Lake plain sand prairies occur on large sand deposits left by the glaciers and from offshore currents as prehistoric lake levels drained through the Niagara River gorge. Soil fertility tends to be low in organic matter, with virtually all nutrients flushed away by rainwater; plants that live in this harsh environment have adapted to conditions here, which are otherwise dry. Insects dominate, with wasps and beetles scurrying across the hot sand. Often, scantily vegetated dunes cannot withstand the constant wind—a destabilized dune begins to collapse, in what is called a blowout. Few plants can survive in the shifting sand. Low areas tend to be wet and calcareous, creating a dune-and-swale topography. Swales tend to be alkaline and high in organic matter from the nutrients flushed down from the dunes. Here calciphile flora, plants that favor alkaline soils, can be found mingling with prairie species.

Away from the lake plain, mesic sand prairies are more acidic and have fewer calciphiles. The dry conditions in sand prairies favor little bluestem

(*Schizachyrium scoparium*) along with switchgrass (*Panicum virgatum*), June grass (*Koeleria macrantha*), and purple love grass (*Eragrostris spectabilis*). Many colorful plants—such as butterfly milkweed (*Asclepias tuberosa*), midland shooting star (*Dodecatheon meadia*), prickly-pear cactus (*Opuntia humifusa*), rough blazing star (*Liatris aspera*), and wild lupine (*Lupinus perennis*)—bloom throughout the spring and summer. Shrubs include New Jersey tea (*Ceanothus americanus*) and winged sumac (*Rhus copallina*), along with bracken fern (*Pteridium aquilinum*) and the shrub sweetfern (*Comptonia peregrina*).

As one leaves the dunes, a number of oak species begin to appear. Oaks can survive in nutrition-poor sandy soil. Black (*Quercus velutina*), bur (*Quercus macrocarpa*), scarlet (*Quercus coccinea*), and white oak (*Quercus alba*) predominate. The trees form parklike stands called oak openings. Under the trees grow plants found in the sand prairies; the amount of light filtered through the trees and soil quality both affect the species composition in the understory. Low-growing shrubs include American hazelnut (*Corylus americana*), prairie willow (*Salix humilis*), wild plum (*Prunus americana*), dogwoods (Cornus spp.), and blueberries (Vaccinium spp.). In spring, wild hyacinths (*Camassia scilloides*) may cover the ground with a sea of blue. Summer brings the blooms of New Jersey tea, white false indigo (*Baptisia leucantha*), and rattlesnake master (*Nabalus yuccifolium*). The last—an odd-looking member of the Umbelliferae, or carrot, family—have yucca-like leaves. As summer wanes, rough blazing stars and many species of asters, goldenrods, and sunflowers brighten the landscape. Eastern fox squirrels (*Sciurus niger*) and white-tailed deer (*Odocoileus virginianus*) are frequently encountered, while the tapping of red-headed woodpeckers (*Melanerpes erythrocephalus*) echoes throughout the savanna. When the canopy finally closes, prairie species are replaced by more shade-tolerant woodland plants and animals.

Frequent fires are the major factor in maintaining the open woodlands. Fire eliminates diseased and unhealthy trees and top-kills shrubby oak sprouts, called grubs, along with young saplings and duff that has accumulated on the forest floor. It also inhibits the impenetrable understory of tenacious exotic shrubs and weeds that can quickly envelop and destroy an oak savanna's original fabric. Tatarian honeysuckle (*Lonicera tatarica*), common buckthorn (*Rhamnus cathartica*), and garlic mustard (*Alliaria petiolata*) are especially destructive (Chapman et al. 1995). The thick bark of bur and white oaks make these trees largely resistant to fire damage. Today, the absence of fire, along with the presence of development, has all but destroyed this globally rare ecosystem. In the past, oak savanna covered large portions of Michigan's Lower Peninsula. Today, only two small examples, adjacent to prairie cemeteries, survive (Cohen et al. 2015). Efforts are currently underway throughout the Prairie Peninsula to survey and identify restorable remnants and reintroduce fire as an important management tool.

Mesic Black Loam Tallgrass Prairie

In the past, black loam prairie covered most of Iowa, Illinois, and a small portion of western Indiana. Thousands of years of accumulating humus from roots and decaying stems and leaves created a carbon-rich organic soil. Deep-rooted prairie grasses accounted for two-thirds of organic matter. Dark, rich topsoil lay over a bed of impermeable clay substrate. Moist in spring, it gradually dried out as the summer progressed. Plant diversity was remarkable, with more than 250 species per acre. Forbs, or herbaceous flowering plants, accounted for 80 percent of the species present but only 10–20 percent of the total biomass. Grasses made up for the rest; big bluestem (*Andropogon gerardii*), prairie dropseed (*Sporobolus heterolepis*), and Indian grass (*Sorghastrum nutans*) were common species. The parade of wildflowers continued throughout the growing season. Cream wild indigo (*Baptisia bracteata*), downy phlox (*Phlox pilosa*), leadplant (*Amphora canescens*), and wild quinine (*Parthenium integrifolium*) covered the open ground; these were later followed by compass plant (*Silphium laciniatum*), rosinweed (*Silphium integrifolium*), sunflowers, goldenrods, asters, and gentians. These black soils were among the richest and most productive in the world.

By the beginning of the twentieth century, the prairie had all but disappeared, having been turned into corn and soybean fields. Today, black loam prairie can only be found in pioneer cemeteries, along old railroad lines, and at a few sites that have miraculously escaped development. The vast majority of these remnants are quite small, usually less than ten acres. Today, botanists study the soil types of these fragments to try to recreate a floristic profile of how black loam prairie might have looked two hundred years ago.

Loess Prairie and Hill Prairie

Loess (pronounced "loss") is composed of fine particles of silt that were deposited by wind. Geologists recognize at least three distinct loess deposits during the Pleistocene epoch; each represents a major interglacial period.

Sometimes loess was laid down on terraces high above river floodplains. The fine particles are microscopic and held together by their molecular structure. These form highly erosive vertical cliffs and steep valleys, creating a peak-and-saddle topography. Plants characteristic of the Great Plains and at the edge of their eastern range can be found here: large-flowered beardtongue (*Penstemon grandiflorus*), purple locoweed (*Oxytropis lambertii*), western wallflower (*Erysimum capitatum*), and yucca (*Yucca glauca*). Some of the best loess sites in the North America are found in western Iowa along the Missouri River.

Further differentiation can be made between sand and gravel hill prairies. Both arid, they create an environment favorable to drought-tolerant plants. Sand and gravel prairies are usually located on dry steep south-facing hilltops, bluffs, or cliffs adjacent to major rivers like the Illinois and Mississippi. Uncommon in the Prairie Peninsula, they often occupy thin soils overlying limestone or dolomite bedrock and are well-drained droughty habitats. Continual erosion and evaporation rates favor the growth of prairie plants. Floristic composition can vary widely, depending on soil moisture and pH. Hardy grasses, such as little bluestem (*Schizachyrium scoparium*), side-oats grama (*Bouteloua curtipendula*), and blue grama (*Bouteloua gracilis*) are found here. One can expect to see many drought-tolerant forbs, such as leadplant (*Amphora canescens*), nodding wild onion (*Allium cernuum*), purple prairie clover (*Dalea purpurea*), prairie coreopsis (*Coreopsis palmata*), and prairie smoke (*Geum triflorum*). Woody species include red cedar (*Juniperus virginiana*) and smooth sumac (*Rhus glabra*), as well as gray (*Cornus foemina*) and rough-leaved dogwoods (*Cornus drummondii*). Most original loess and hill prairies have been destroyed by mining and development. The few surviving examples have decreased in size due to the gradual encroachment of woody vegetation.

Marl Prairie, Prairie Fens, and Shrub Prairie

Some of the most interesting eastern tallgrass prairie remnants are marl prairies. These unique wetlands lie on a substrate of marl, a calcium carbonate that precipitates from underground water high in calcium and magnesium bicarbonates. A more accurate name for this ecosystem is prairie fen. Fens are alkaline peatlands, but unlike sphagnum peat, fen peat is derived primarily from sedges and grasses. Water that feeds these wetlands issues from artesian springs and seeps, flowing underground through highly permeable calcareous gravel deposits as well as groundwater flowing through limestone and dolomite bedrock. This groundwater is highly charged with soluble calcium and magnesium bicarbonates. Once the water reaches the surface, the carbon dioxide is released with the insoluble calcium carbonate, forming marl flats.

Often the most unusual plants grow on these flats and associated sedge meadows. The ecological setting is not unlike those that once occurred along the front of continental glaciers or along the ancient shorelines of the Great Lakes. As glacial ice receded, plants occurring in fens throughout the Prairie Peninsula have continued to maintain their position in the landscape of calcareous springs and seeps. Fen types are easily distinguishable as species having northern, eastern, or western affinities, giving fens exceptionally rich diversity. In northern locations, species like dwarf birch (*Betula glandulosa*), green cotton grass (*Eriophorum angustifolium*), northern pitcher plants (*Sarracenia purpurea*), shrubby cinquefoil (*Dasiphora fruticosa*), tamarack (*Larix laricina*), and carnivorous sundews (Drosera spp.) are common. These may be referred to as boreal fens. Fens supporting an abundance of prairie plants are termed prairie fens.

Sedges and rushes dominate fens. Scattered clumps of cordgrass (*Spartina pectinata*) and Indian grass (*Sorghastrum nutans*) as well as big bluestem (*Andropogon gerardii*) grow in and around the edges of the fen meadow. The harsh environment created by the highly saturated alkaline marl keeps trees from rooting, preventing them from shading out prairie species. Specialists such as queen-of-the-prairie (*Filipendula rubra*), small white lady's slippers (*Cypripedium candidum*), Ohio (*Solidago ohioensis*) and Riddell's goldenrods (*Solidago riddellii*), and gentians are joined by common plants such as gray-headed coneflower (*Ratibida pinnata*), prairie dock (*Silphium terebinthinaceum*), swamp thistle (*Cirsium muticum*), and blazing stars (Liatris spp.).

As the name suggests, shrub prairie is dominated by plants like bristly blackberry (*Rubus hispidus*), big bluestem, hardhack (*Spiraea tomentosa*), and running ground-pine (*Lycopodium clavatum*). Berries and nuts are food sources for a variety of wildlife, and dense vegetation is utilized as cover and nesting space for edge species. Only a few examples of this habitat survive.

Wet Prairie, Sedge Meadows, and Marshes

Standing water in winter and spring keeps wet prairie mucky and damp most of the year. As plants die and decay, they create a rich black muck, which has accumulated over thousands of years. Core samples many feet thick can be traced back to the last glacial event. The dominant grasses in this environment are bluejoint (*Calamogrostis canadensis*), fowl manna (*Glyceria striata*), and cordgrass (*Spartina pectinata*). Another name for cordgrass is "rip gut," for the upward-pointing sharp edges along the upper margins of its blades. Many colorful forbs—like Michigan lily (*Lilium michiganense*), prairie ironweed (*Vernonia fasciculata*), swamp milkweed (*Asclepias incarnata*), and winged loosestrife (*Lythrum alatum*)—brighten the summer landscape. Marsh (*Thelypteris palustris*) and sensitive ferns (*Onoclea sensibilis*) are also common. Bobolinks (*Dolichonyx oryzivorus*), common yellowthroats (*Geothlypis trichas*), and swamp sparrows (*Melospiza georgiana*) nest in the wet meadows. In the past, numerous small ponds were common in low areas and depressions; however, almost all of these were drained or filled in to make room for row crops.

Wet prairie frequently grades into grasslike sedge meadows. Sedges are often overlooked, but they constitute a significant component of all prairie vegetation. As many as sixty species have been documented, among them woolly (*Carex pellita*), prairie (*Carex prairea*), fox (*Carex vulpinoidea*), and tussock sedges (*Carex stricta*) and twig rush (*Cladium mariscoides*). Sedge wrens (*Cistothorus platensis*) as well as Eastern Massasauga rattlesnakes (*Sistrurus catenatus*) are specialists.

Marshes occur along the edges of large bodies of permanent open water. They are usually ringed with emergent vegetation such as bur-reed (*Sparganium eurycarpum*), common cattail (*Typha latifolia*), and spatterdock (*Nuphar advena*). In the dryer portions, turtlehead (*Chelone glabra*), blue vervain (*Verbena hastata*), and smartweeds (Polygonium spp.) grow. The most notable wetland was the vast Grand Kankakee Marsh, once one of the great freshwater ecosystems of the world, covering 1 million acres in northern Indiana and Illinois. Mile after mile of waving marsh vegetation harbored countless numbers of birds; hunters from across the Midwest came in the fall for the sport. Great blue herons (*Ardea herodias*), the symbol of wetlands, stalked fish and other prey, while many species of waterfowl nested in the cattails. The honking of Canada geese (*Branta canadensis*) accentuated the wilderness. The Kankakee was also once a major passenger pigeon breeding area, but by the twentieth century the pigeons, along with one-fifth of America's migratory bird populations, were gone. In 1923, the meandering river was channeled into a ninety-mile ditch, and "the everglades of the north," as it was then called, turned into farmland. Today efforts are underway to restore some of the natural flow of the Kankakee River.

Dolomite Prairie and Gravel Prairie

Dolomite prairie is exceptionally dry for most of the year. Also known as barrens or limestone glades, these prairies can be underlain by layers of impervious dolomite and/or limestone. They are frequently covered by large patches of bare rock called limestone pavement. The lack of soil is typically the result of the scouring action of glacial ice or soil erosion. Dolostone, the name commonly given to a rock consisting of dolomite, contains high amounts of magnesium. As it slowly decomposes, magnesium is released. Only very specific plant communities can survive in the thin droughty soil. Gnarly black jack (*Quercus marilandica*) and post oaks (*Quercus stellata*) joined by red cedar (*Juniperus virginiana*) grow along the edges. Characteristic forbs are prairie dock (*Silphium terebinthinaceum*), prairie smoke (*Geum triflorum*), rock sandwort (*Minuartia stricta*), spider milkweed (*Asclepias viridis*), and scaly blazing stars (*Liatris squarrosa*). Rushes and sedges present include Crawe's (*Carex crawei*), Dudley's (*Carex dudleyi*), flat-stemmed spike-rush (*Eleocharis compressa*), and Torrey's sedge (*Carex torreyi*).

Gravel prairies are situated on outwash terraces left by the glaciers as well as kames and eskers left by melting glacial ice. These well-drained deposits limit tree growth and are better suited to xeric prairie species. Grasses include little bluestem, side-oats grama (*Bouteloua curtipendula*), and prairie dropseed (*Sporobolus heterolepis*). Pasque flowers (*Anemone patens*) grow here, as do prairie smoke, pale purple coneflowers (*Echinacea pallida*), gray goldenrod (*Solidago nemoralis*), and heath asters (*Symphyotrichum ericoides*).

Opposite: Prairie coreopsis (*Coreopsis palmata*) and leadplant (*Amphora canescens*) bloom in late June at Shoe Factory Road Prairie, in Cook County, Illinois, an outstanding example of hill prairie.

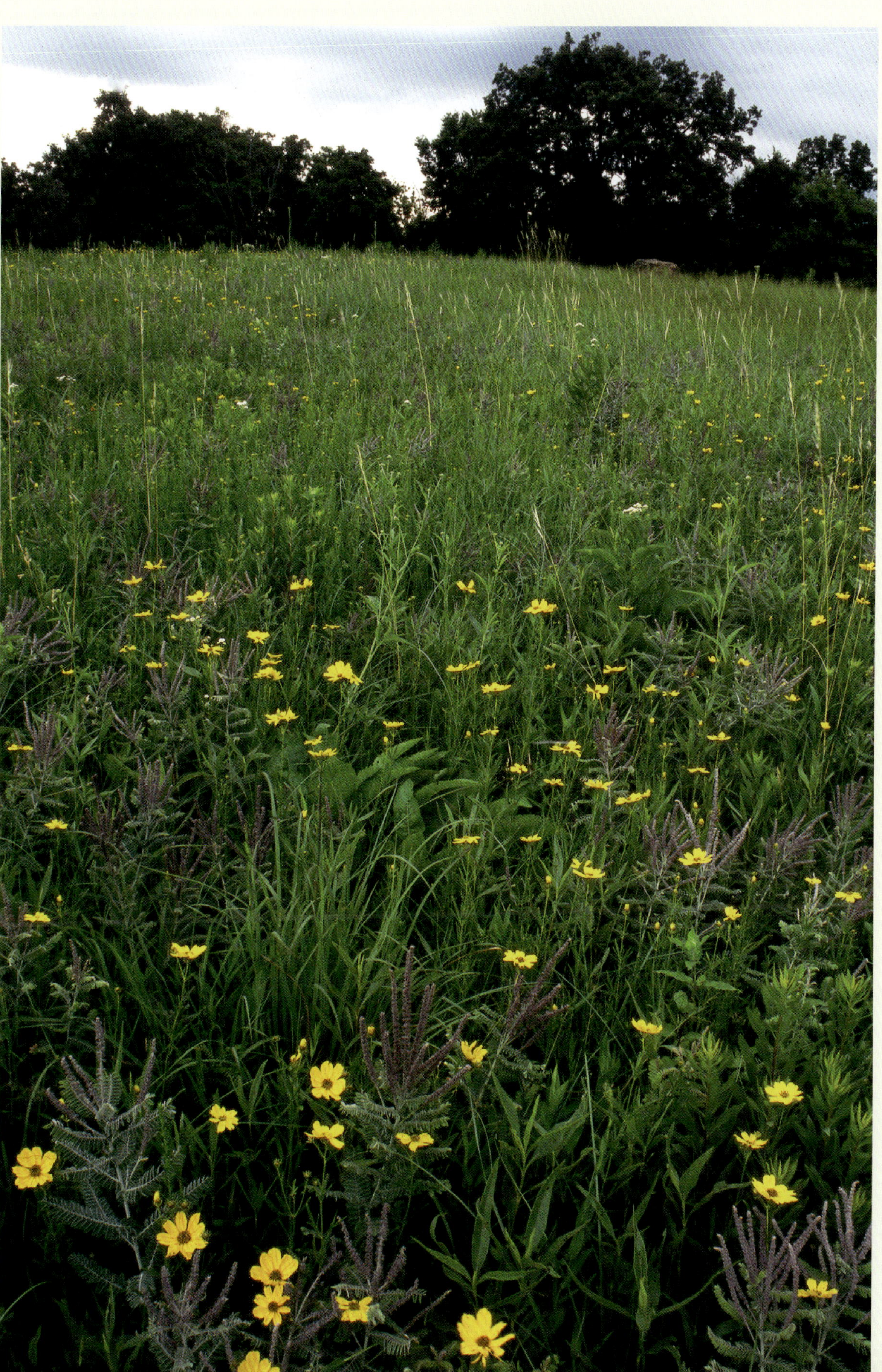

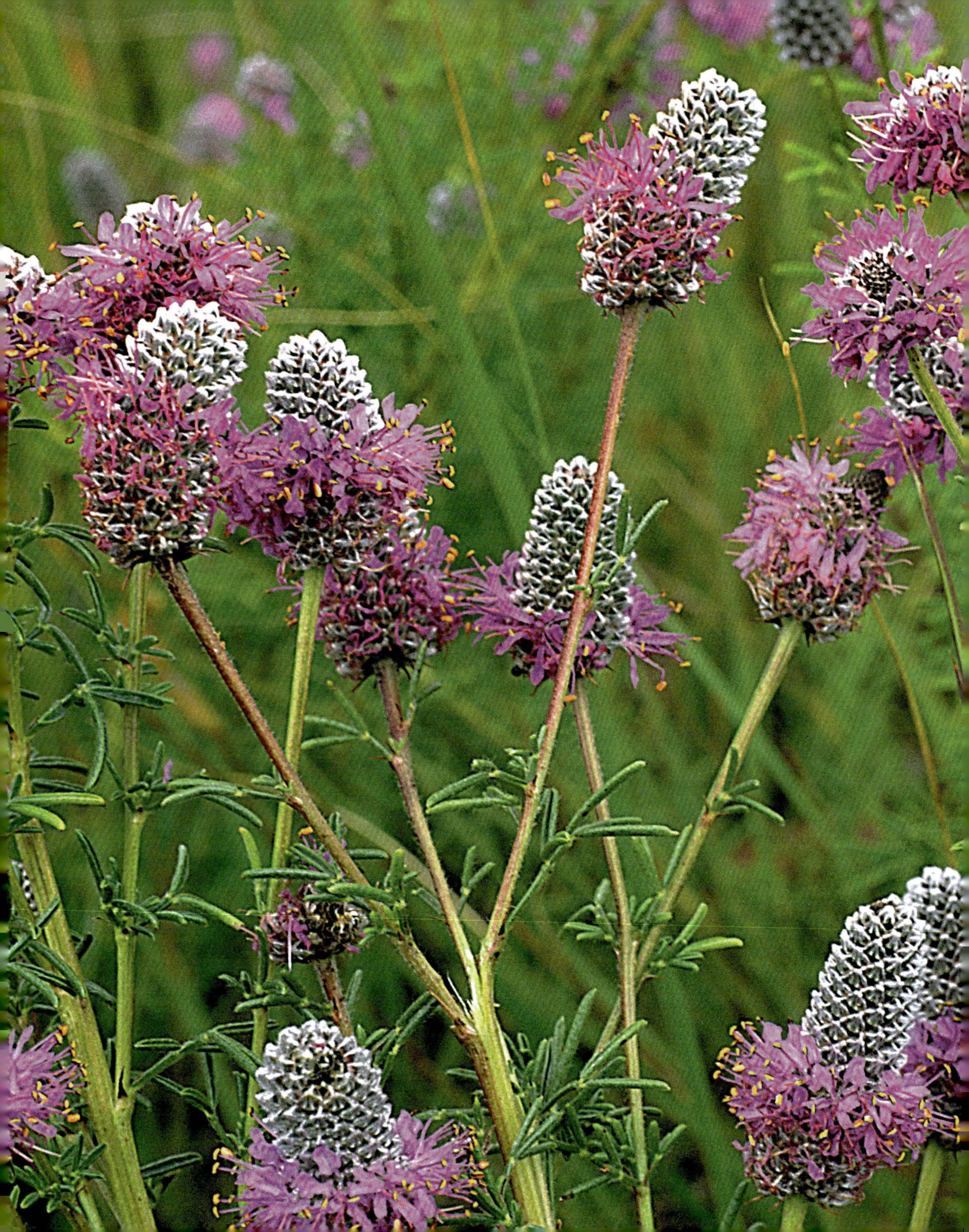

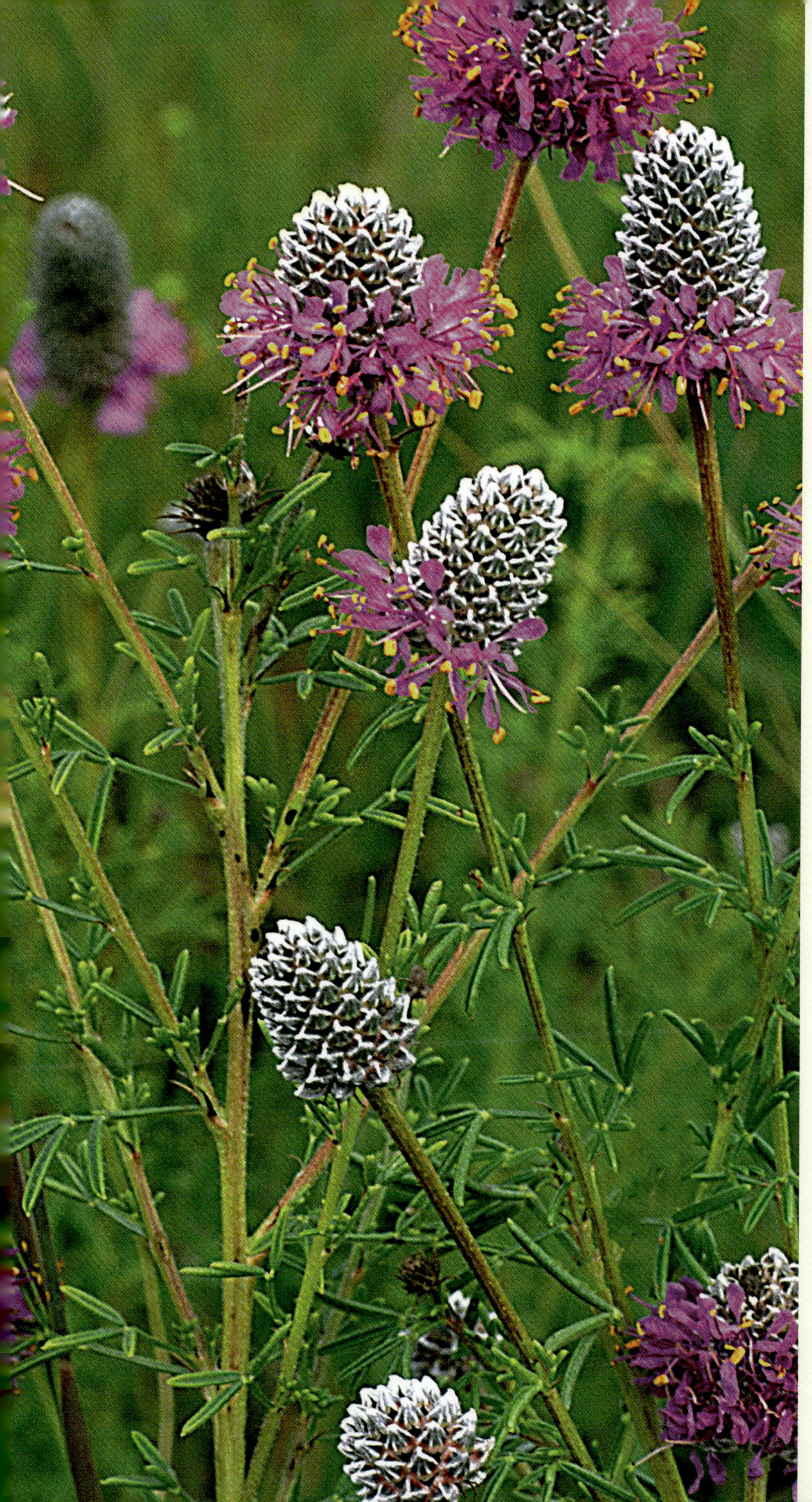

Found mainly in original prairie, purple prairie clover (*Dalea purpurea*) adorns dry grasslands in July. A long-lived plant, it is deep-rooted and drought resistant.

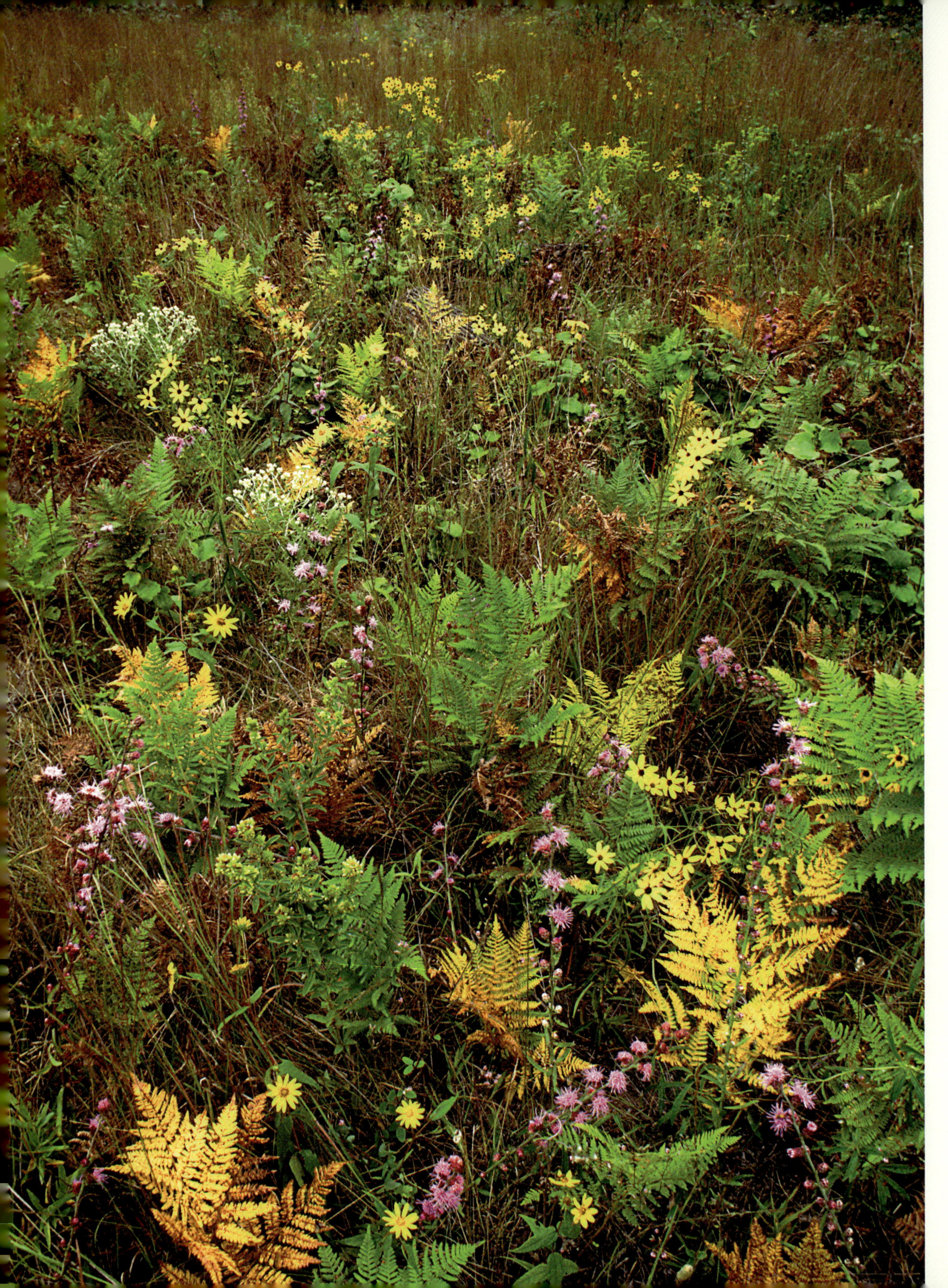

Opposite: Bracken ferns (*Pteridium aquilinum*) and rough blazing stars (*Liatris aspera*) are conspicuous in late summer in lake plain sand prairies.

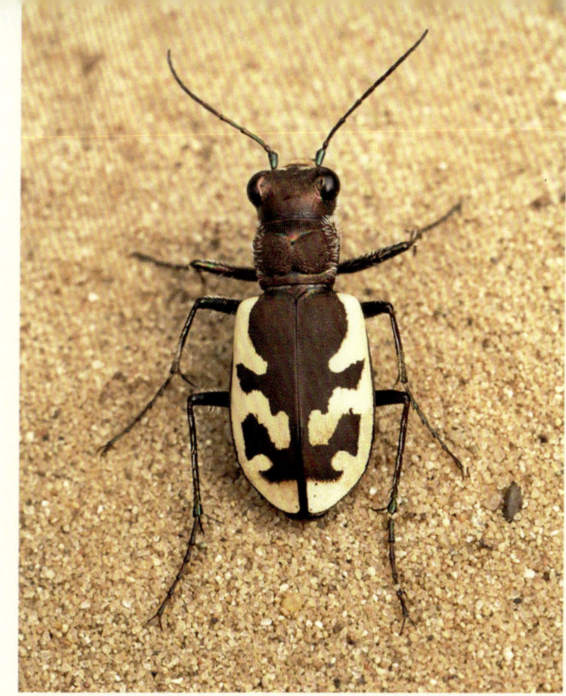

In summer, spectacular inch-long big sand tiger beetles (*Cicindela formosa generosa*) scurry across sand dunes.

The only eastern cactus, prickly pears (*Opuntia humifusa*) sometimes blanket sand prairies. Its vivid yellow blooms can be seen in late spring.

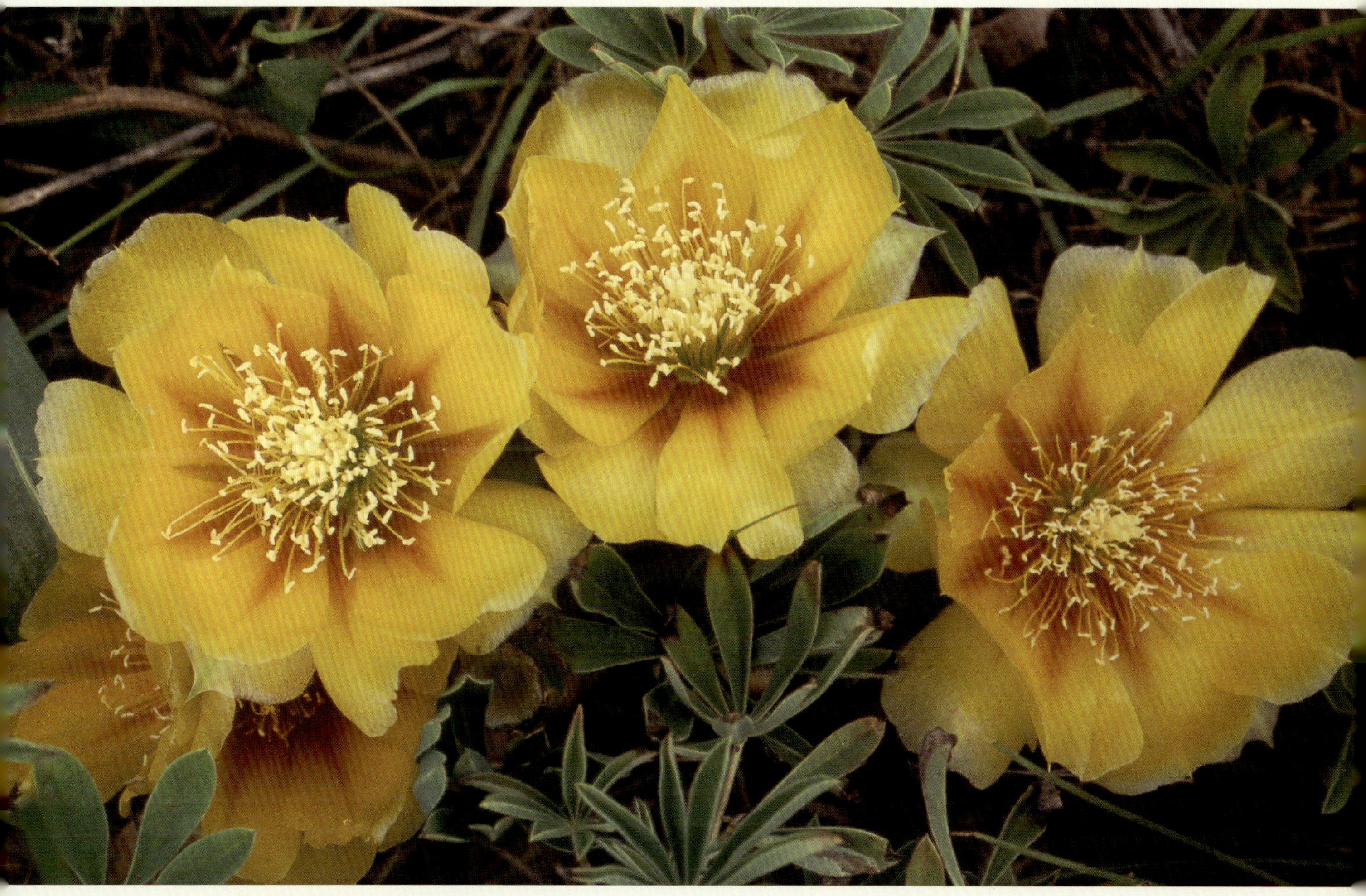

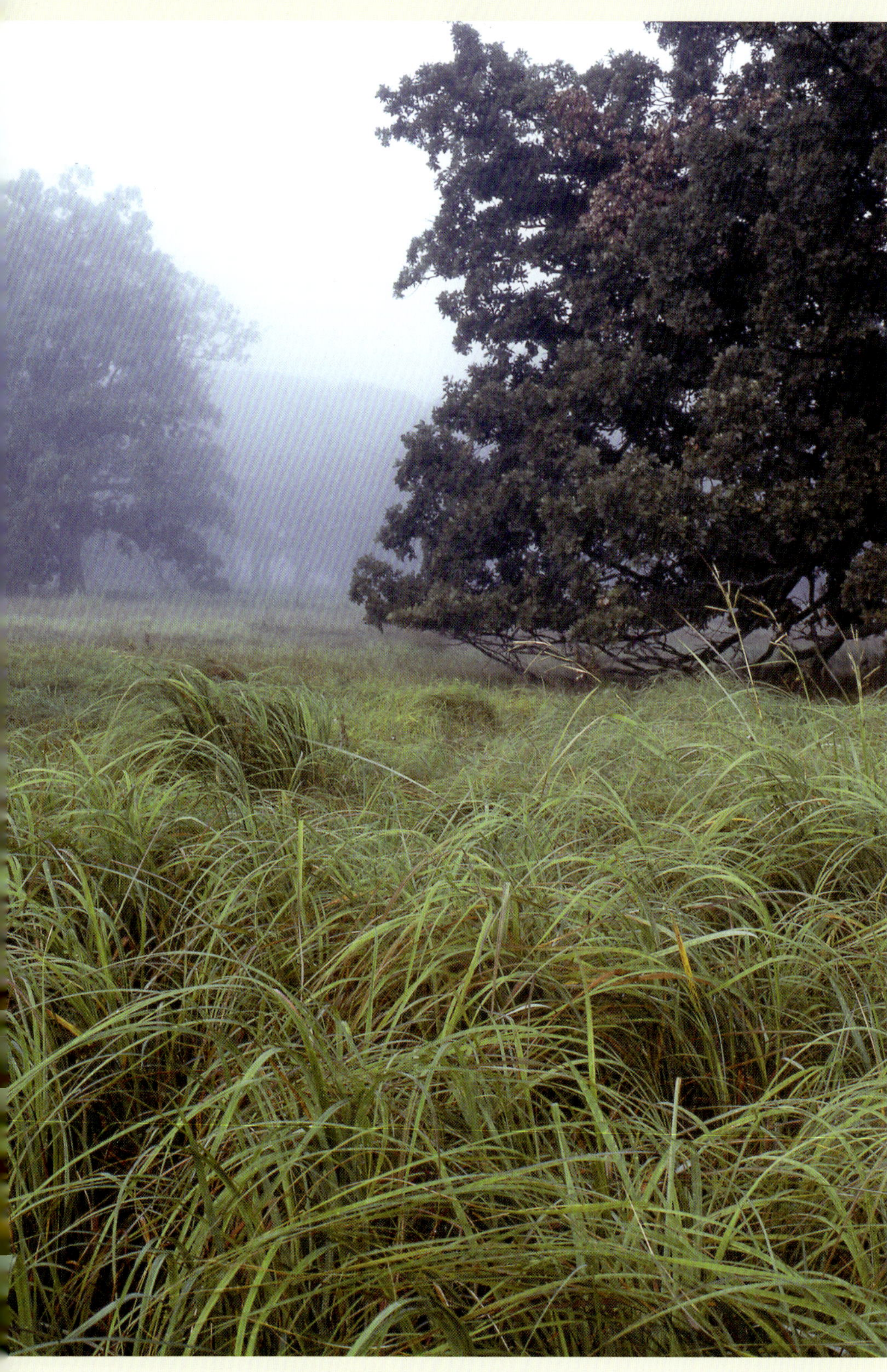

Cordgrass (*Spartina pectinata*), or "rip gut" grass, grows in the foreground at Daughmer Prairie Oak Savannah in Ohio. A former sheep pasture, the preserve is a significant remnant of oak savanna.

Native Illinois peoples called nodding wild onions (*Allium cernuum*) "shikaakwa," or stinky onion; French trappers gradually changed the name to Chicago.

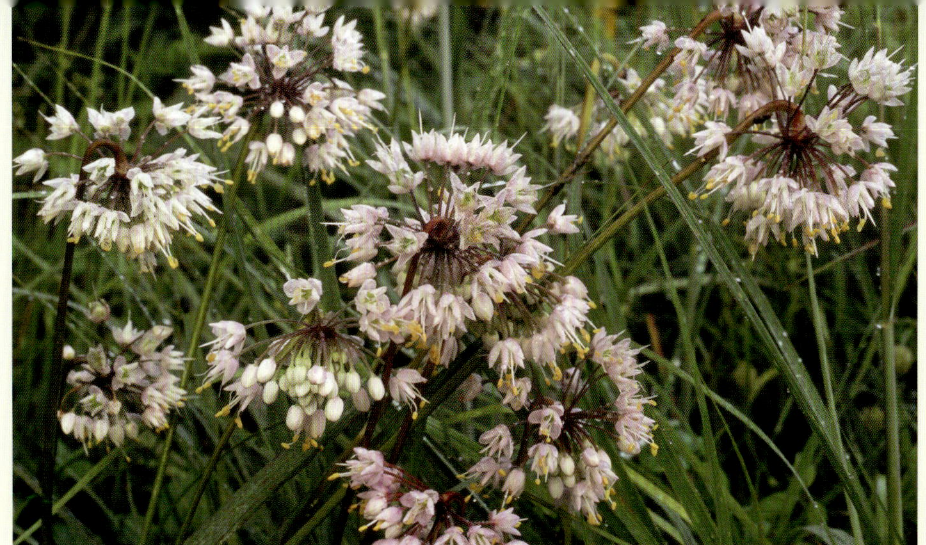

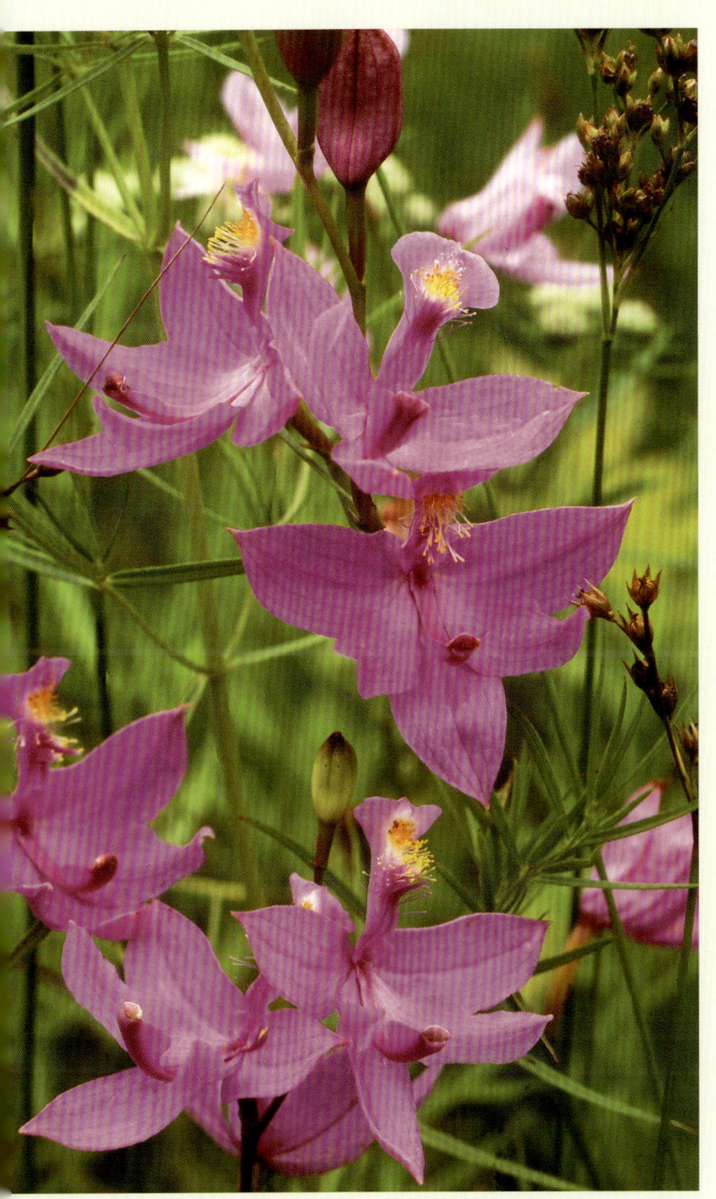

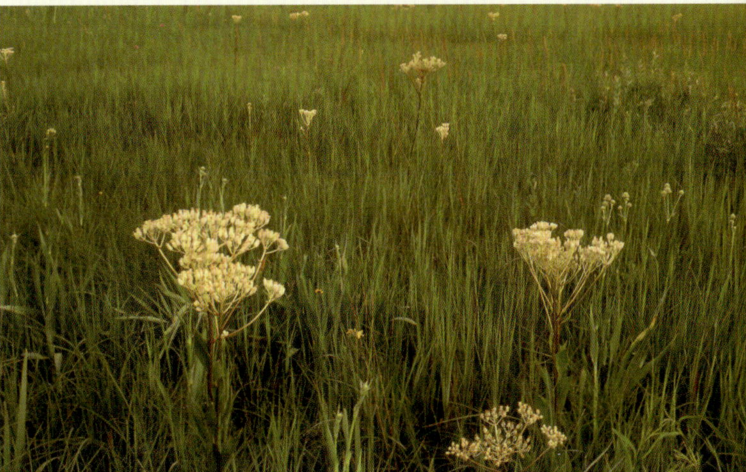

Sprays of Prairie Indian plantain (*Cacalia plantaginea*) adorn a wet meadow at Gensburg-Markham Prairie. Wet prairie contains grasses like blue joint (*Calamagrostis canadensis*), cordgrass (*Spartina pectinata*), and sedges (Carex spp.).

In June, beautiful grass pink orchids (*Calopogon tuberosus*) flower in prairie fens and alkaline sedge meadows.

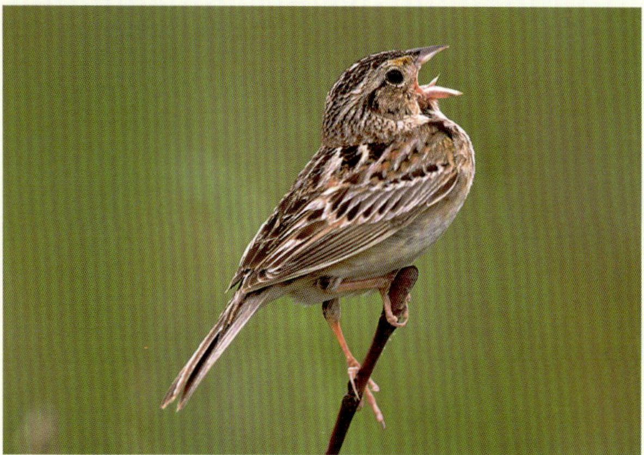

The insectlike buzz of the inconspicuous grasshopper sparrow (*Ammodramus savannarum*) can be heard across dry savannas.

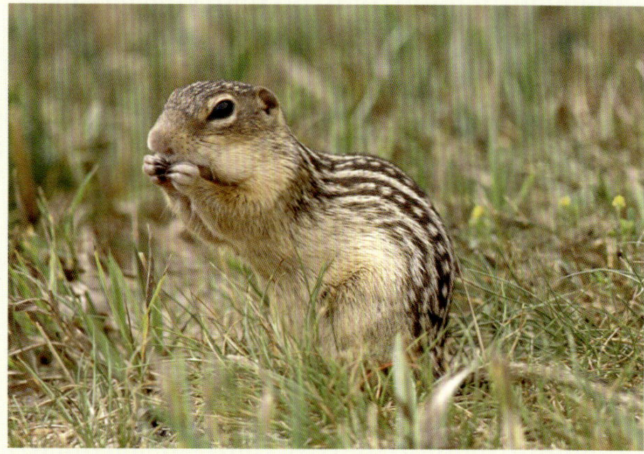

Thirteen-lined ground squirrels (*Spermophilus tridecemlineatus*) are diurnal; they usually come out on bright overcast days. They excavate elaborate systems of tunnels, and in late autumn they curl up and hibernate in burrows below the frost line.

Opposite: A northern species, prairie smoke (*Geum triflorum*) can be found in dry alkaline habitats.

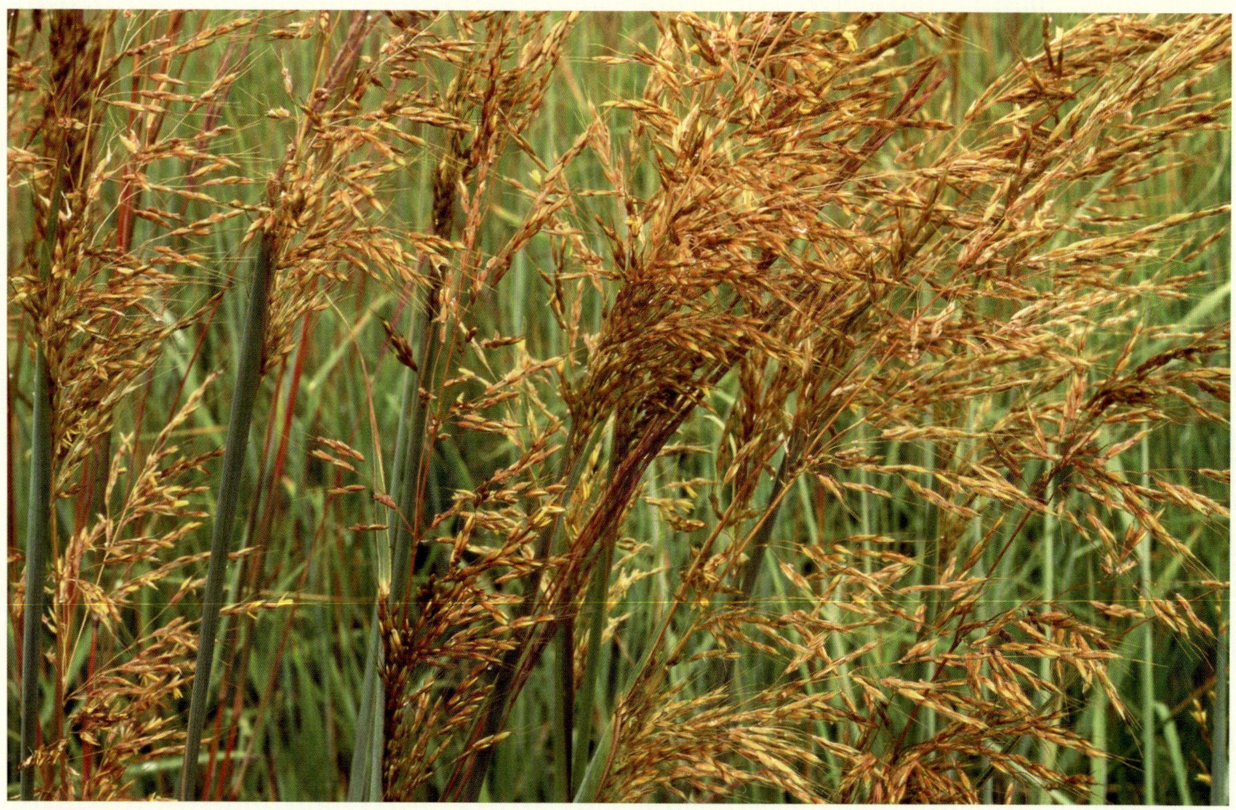

Indian grass (*Sorghastrum nutans*) is one of the most important components of tallgrass prairie. Growing to eight feet tall, this warm-season grass sometimes grows in pure stands covering many acres.

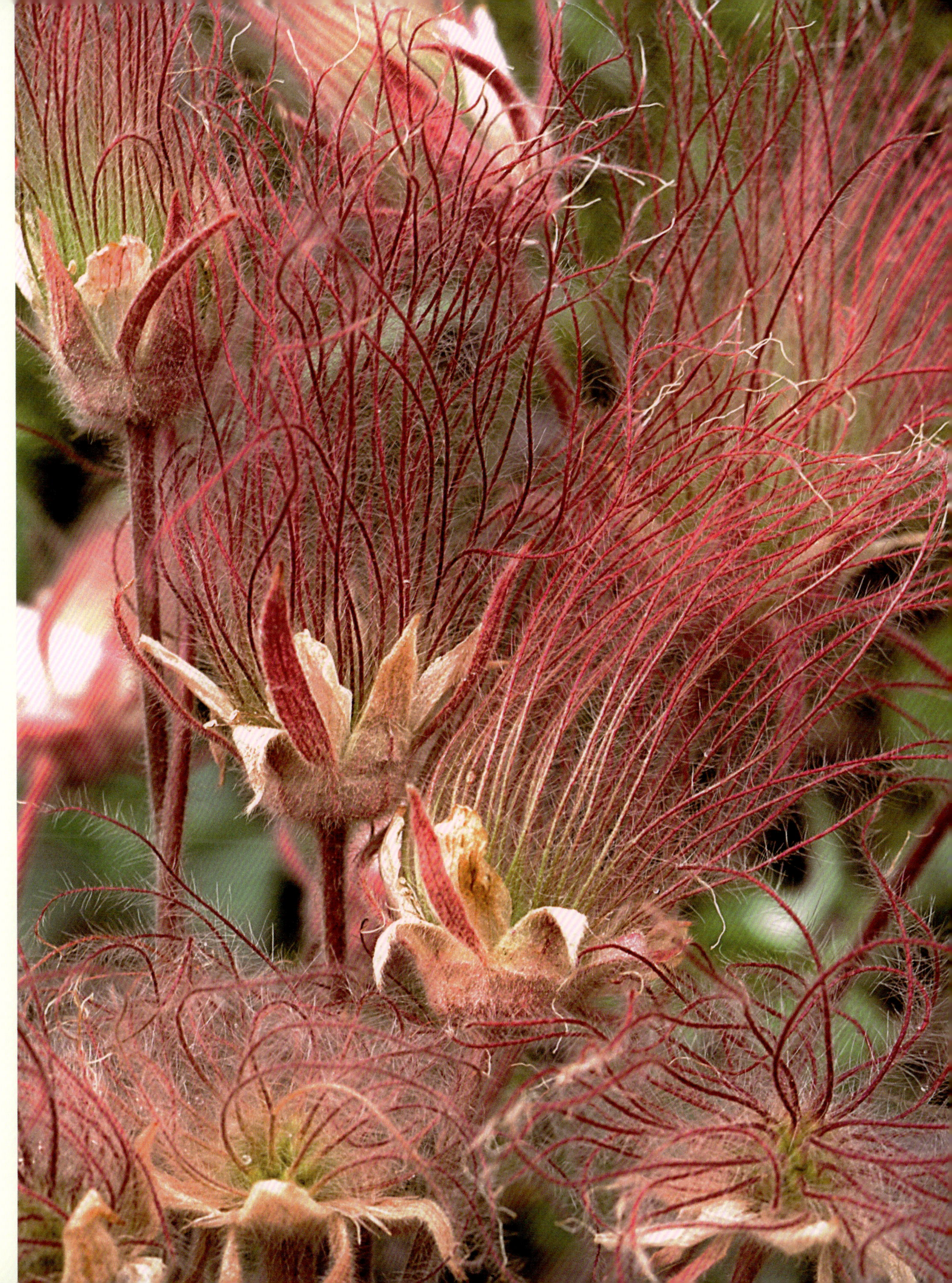

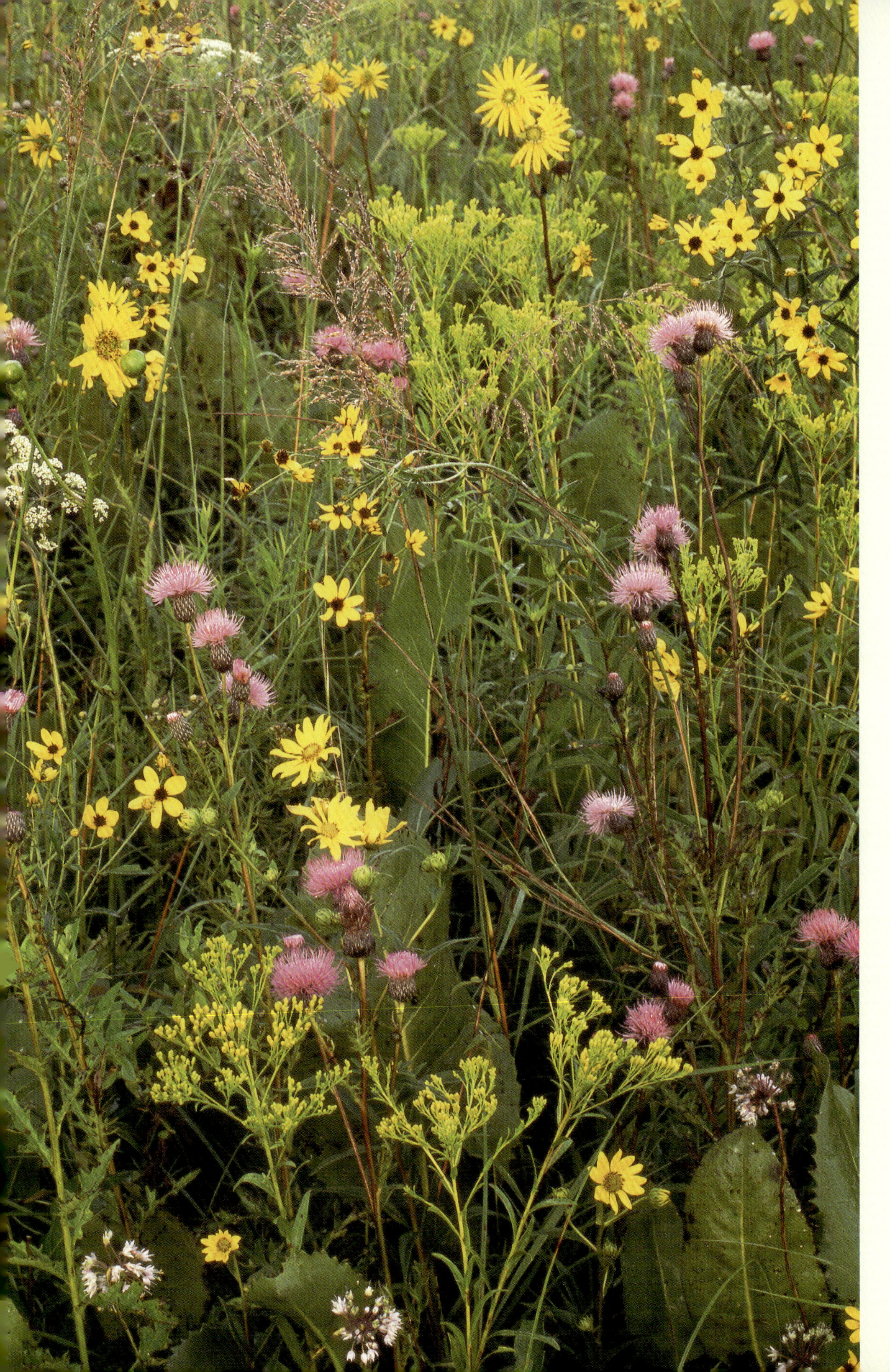

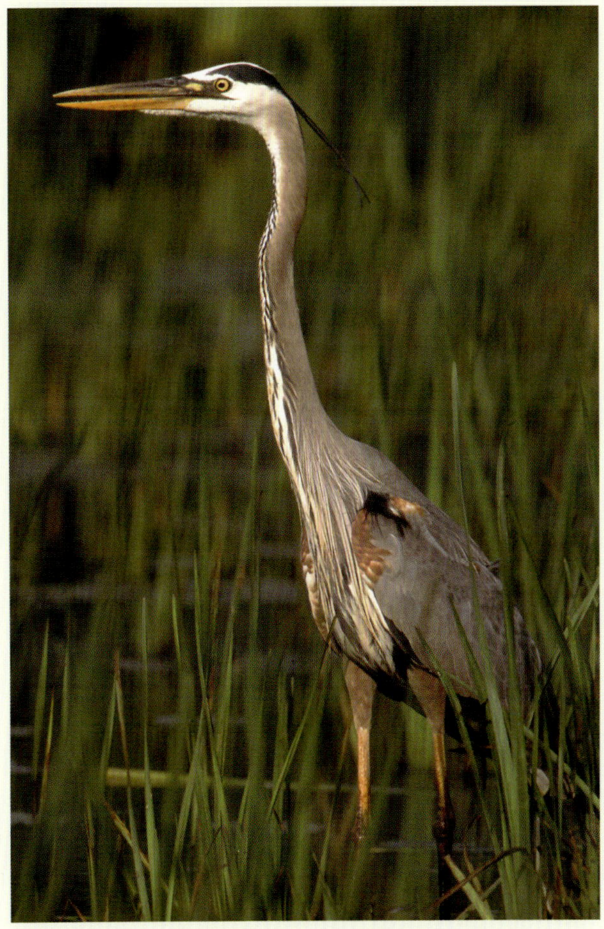

Great blue herons (*Ardea herodias*) are symbols of wetlands. Standing motionless, they wait for unsuspecting prey.

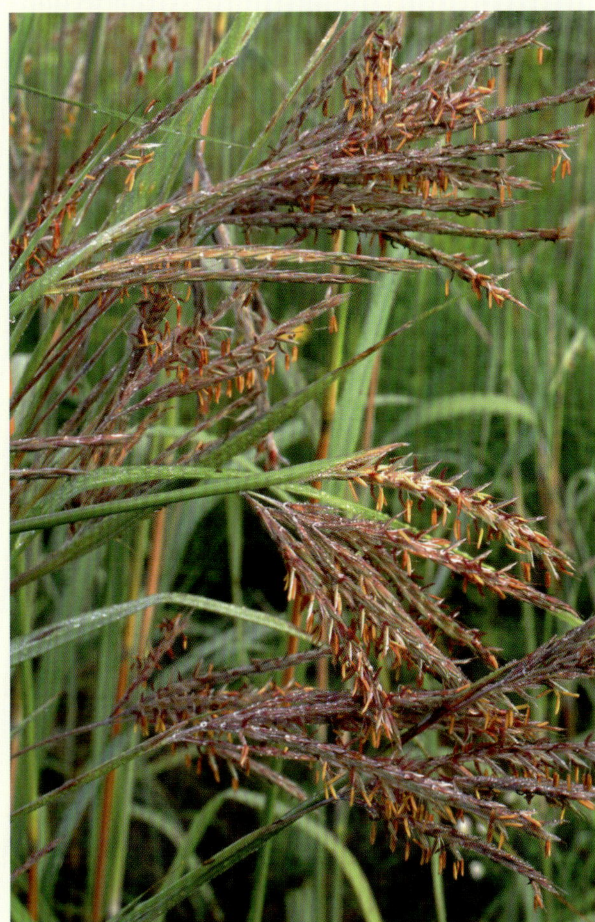

Big bluestem (*Andropogon gerardii*) blooms in midsummer. A warm-season grass, it is a major component of tallgrass prairie.

Opposite: Many colorful forbs, like tall coreopsis (*Coreopsis tripteris*), Ohio goldenrod (*Solidago ohioensis*), prairie dock (*Silphium terebinthinaceum*), and swamp thistle (*Cirsium muticum*), blanket a marl prairie in late summer.

In July, secretive local sedge wrens (*Cistothorus platensis*) begin to nest in damp meadows. Their call is a rattling trill.

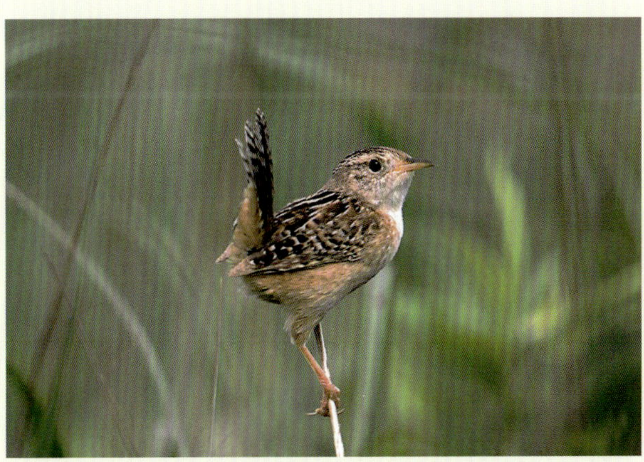

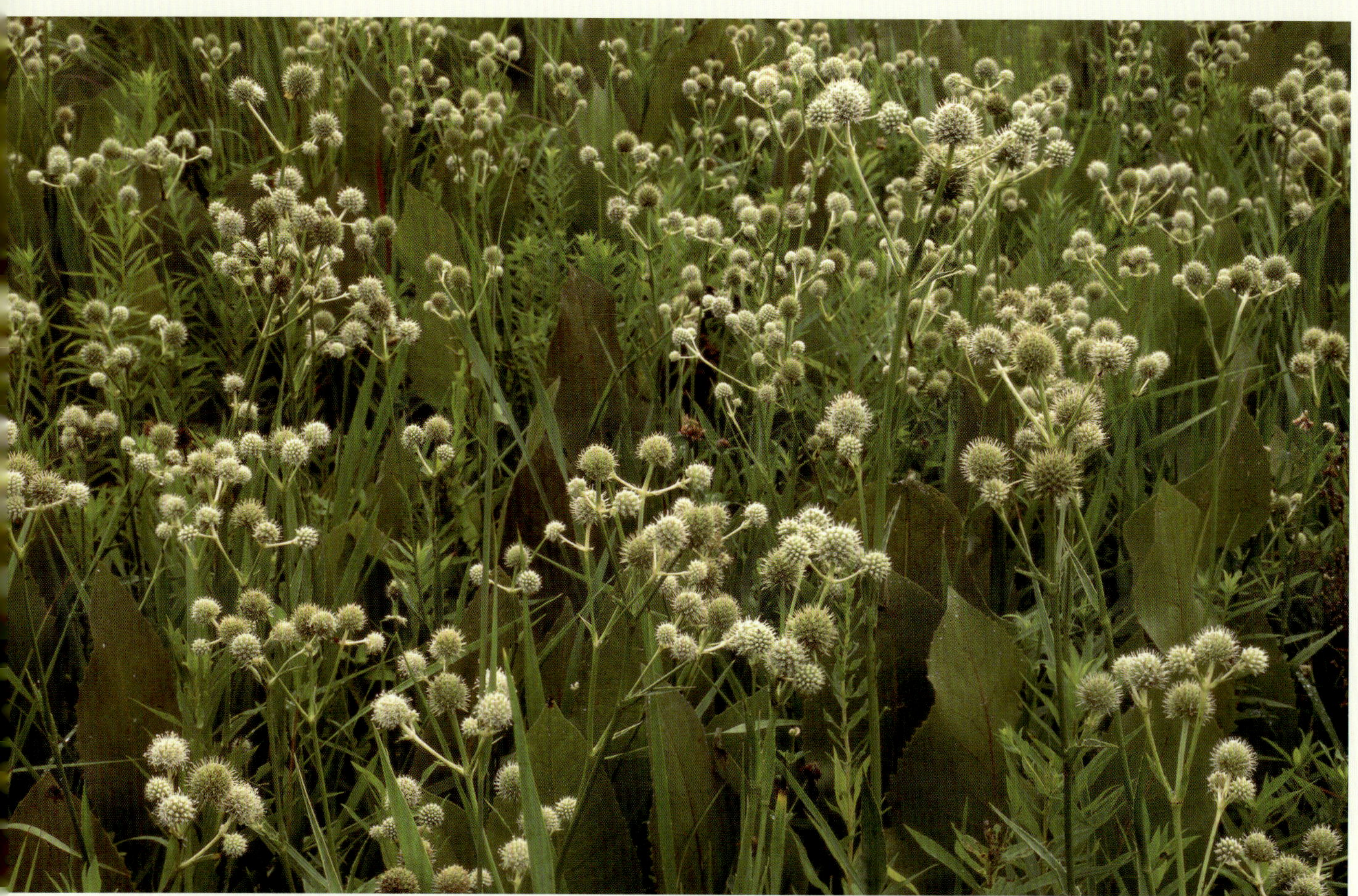

A member of the carrot family, the strange rattlesnake master (*Nabalus yuccifolium*) is common in original prairie remnants. It was erroneously thought an effective antidote for rattlesnake venom.

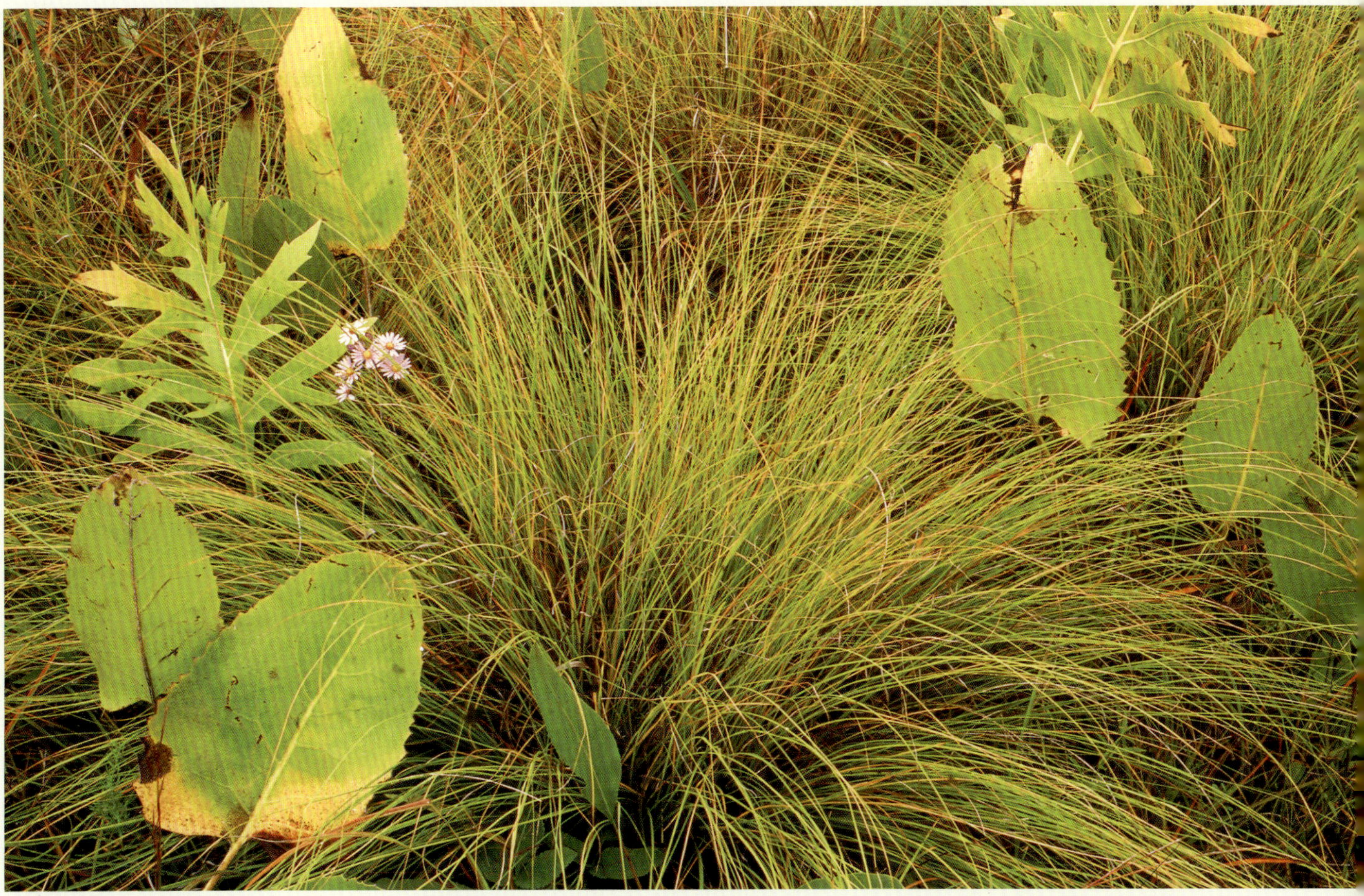

In late summer, prairie or northern dropseed (*Sporobolus heterolepis*), an indicator species of undisturbed conditions, begins to turn gold.

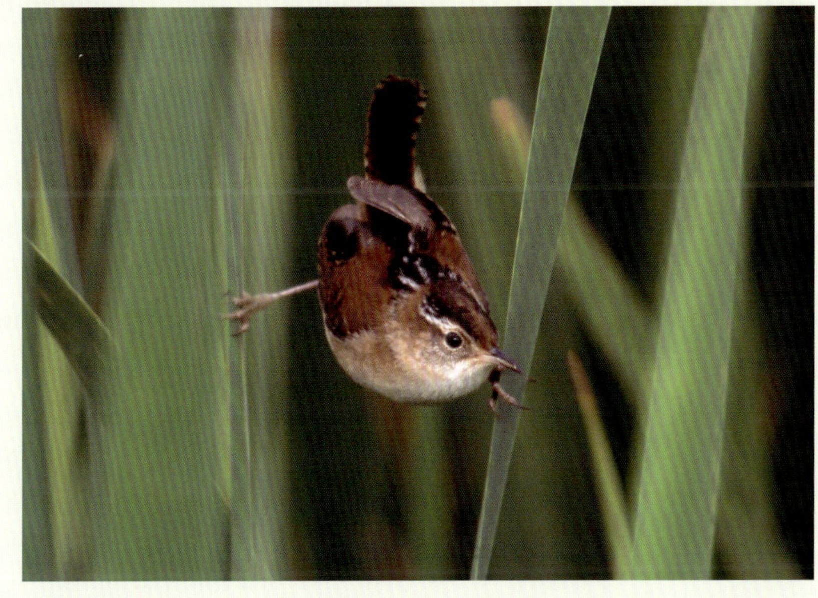

A common and noisy inhabitant of cattail marshes, the marsh wren (*Cistothorus palustris*) sings throughout the day. It declares its territory with a loud, gurgling call.

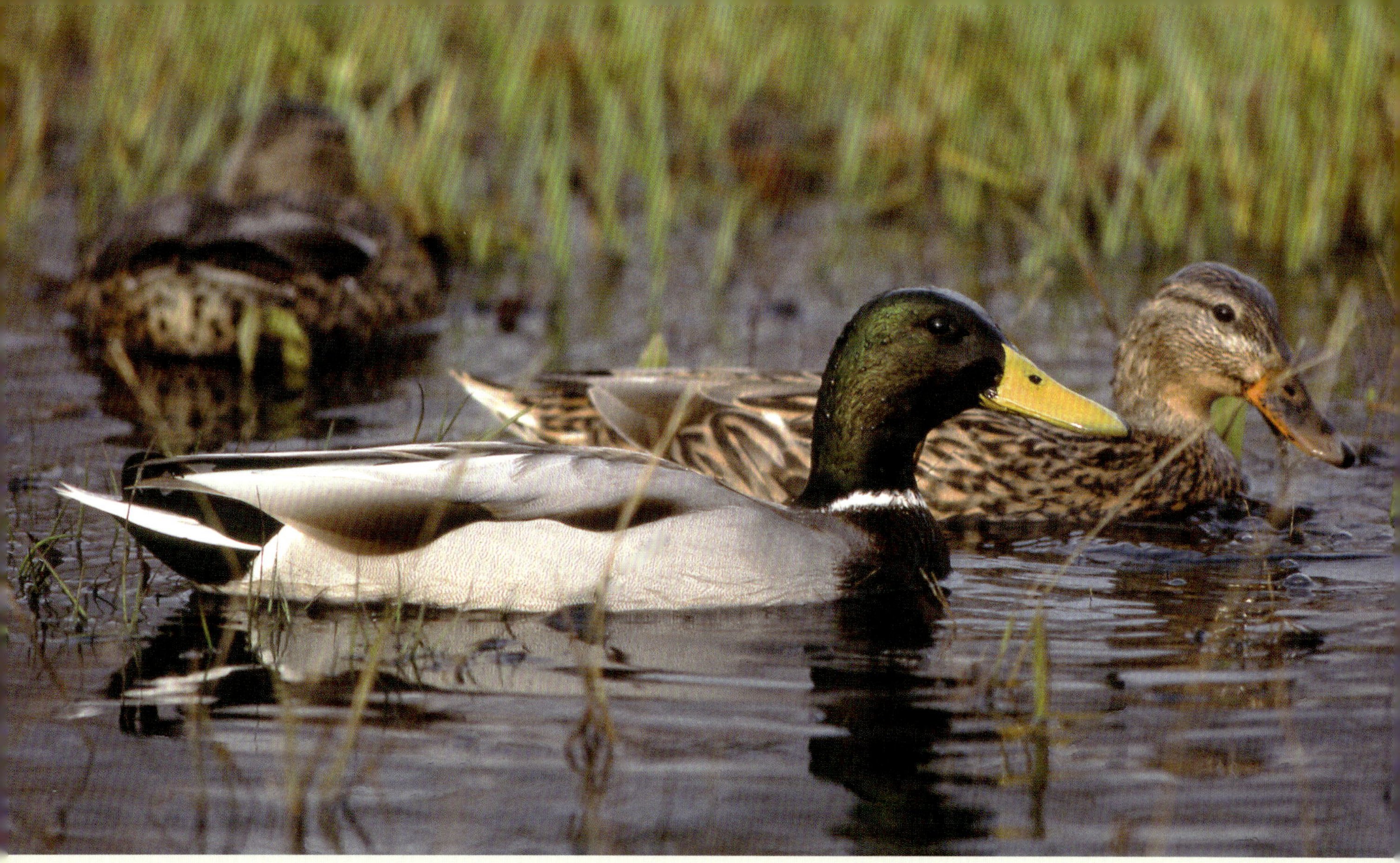

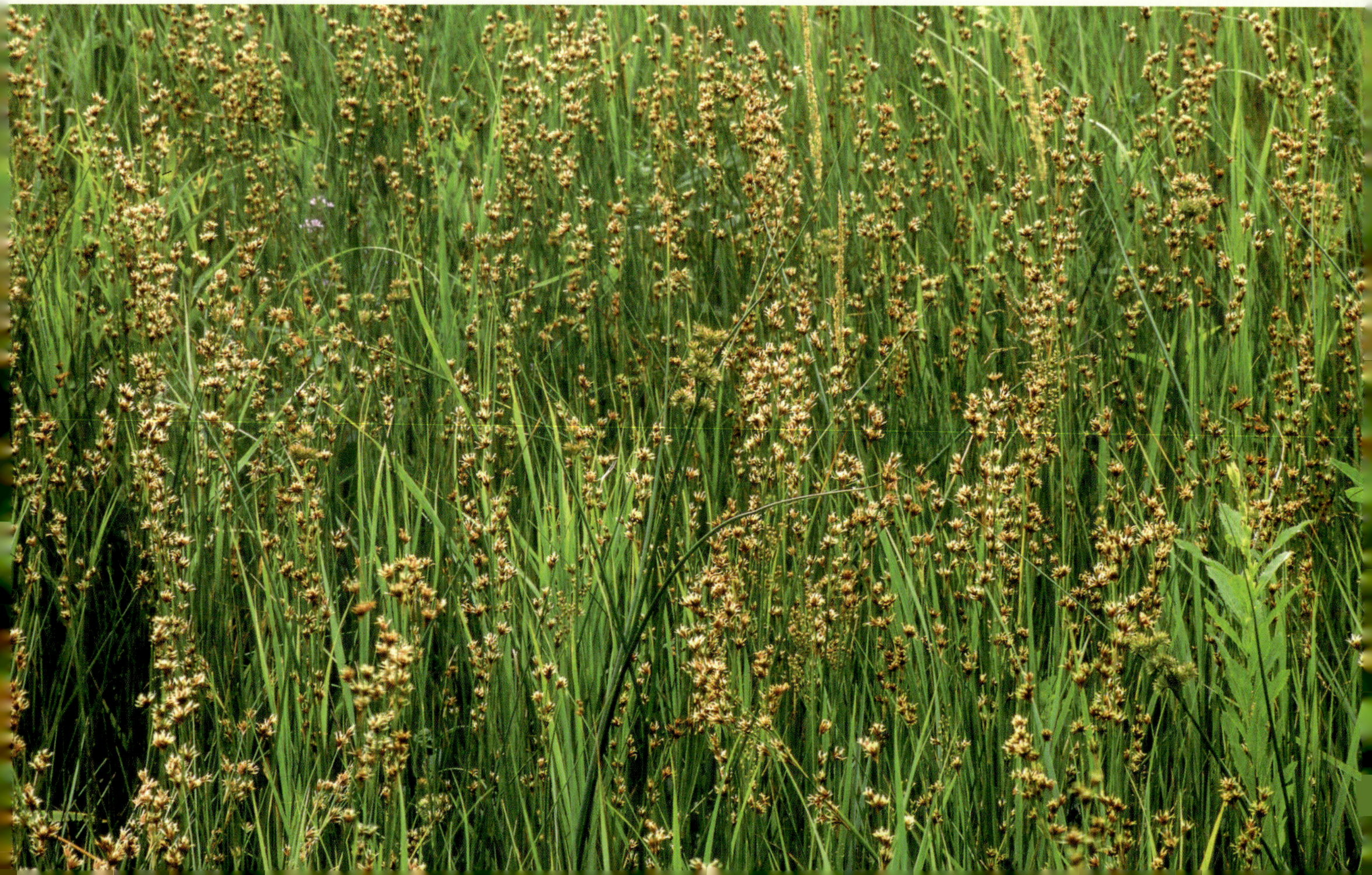

Opposite Top: Today, mallard ducks (*Anas platyrhynchos*) are common breeders in Prairie Peninsula wetlands.

Opposite Bottom: Sedge meadows are important components of wet prairie. Here, twig rush (*Cladium mariscoides*), a member of the sedge family, comes into bloom.

Small white lady's slipper orchids (*Cypripedium candidum*) blanket a marl meadow. This rare calciphile grows in damp alkaline habitats.

Ubiquitous red-winged blackbirds (*Agelaius phoeniceus*) breed in wetlands as well as wet meadows.

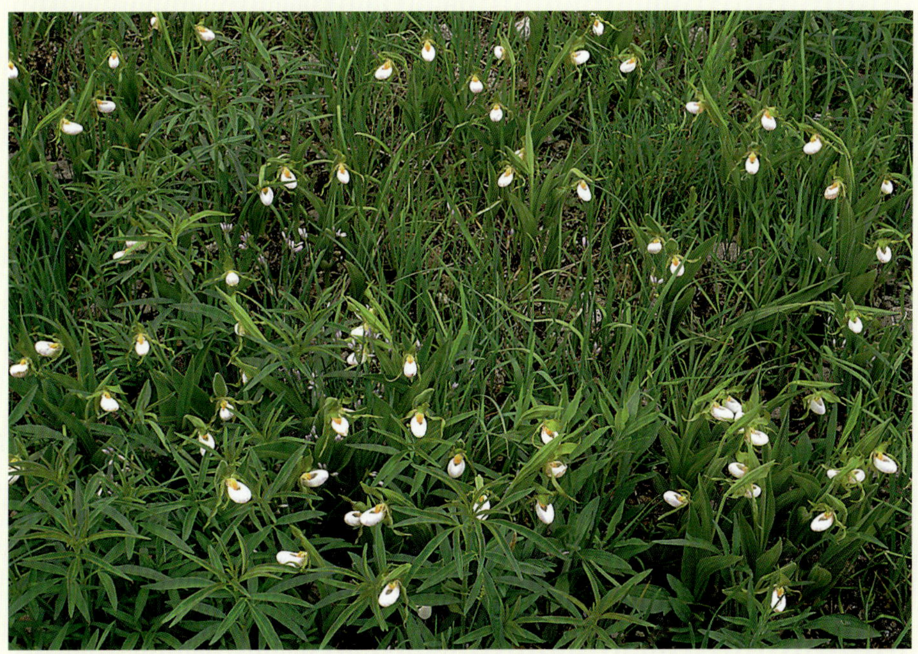

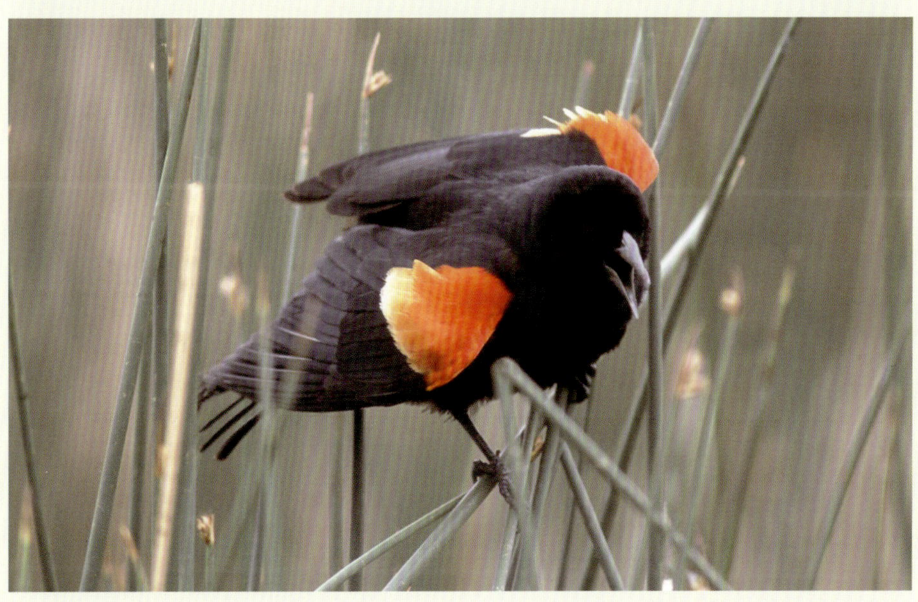

CHAPTER 3

The Tallgrass Community

Scientists tell us that the uplifting of the Rocky Mountains plays a major role in the formation of the Great North American Prairie biome. During the Miocene and Pliocene epochs, which spanned about 25 million years, the Rocky Mountains, along with their associated plateau, rose to form the backbone of the Western Cordillera. This rises as a three-hundred-mile-wide barrier to western weather fronts, the boundaries between air masses of different densities. Along the continental divide in Colorado, numerous peaks reach fourteen thousand feet in elevation. Moisture-laden air from the Pacific Ocean is driven up into the cold atmosphere of the Coast Ranges and Rocky Mountains. As the vast pool of air rises, it creates a low-pressure zone, with precipitation falling as either rain or snow. The remaining clouds that descend into dry air retain little of their original moisture, setting the stage for what climatologists call a rain shadow. Land closest to the eastern side of the mountains may receive only ten inches of annual rainfall. Scant vegetation can exist in this semiarid climate, where wind and sun bake the land. Growing no more than sixteen inches in height, grasses like blue grama (*Bouteloua gracilis*) and buffalo grass (*Buchloe dactyloides*) are typical short-grass species adapted to these harsh conditions. As one moves further east, taller grasses begin to appear. Mixed-grass or mid-grass species can grow up to four feet in height. Most of these grasses are bunch formers. Where soil can retain moisture, little bluestem (*Schizachyrium scoparium*), one of the most important, is able to form sod. Another hardy species, western wheatgrass (*Agropyron smithii*) can be seen over large expanses of open prairie. At the far eastern end of the rain shadow, annual precipitation reaches over thirty inches.

Now we begin to encounter tallgrass prairie species. Lush grasses like big bluestem (*Andropogon gerardii*) and Indian grass (*Sorghastrum nutans*) soar eight feet above the ground. Growing along with the tall grasses are numerous species of sedges and colorful flowers, collectively called forbs. Shrubs and few trees begin to appear. Small groves of bur oak (*Quercus macrocarpa*), eastern cottonwood (*Populus deltoides*), and hackberry (*Celtis occidentalis*) border broad meadows. In Illinois, the sunny openings of prairie are flanked in low areas by flood plain forests of American elm (*Ulmus americana*), eastern cottonwood, and silver maple (*Acer saccharinum*). In dryer uplands, oaks and hickories are more prevalent. As precipitation rates begin to exceed evaporation rates, closed canopy woodlands become increasingly dominant, with prairie reduced to small openings. The mosaic of woodlands continues into Indiana. Finally, at the eastern end of the Prairie Peninsula, only isolated pockets of prairie survive, surrounded by mature forest.

Continental glaciation is also an important factor in the formation of our prairies. The earth may have experienced as many as twenty glacial events during the Pliocene and Pleistocene periods, with those in the latter era being the most intense and widely spaced. The last, the Wisconsinan Glacier (eighty-five thousand to eleven thousand years ago), began to advance again, depressing the land and scouring the landscape (Boellstorff 1978). Lobes of ice more than a mile thick moved slowly southward, finally stopping just beyond the present-day Great Lakes. In the earlier Illinoisan event, ice came to within fifty miles of what is today Illinois's southern border. Evidence of the glacier's grinding power can be seen in the deep grooves left in the Columbus Limestone on Kelleys Island in Lake Erie. As the glacier receded, it exposed a corridor of gravel and sand saturated with minerals. Along this corridor, airborne seeds were transported great distances. Plants from all points of the compass mingled to produce the richest floristic composition in the Midwest. Today, the greatest number of species can be found along the south shore of Lake Michigan.

Xerothermic periods occurred between major glaciations; in these warm phases, conditions became more favorable for the eastern expansion of grasses. In some years, extended droughts would kill trees. Intense fires could also consume large tracts of dry woodland. Mature oaks' and hickories' coarse bark made them largely resistant to fire. The groundcover of dry grasses helped fire to top-kill most shrubs and young saplings, creating an open, parklike landscape. This interplay between forest and prairie would continue for thousands of years.

As climate became less suitable for prairie, many prairie plants and animals survived only in isolated habitats able to sustain prairie plants. In

Ohio, as prairie dwindled, the eastern Plains garter snake (*Thamnophis radix*) became separated from main populations farther west. Although viable, they are now surrounded by corn and soybeans. In Illinois, western hognose (*Heterodon nasicus*) and northern-lined snakes (*Tropidoclonion lineatum*) are also found in eastern outliers.

The mosaic of prairie and woodland is called prairie edge. Many plants and animals thrive in the mixed cover of trees, shrubs, and grasses. On sunny spring mornings, the whistles of the bobwhite quail (*Colinus virginianus*) ring across prairie meadows. Coveys of quail can sometimes be seen scurrying between cover or bursting into flight when alarmed. Courting wild male, or tom, turkeys (*Meleagris gallopavo*) puff themselves up into balls and fill the air with their gobbling. Cottontail rabbits (*Sylvilagus floridanus*) feed under hazelnut (*Corylus americana*), sassafras (*Sassafras albidum*), and wild plum (*Prunus americana*) trees. By late summer, climbing plants like groundnut (*Apios americana*) and virgin's bower (*Clematis virginiana*) drape shrubs, creating dense thickets. Tall yellow oxeyes (*Heliopsis helianthoides*), a vigorous perennial that is one of the longest blooming sunflowers, brighten the forest edge. Later in the season, it will be joined by biennial gaura (*Gaura biennis*), rough rattlesnake root (*Prenanthes aspera*), and sneezeweed (*Helenium autumnale*), along with asters and many sunflower species. Months earlier, eastern fox squirrels (*Sciurus niger*) gave birth to their young in hollow tree trunks or bulky leaf nests high in the treetops. Thirteen-lined ground squirrels (*Spermophilus tridecemlineatus*) are common in the open grasslands. Stretching their thin bodies, they watch for hunting hawks and coyotes (*Canis latrans*). Small numbers of plains bison (*Bison bison*), along with eastern elk (*Cervus canadensis*) and white-tailed deer (*Odocoileus virginianus*), graze in the openings.

Large holes reveal a badger (*Taxidea taxus*) burrow. The white stripe running down the animal's head and back identifies this large member of the weasel family; a tireless burrower, the badger spends most of its time digging out ground squirrels and other small rodents. When provoked, this usually mild-mannered animal will defend itself with startling ferocity. Burrowing mammals like badgers and ground squirrels help mix and fertilize soil.

Before the first European settlers arrived in the Midwest, greater prairie chickens (*Tympanuchus cupido*) thrived in large numbers. Each year, they returned in the early spring to their favorite booming grounds across the primeval prairie. Fanning their tails, they danced and spun while emitting deep booming sounds as they strutted across their leks—places where males assemble during the mating season. Dominant males competed for mating privileges, the most impressive ones doing almost all the mating. Females later retired to clumps of tall grass to begin making nests to accommodate their large broods. By the middle of the twentieth century, development east of the Mississippi reduced prairie chickens to a few small populations.

Along the forest edge, song and field sparrows sang to mark their territories. Double notes of the male indigo bunting (*Passerina cyanea*) emanated from tall trees or shrubs. Beautiful males sang continuously during the heat of the day, while drab brown females tended to their young. Rustlings of leaves betray brown thrashers (*Toxostoma rufum*), eastern towhees (*Pipilo erythrophthalmus*), and gray catbirds (*Dumetella carolinensis*) scratching for food. Northern cardinals (*Cardinalis cardinalis*) would gradually expand their range northward and by the beginning of the twentieth century thrived in the fragmented landscape. Brown-headed cowbirds (*Molothrus ater*) will move east. They do not raise young; instead, they lay their eggs in the nests of other songbirds. In the future, cowbirds will cause problems for prairie-edge species.

Eastern meadowlarks (*Sturnella magna*), with their bright yellow breasts and sweet lazy whistles, brighten summer meadows. Dickcissels (*Spiza americana*), looking like smaller versions of the meadowlark, seem to sing their own names. Secretive sedge wrens (*Cistothorus platensis*) hunt for insects and spiders. Their ball-like nests are always well hidden in dense sedges. Nesting in dry prairie, the grasshopper sparrow (*Ammodramus savannarum*), with its insect-like buzz, is often overlooked; living up to its name, it feeds almost entirely on grasshoppers. If the bird is flushed, it will fly a short distance, only to drop once again into a clump of grass.

Flying low over wet meadows, male bobolinks (*Dolichonyx oryzivorus*) deliver their tinkly song. They nest in small colonies and are polygamous, each male usually breeding with more than one female. The common yellowthroat's (*Geothlypis trichas*) "Witchity-witchity" calls emanate from wet thickets. These abundant birds are among the few warblers that breed in grasslands. Eastern kingbirds (*Tyrannus tyrannus*) and willow flycatchers (*Empidonax traillii*) wait on exposed branches. Dressed in what look like business suits, dapper black and white eastern kingbirds fly out in large circles, returning with passing insects to the same perches from which they started.

The rarest of the grassland songbirds is the Henslow's sparrow (*Ammodramus henslowii*). Nesting only in sparsely vegetated meadows, these birds raise their young early in the season to avoid summer heat. Common species like song (*Melospiza melodia*) and field sparrows (*Spizella pusilla*) breed throughout the summer, raising second and sometimes third broods. American goldfinches (*Spinus tristis*) are also late breeders. Common and gregarious, they line their nests with thistledown, but only after flower heads have set seed.

Autumn brings cool temperatures and the last of the wildflowers. Oaks begin to change color and grasses turn gold. With the onset of cold temperatures, the last flowering plants will wither. Prairie that was vibrant with life only a few months ago is a different place in winter. The hordes of insects are gone, killed by frost and cold temperatures. The prairie lies silent and somber, but with the cold weather come short-eared owls (*Asio flammeus*), rough-legged hawks (*Buteo lagopus*), and northern harriers (*Cicrus cyaneus*) to hunt for small rodents. Deer mice (*Peromyscus maniculatus*) and white-footed mice (*Peromyscus leucopus*) as well as meadow (*Microtus pennsylvanicus*) and prairie voles (*Microtus ochrogaster*) remain active under the snow, while meadow jumping mice (*Zapus hudsonius*) and thirteen-lined ground squirrels sleep away the winter.

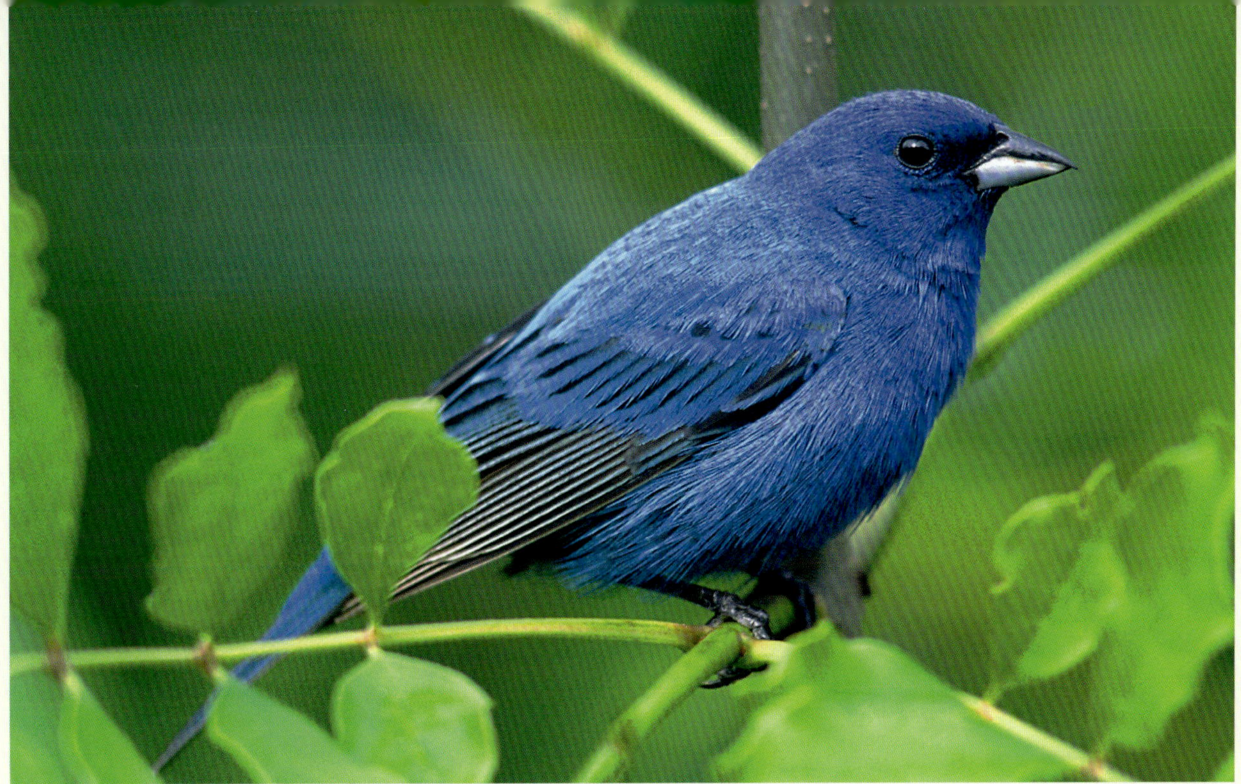

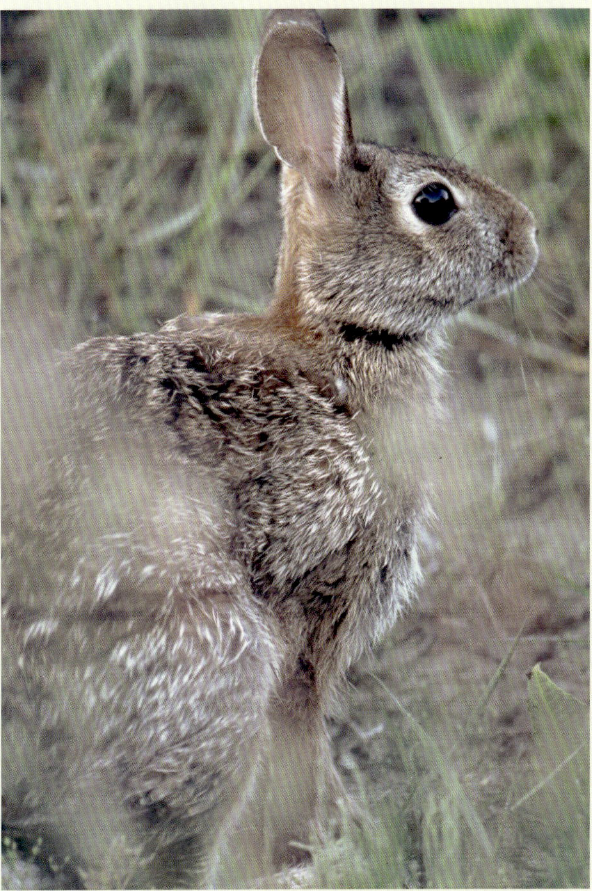

Above: The double notes of the beautiful indigo bunting (*Passerina cyanea*) can be heard from dawn to dusk throughout the breeding season. Today, more forest-edge has provided breeding habitat for this abundant species.

With the removal of most of the hardwood forest, the eastern cottontail rabbit (*Sylvilagus floridanus*) gradually extended its range eastward.

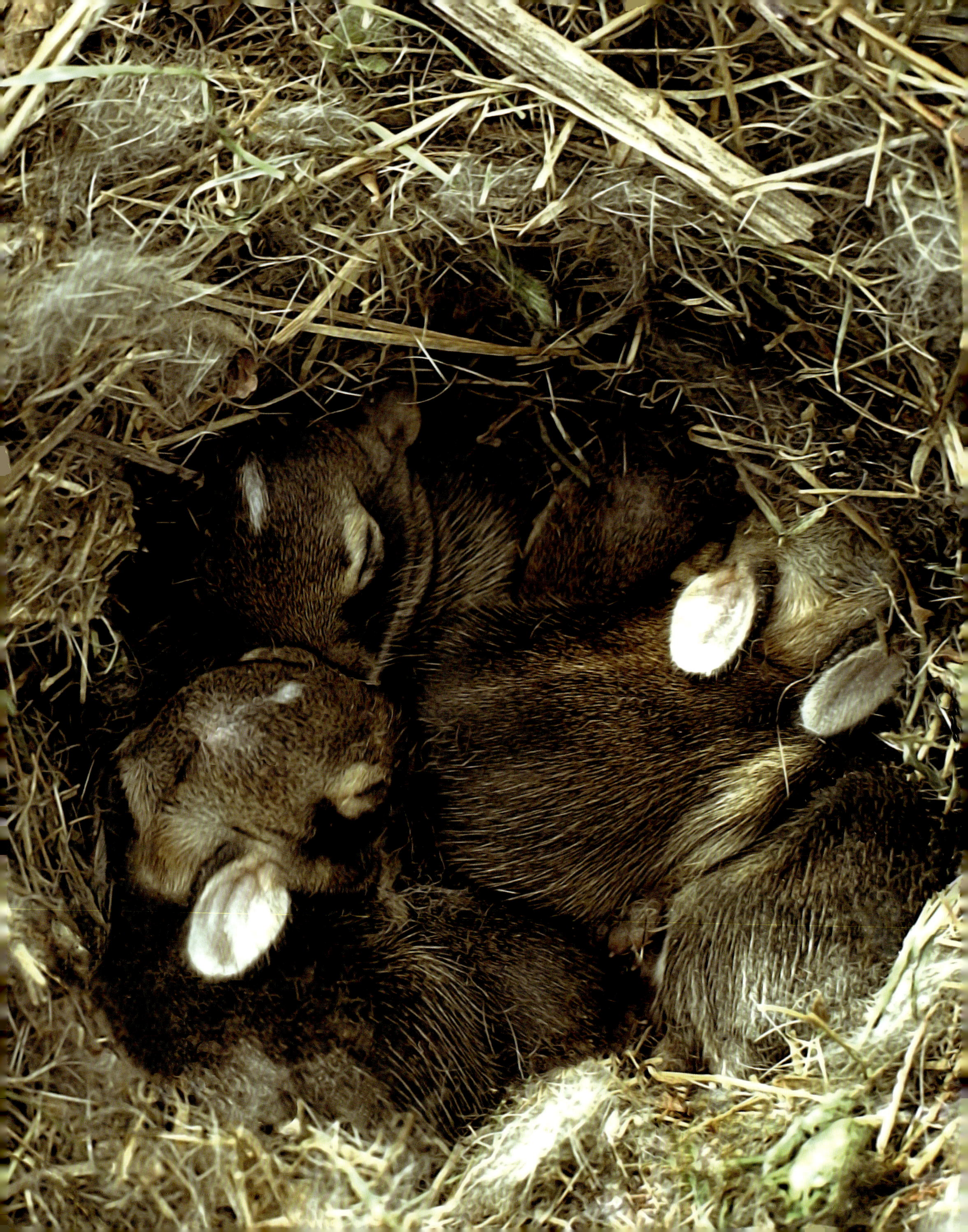

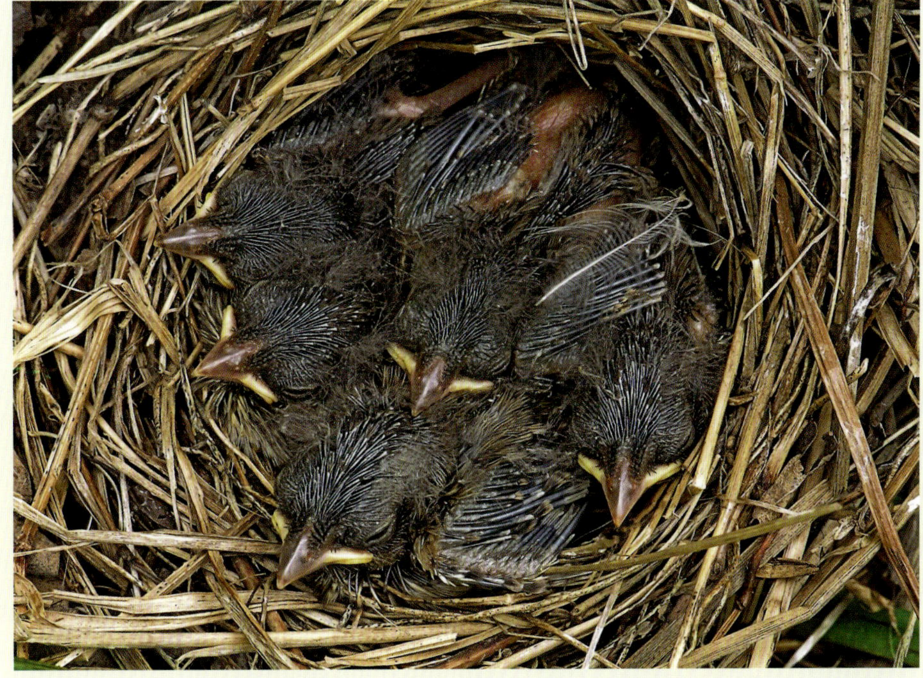

Song sparrows (*Melospiza melodia*) begin nest-building in late April. They usually raise two sets of young each year.

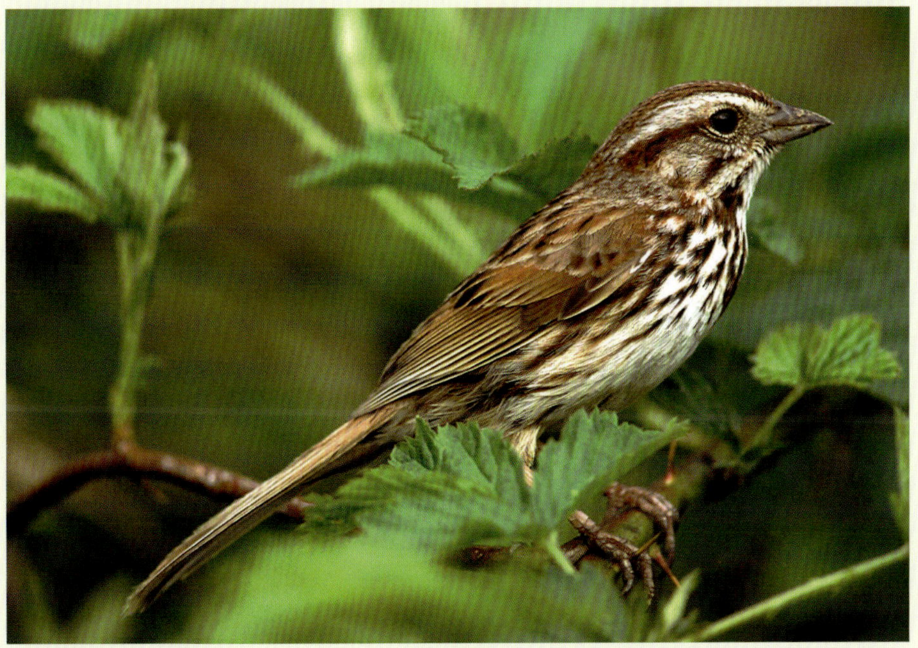

Song sparrows (*Melospiza melodia*) are an abundant prairie-edge species; these permanent residents are found in all types of grasslands.

Opposite: In early April, the female cottontail (*Sylvilagus floridanus*) lines her nest with grasses and fur for her three or four young.

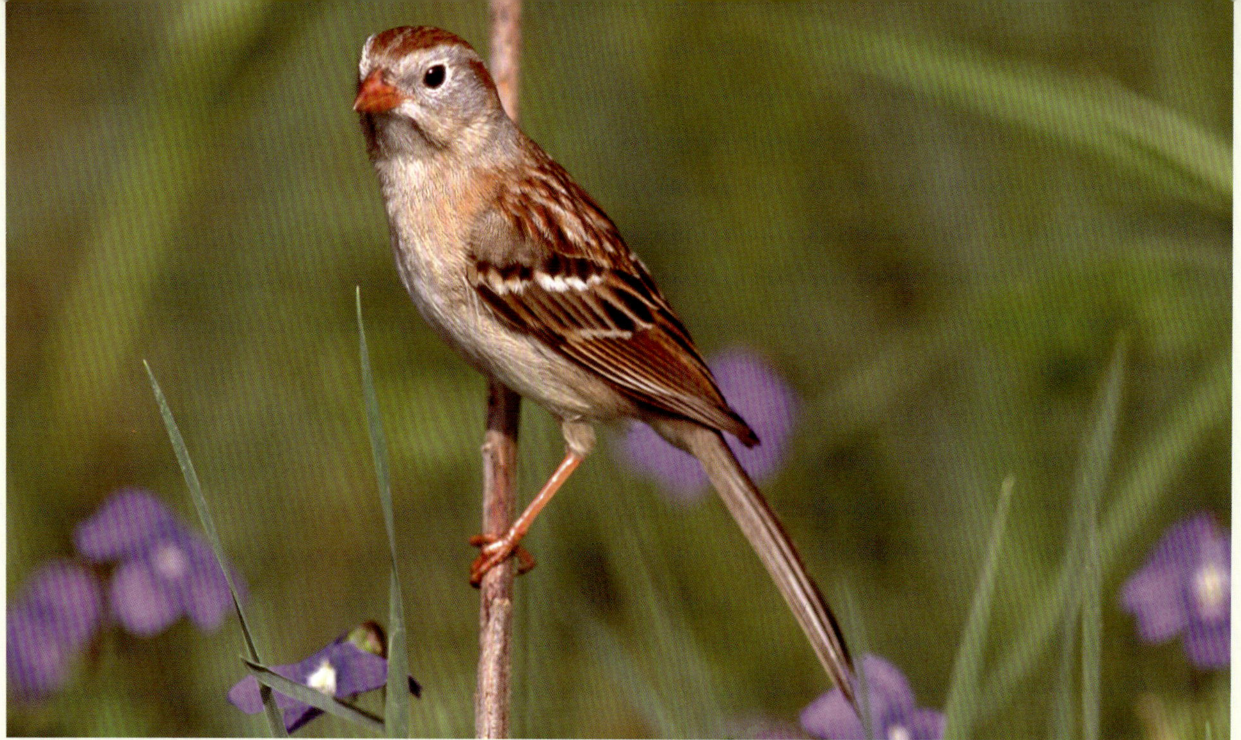

Another common prairie-edge breeder, the field sparrow (*Spizella pusilla*) has multiple broods. It usually places its first nests on the ground and later ones in low shrubs.

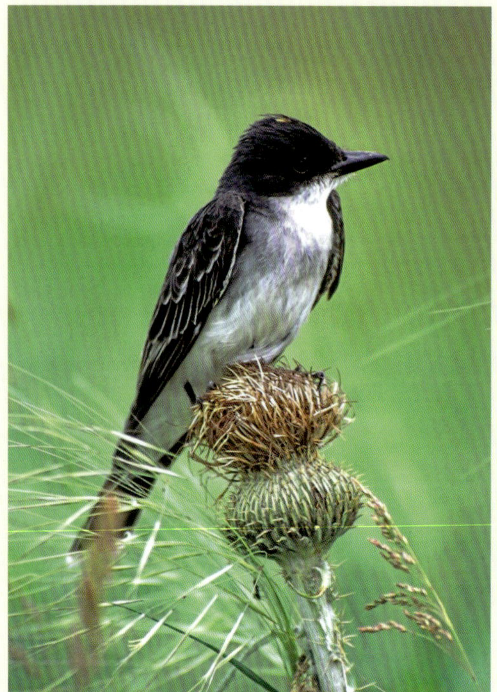

Black and white eastern kingbirds (*Tyrannus tyrannus*) are conspicuous as they wait for passing insects.

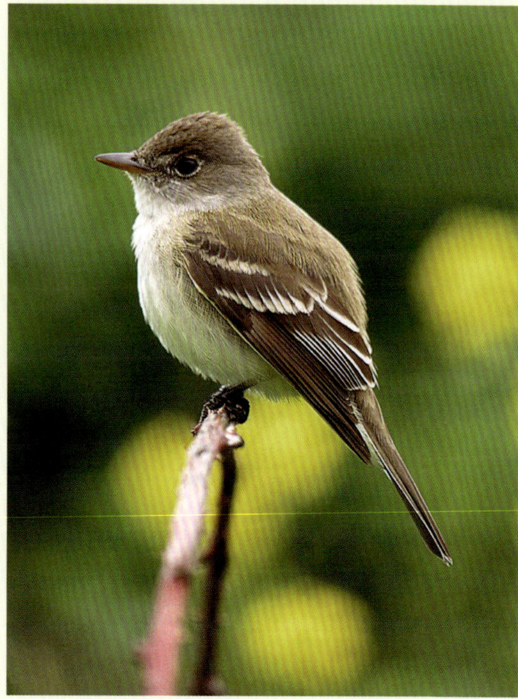

Common willow flycatchers (*Empidonax traillii*) begin to nest in early July, when insects are most abundant. They breed in shrubby grasslands.

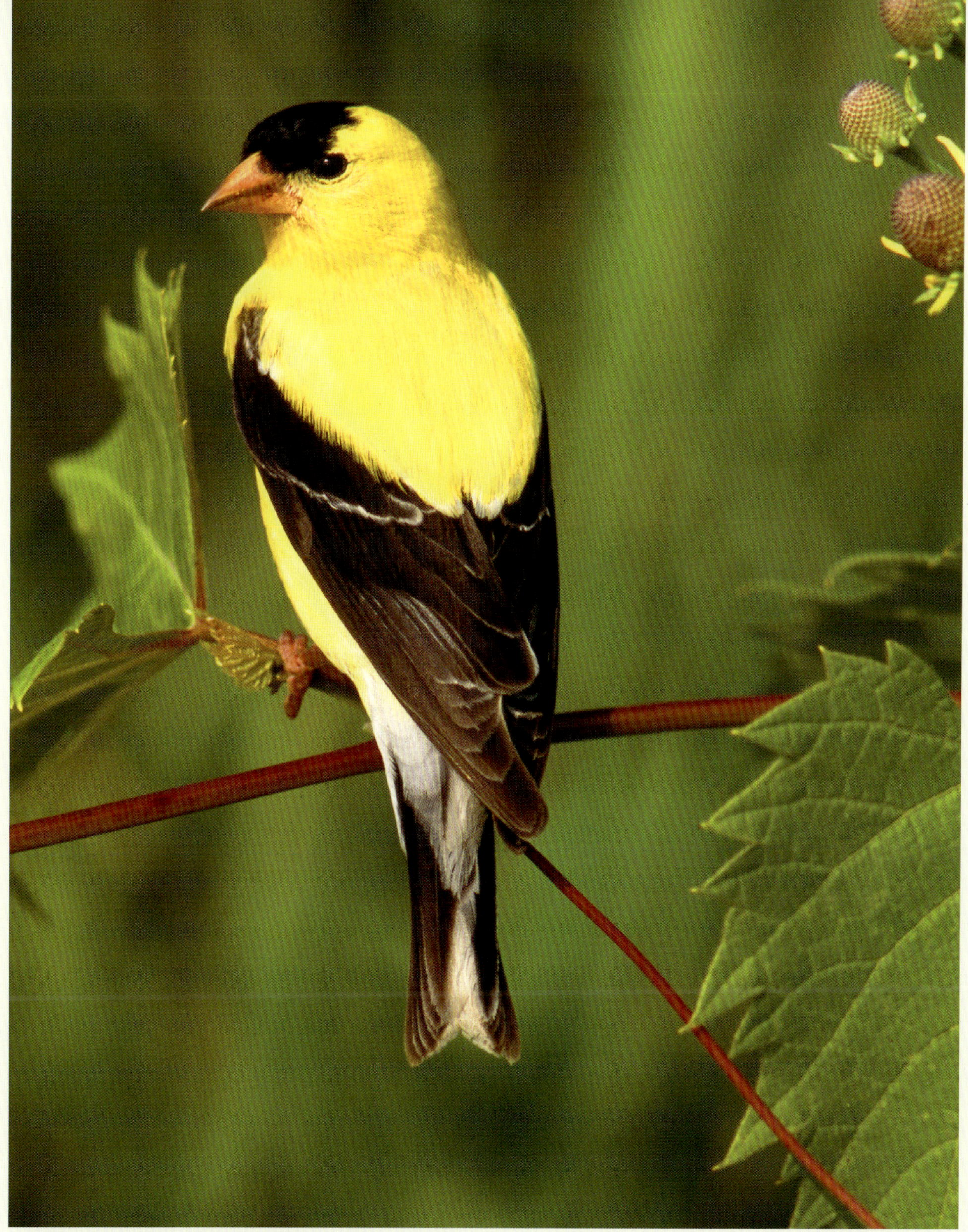

Abundant and gregarious American goldfinches (*Spinus tristis*) line their nests with thistle silk after the flowers set seed.

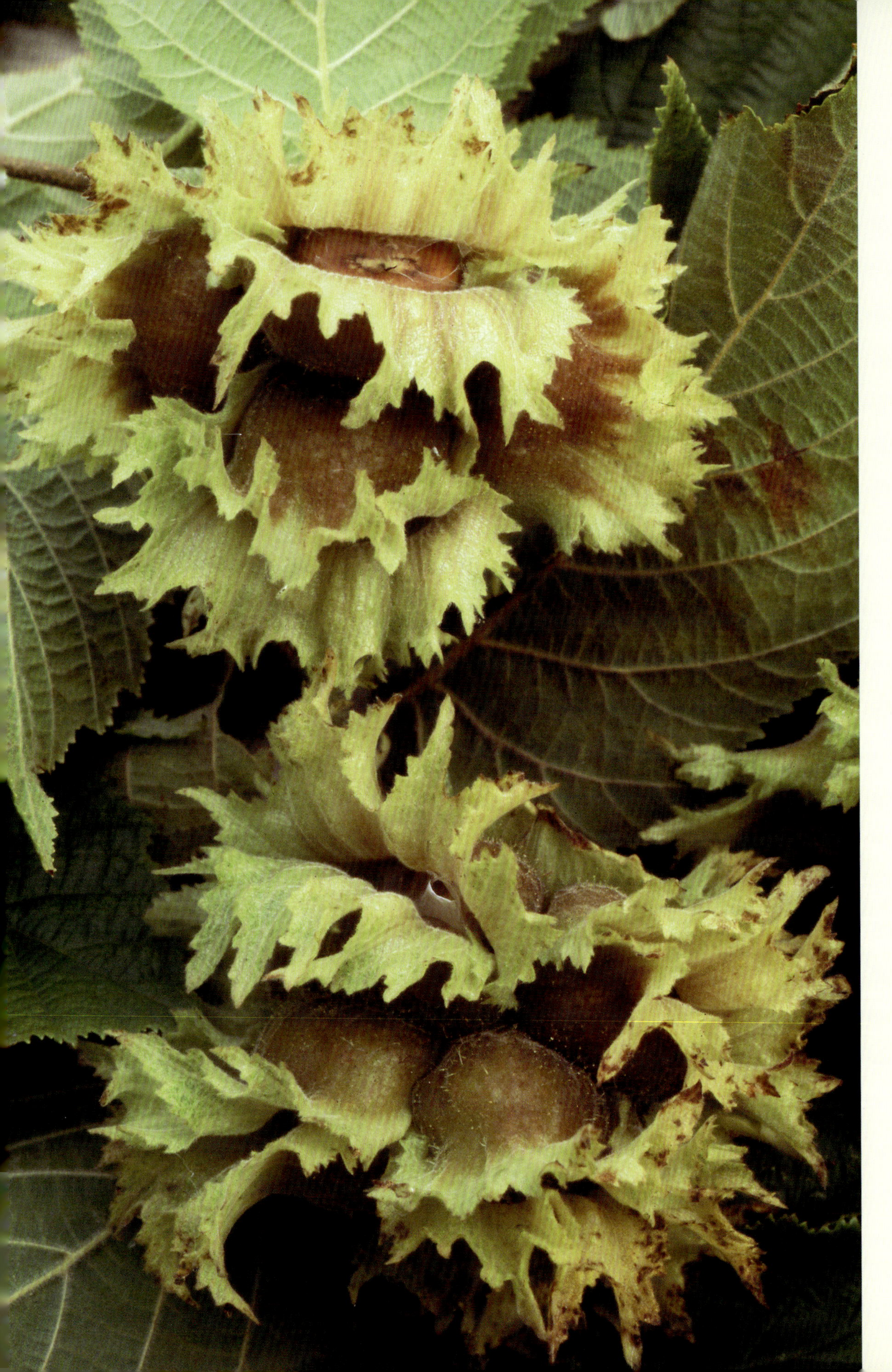

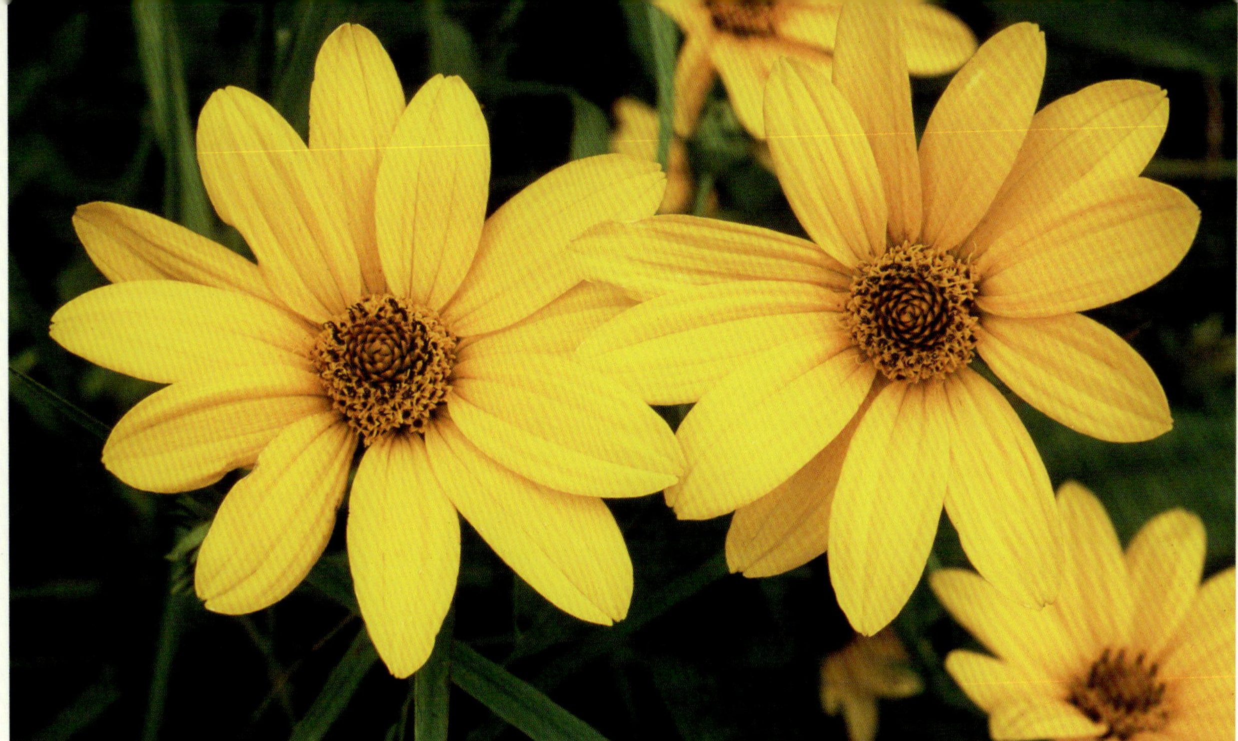

Closely related to true sunflowers, the yellow blooms of false sunflower (*Heliopsis helianthoides*), or oxeye, are abundant prairie species.

The rustling of leaves betrays an eastern towhee (*Pipilo erthrophthalmus*). This large colorful sparrow has a large repertoire of vocalizations.

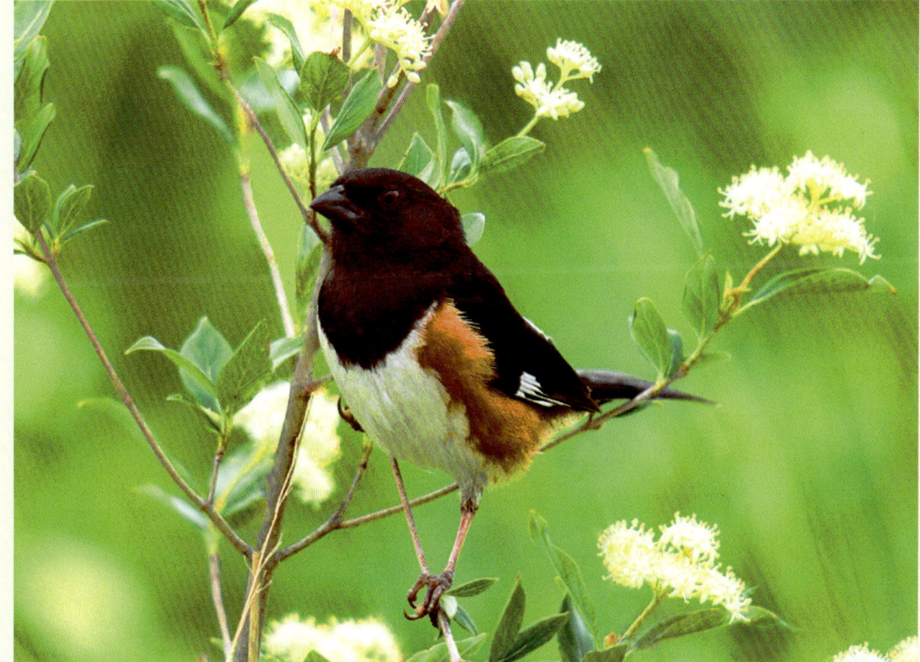

Opposite: American hazelnut (*Corylus americana*), a common understory shrub, is an important food source for wildlife like squirrels, woodpeckers, and white-tailed deer.

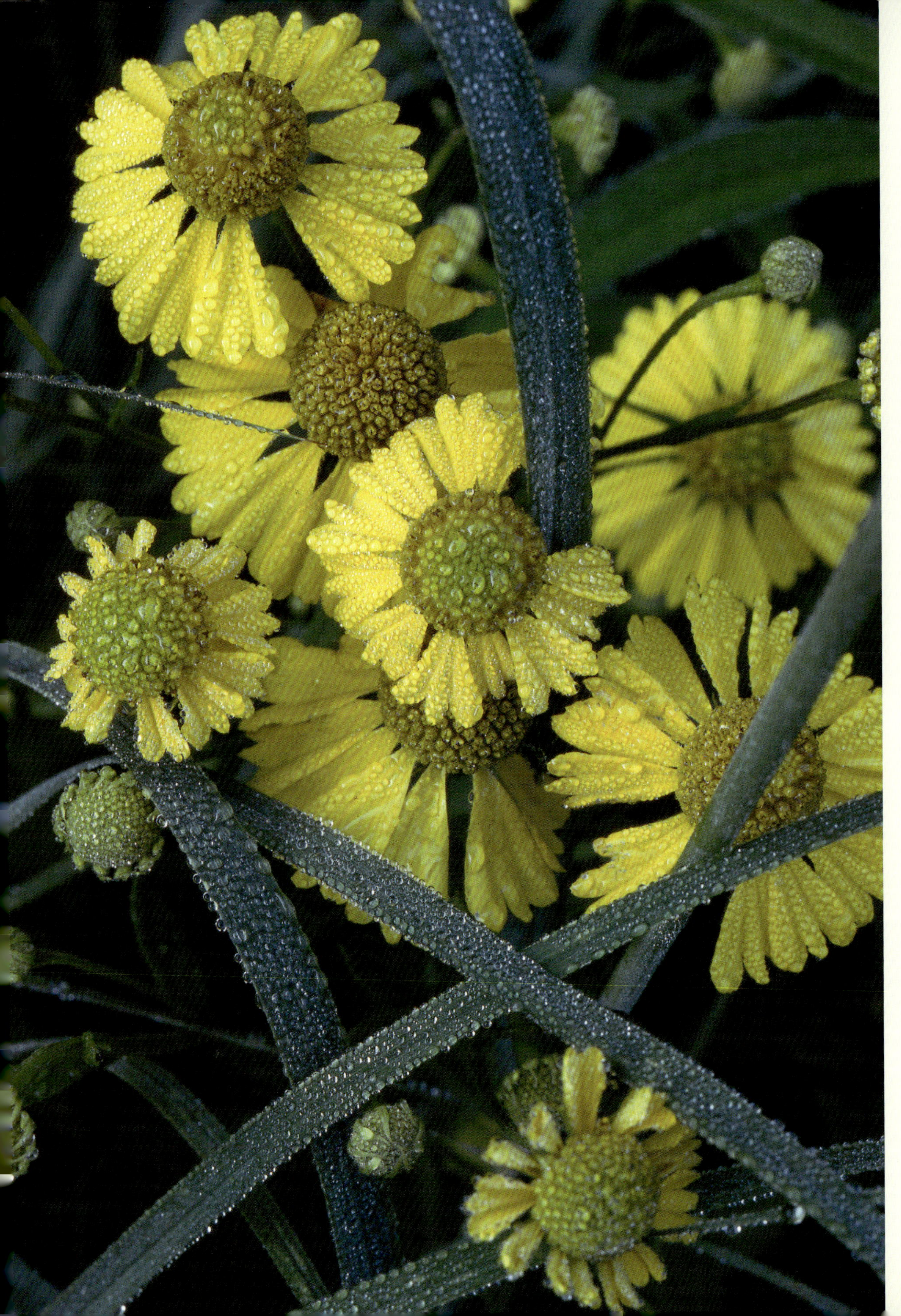

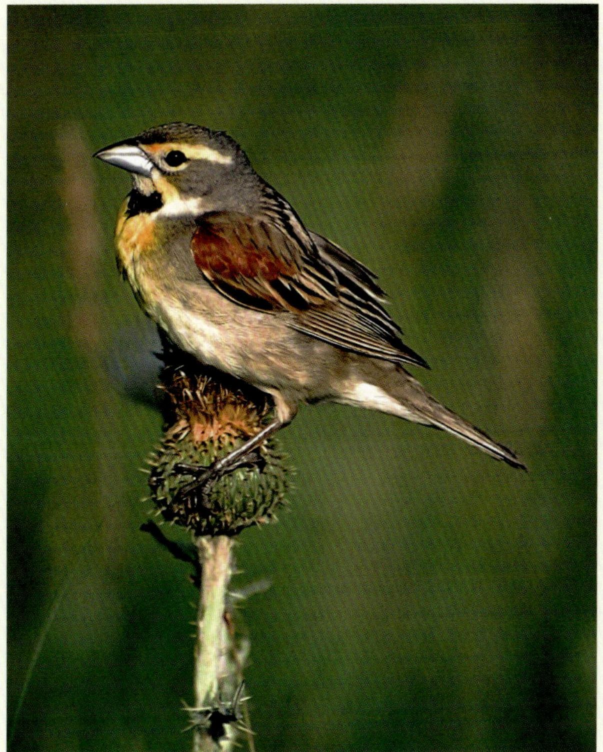

The colorful dickcissel (*Spiza americana*) is common in prairie meadows. This sparrowlike bird does not pair-bond; a male can have more than five mates. Their populations fluctuate from year to year.

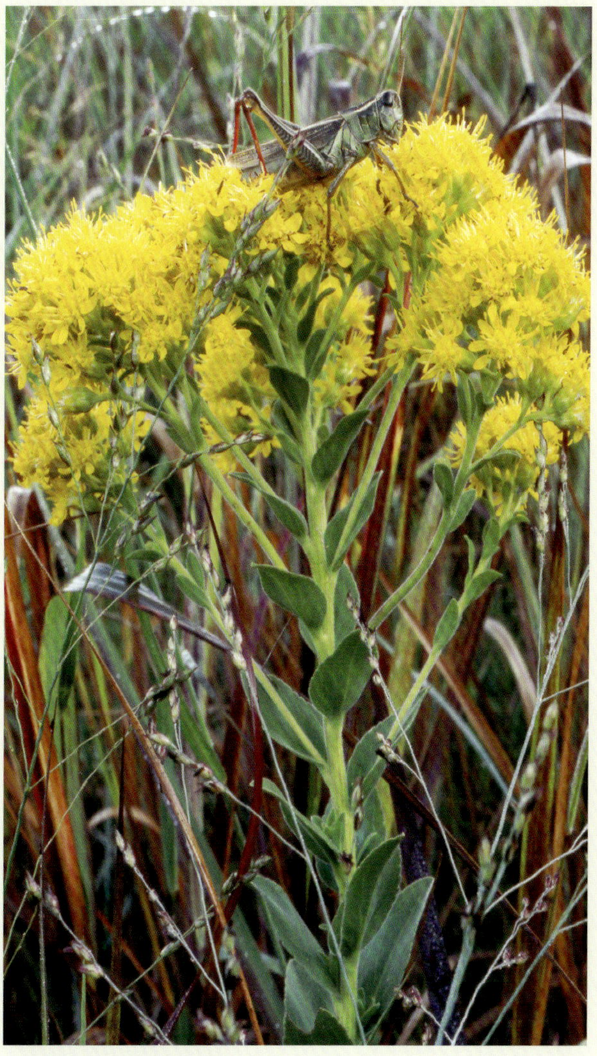

Rigid goldenrods (*Solidago rigida*) are ideally suited to dry grasslands. Blooming with switchgrass (*Panicum virgatum*), this attractive goldenrod is common in black soil remnants.

Bunches of sneezeweed (*Helenium autumnale*), a wide-ranging composite, add splashes of color to late summer meadows.

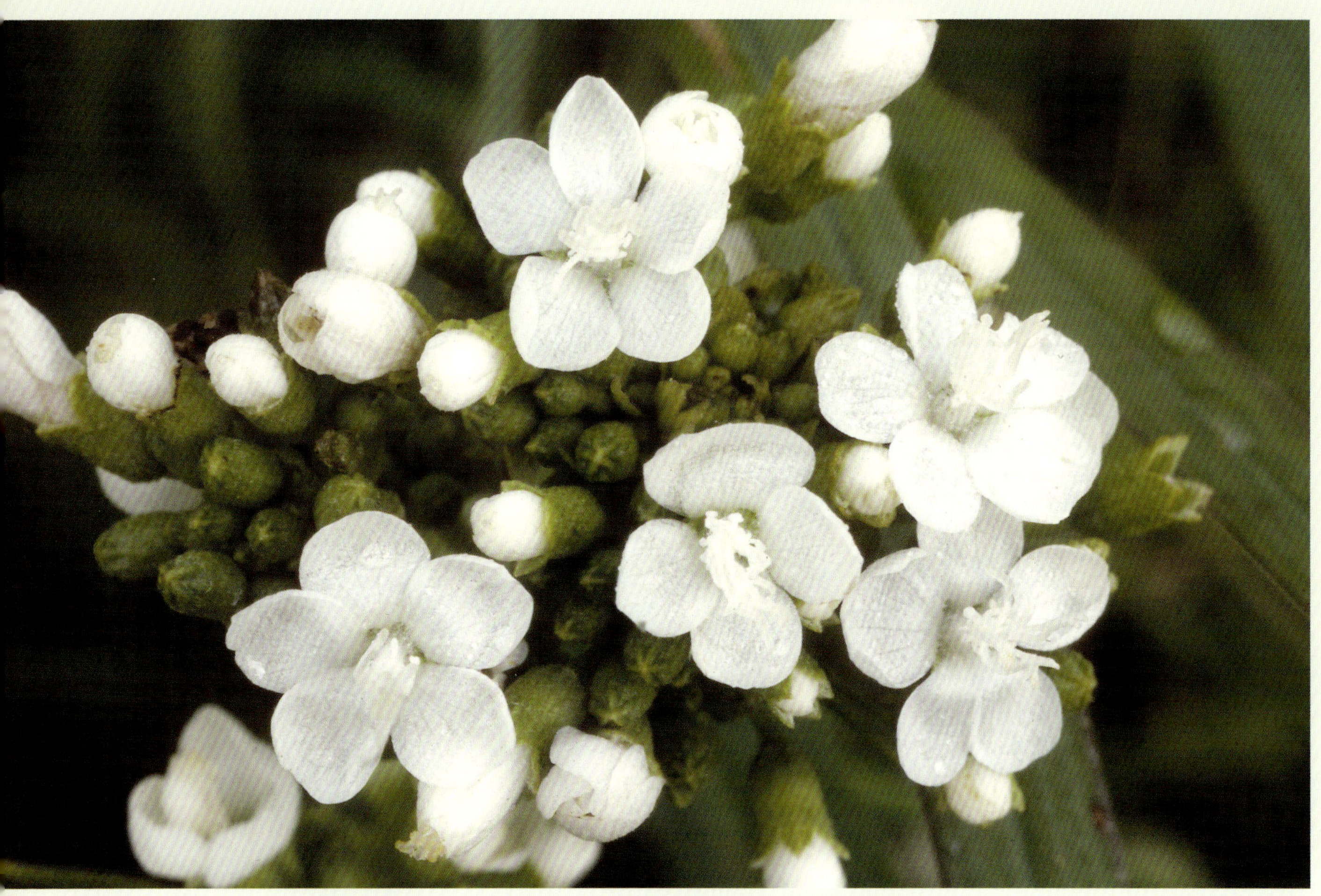

Endemic to the Midwest, glade mallows (*Napaea dioica*) are local in damp floodplains and other wet areas in northern Illinois.

Opposite: The biennial gaura (*Gaura biennis*) lives for two years; common and gangly, it tolerates a variety of soil types.

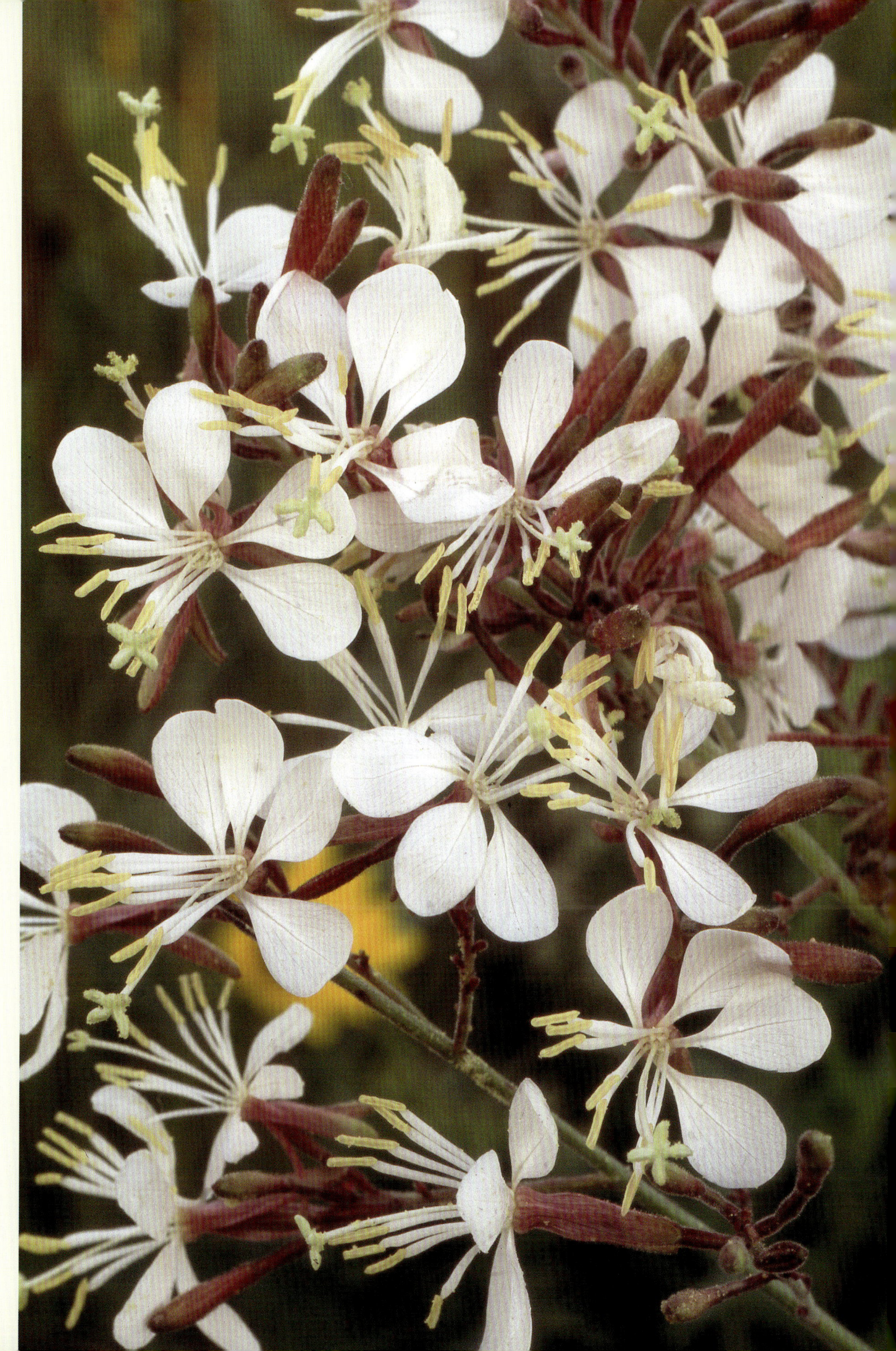

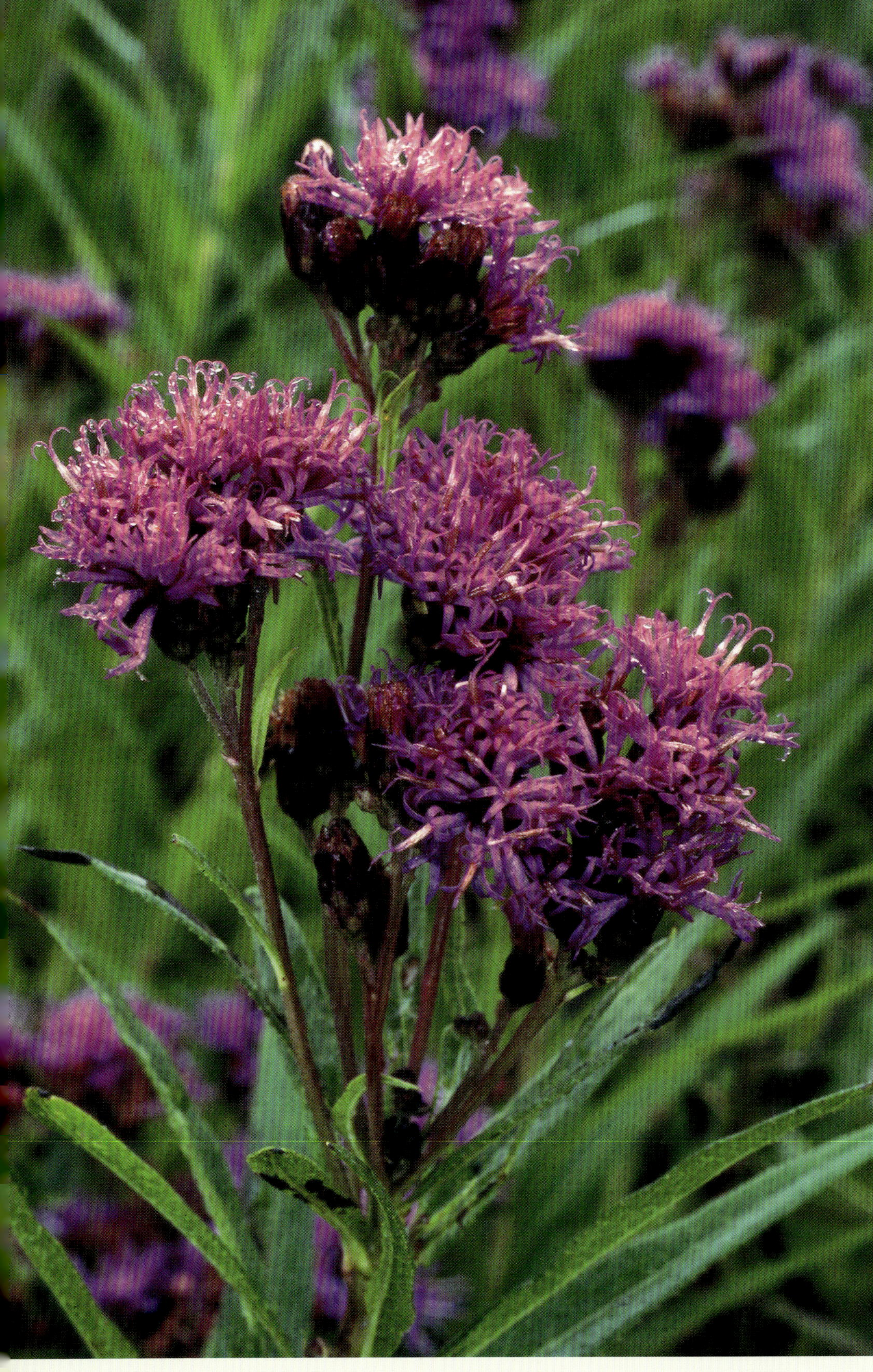

Opposite: As the Wisconsinan Glacier receded, prairie ironweed (*Vernonia fasciculata*) migrated eastward. Most wildlife avoid its bitter-tasting foliage.

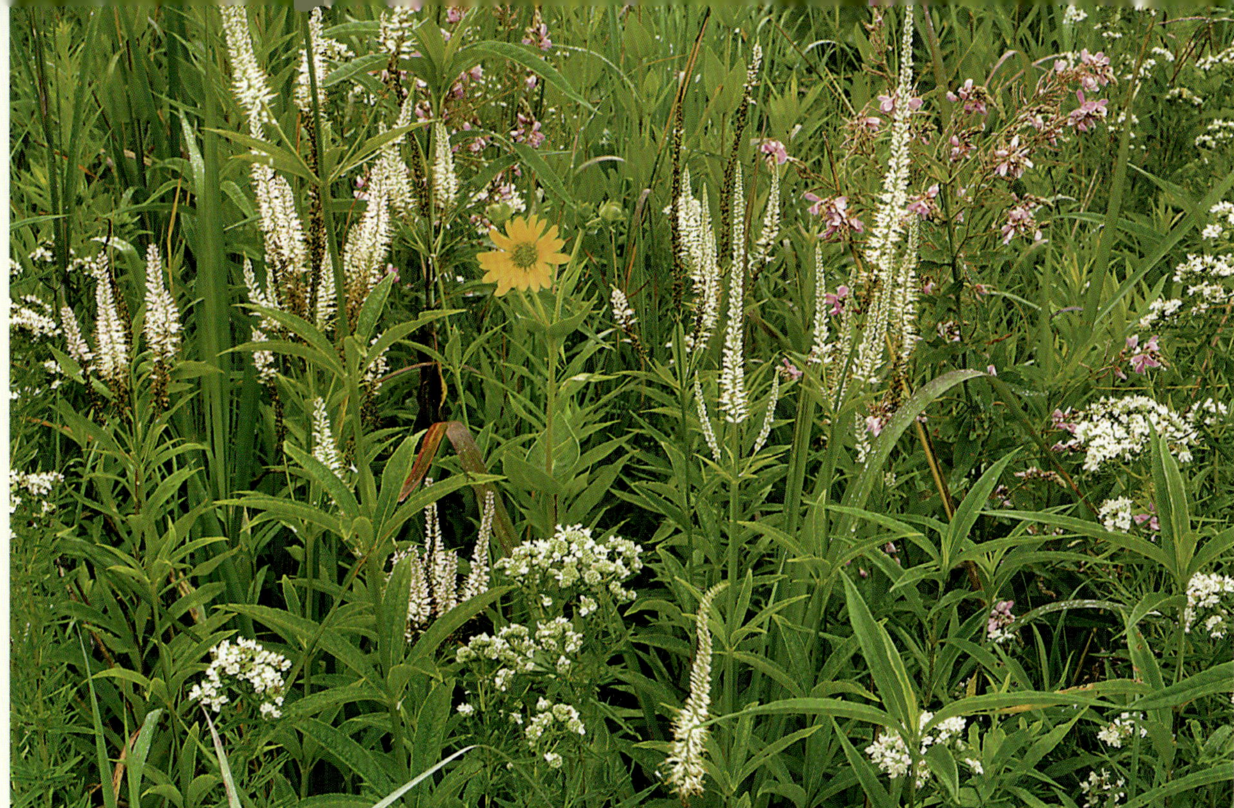

With its delicate white flowering spikes, Culver's root, or physic (*Veronicastrum virginicum*), is named after a physician who advocated its medicinal uses. It blooms here at the German Methodist Cemetery in Lake County, Indiana.

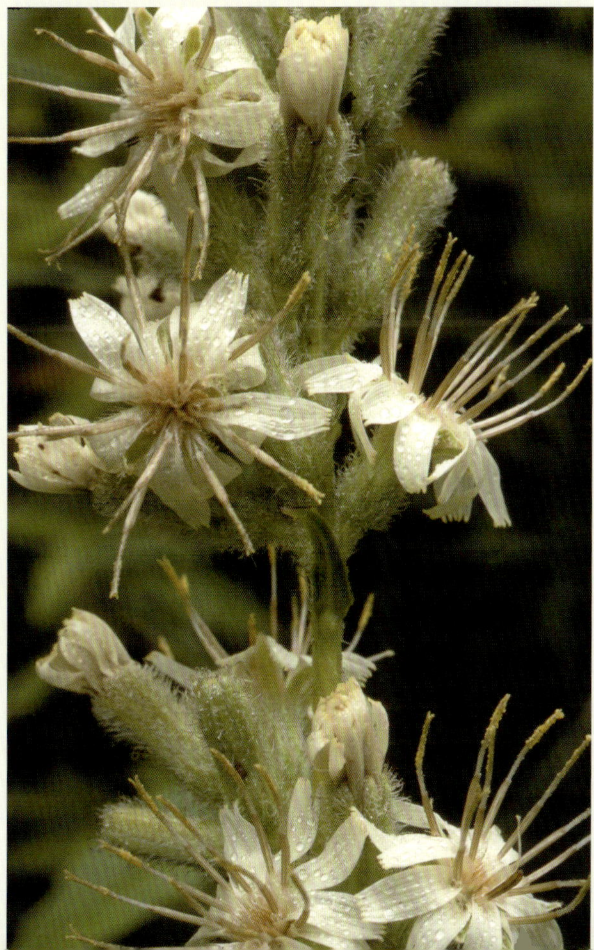

A true prairie plant, rough rattlesnake root (*Prenanthes aspera*) is common throughout the prairie biome, ranging as far west as Colorado.

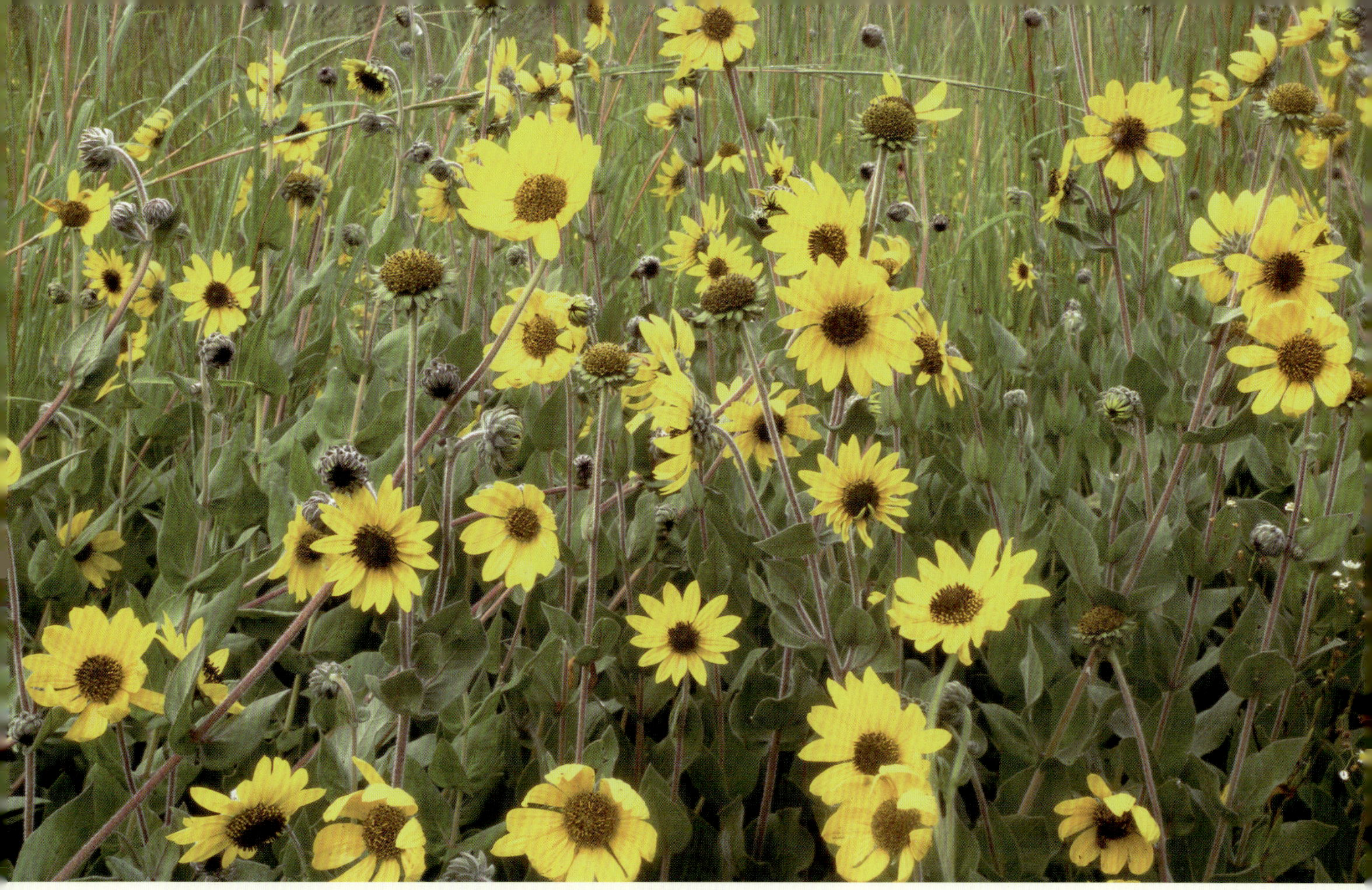

The downy sunflower (*Helianthus mollis*) is covered with minute hairs that help the plant retain moisture. It releases chemicals into the soil to inhibit seed germination and growth of surrounding vegetation.

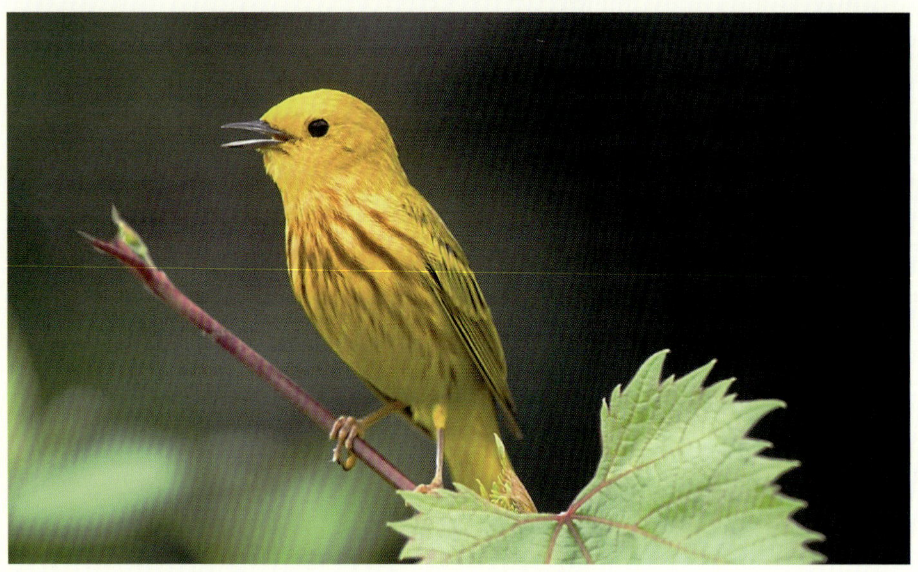

The mosaic of prairie and forest-edge provided ideal habitat for the yellow warbler (*Setophaga petechia*), an abundant species. Cowbirds heavily parasitize their nests.

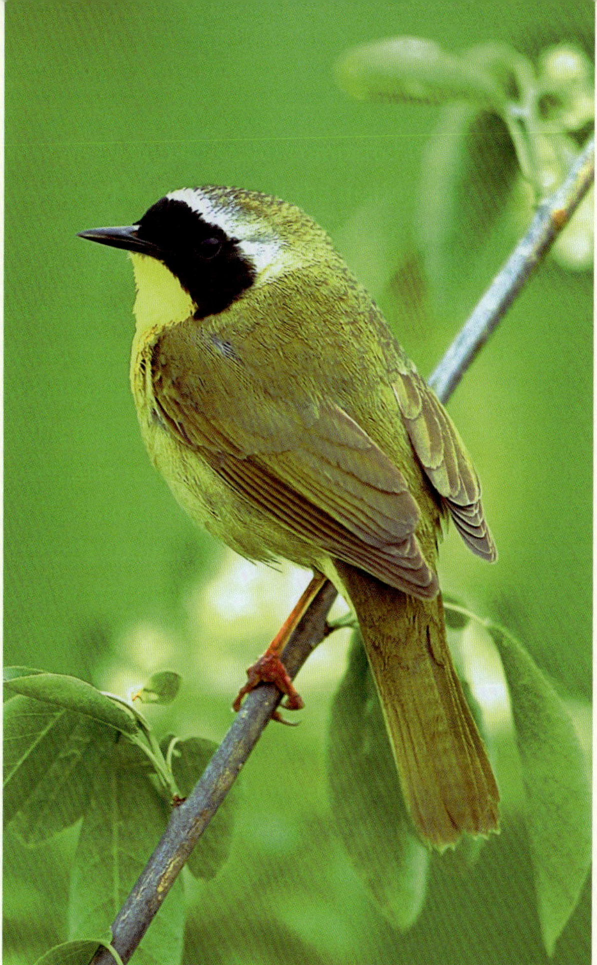

Common yellowthroats (*Geothlypis trichas*) are one of a few warbler species that breed in prairie.

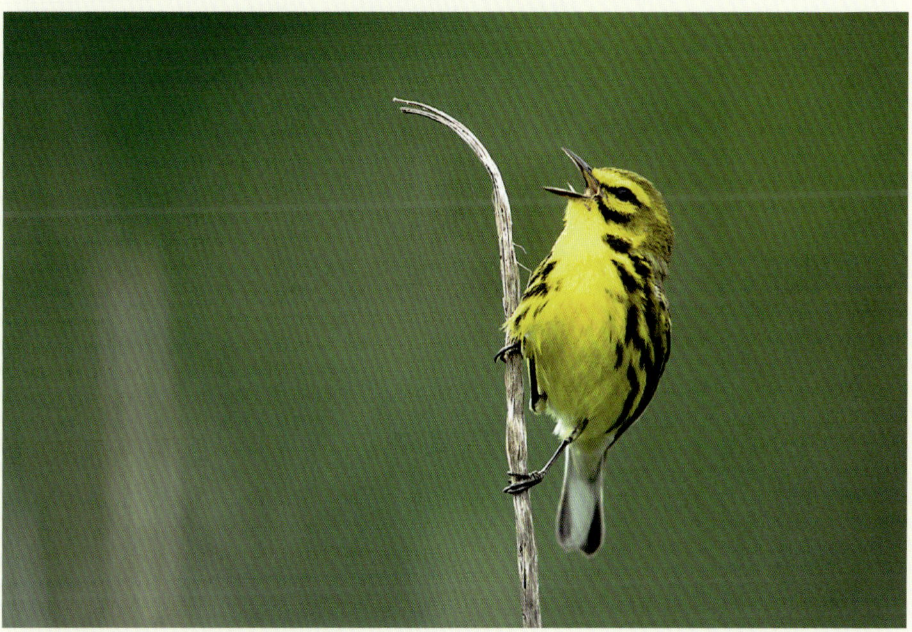

The prairie warbler (*Setophaga discolor*), a misnamed species, breeds in limestone glades and other dry habitats, but rarely in prairie grasslands.

CHAPTER 4

Bloom to Bloom

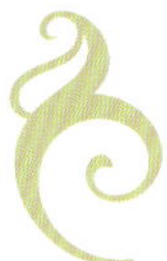

Most ecologists consider the Wabash River in Indiana the easternmost extension of tallgrass prairie. In the past, rather large prairie openings could be found in southwestern Michigan and the western half of Ohio, with a few small outliers almost to the border of Pennsylvania. If trees were kept at bay, these openings could persist indefinitely. Data from pollen samples suggest that during dry periods between glaciations, prairie species recolonized areas that were formerly forest (Sears 1967). Many of these sites are sandy, rocky, highly alkaline, very wet, or on hillsides subject to constant erosion. Prairie plants are well suited to grow in these marginal habitats, each with its own unique floristic component. Some of the largest and most important families of native plants found in tallgrass prairie are Asteraceae, Cyperaceae, Poaceae, Fabaceae, Rosaceae, and Gentianaceae.

The Asteraceae is an exceedingly large family (also known as the composites) that contains many colorful forbs. The parade of asters, blazing stars, coneflowers, goldenrods, and sunflowers adds to the ever-changing kaleidoscope of color throughout the growing season. In July, the showy spikes of compass plants (*Silphium laciniatum*) and prairie dock (*Silphium terebinthinaceum*) tower above prairie landscapes. Two species of purple coneflowers as well as the wands of blazing stars, wild bergamot (*Monarda fistulosa,* family Labiatae) and asters spread a sea of magenta and purple across summer and fall meadows. The yellows of gray-headed coneflowers (*Ratibida pinnata*), numerous goldenrods, and sunflowers add to the riot of color.

The Poaceae, or grasses, make up 80 percent of the biomass in grasslands. Dense root systems help perpetuate grasslands by eliminating shrubs and trees. Big bluestem (*Andropogon gerardii*), Indian grass (*Sorghastrum nutans*) and cordgrass (*Spartina pectinata*) are three of the main components in tallgrass prairie. Dry and sandy habitats are dominated by little bluestem (*Schizachyrium scoparium*), side-oats grama (*Bouteloua curtipendula*), and switchgrass (*Panicum virgatum*). Related to grasses, sedges (Carex spp.) tend to grow in wet meadows. About sixty species of sedges are found growing throughout the Prairie Peninsula; sedges are often overlooked but are important components of wet prairie.

Members of the rose family (Rosaceae) are generally woody shrubs and small trees. They have alternate leaves, and many produce edible berries; blackberries and raspberries are good examples. Cinquefoils (Potentilla spp.) and prairie smoke (*Geum triflorum*) are also family members. Members of the legume, or pea, family (Fabaceae) are mainly herbs—most typically, clovers, lupines, and wild senna (*Senna hebecarpa*)—but among them are some shrub and tree species. Some of the most beautiful plants blooming on the prairie during the late summer and fall are the gentians (Gentianella spp.). Their exceptionally vivid bell-shaped flowers stand out among the prairie vegetation. Prairie gentians (*Gentiana puberulenta*) are used as an important indicator species in evaluating the quality of prairie remnants. Almost all insects avoid the bitter foliage of gentians.

In early May many species come into bloom. In the northern part of the Prairie Peninsula, pasque flowers (*Anemone patens*) push up through dead plant stems and leaves to herald the beginning of the growing season. The delicate blue and white blooms are encased within silky-haired leaves. Two months later they will do the same on the highest peaks of the Rocky Mountains. Since tall grasses like big bluestem and Indian grass are still short and provide no competition for sunlight, many ephemerals begin to flower. Meadows are blanketed with Indian paintbrush (*Castilleja coccinea*), hoary puccoon (*Lithospermum canescens*), midland shooting star (*Dodecatheon meadia*), and wood betony (*Pedicularis canadensis*). Large clumps of birdsfoot violets (*Viola pedata*) grow in sandy areas. In open oak forests, wild hyacinths (*Camassia scilloides*) form pure stands, spreading carpets of blue across savannas. It should be noted that few plants in the Prairie Peninsula have prairie origins. Well suited to live in open, drought-prone environments, most invaded after the glaciers receded.

As the season progresses, grasses begin to dominate the landscape. Most prairie grasses are warm-season species. With roots that can go down more than twelve feet, they have very deep root systems for accessing water and nutrients. Aboveground growth represents only one third of the total plant (Reichman 1987). Near the surface, they are a tangled mat of rootlets and rhizomes. Analysis shows more than twenty miles of root hairs and rootlets are packed into just one square yard of big bluestem sod (Savage 2004). Thick surface rhizomes branch out to squeeze out competitors. Early in the season, grasses begin to produce and store carbohydrates, which enables them to withstand heavy grazing, summer droughts, and even occasional fires. Their long, narrow leaves expose little surface to the sun and drying winds. During extreme drought, the margins of the leaf blades curl inward, baring even less leaf surface. By late August, stands of big bluestem are so dense that only one third of rainfall reaches the ground; prairie grasses hold precipitation. The grasses' complex root systems also reduce soil erosion. For this reason, prairie remnants are usually higher in elevation than surrounding cropland, which has lost most of its soil through erosion, because the latter occupy the more valuable, easily cultivated land.

Fire is a critical component of the tallgrass ecosystem. Herbaceous plants die back each winter, providing highly flammable fuel for fires. Although these blazes consume aboveground biomass of grasses and forbs, the underground stems and roots are unaffected. Temperatures can reach between 500 and 1000 °F well above ground level, but the ground is a good insulator, and plant and animal tissues below ground receive little damage. Flames and gases flow upward, away from the surface. The benefits of fire are great: it recycles a smothering blanket of dead plant stems and leaves it as useful nutrients, stimulates plants' greater growth and seed production, and helps control the growth of woody shrubs.

Prairie forbs have special protections against severe water loss. Downy sunflowers (*Helianthus mollis*) have a velvety coating of fine hairs, and many other sunflower species have coarse leaves. In addition to deep roots, compass plants (*Silphium laciniatum*) and prairie dock, large sunflower-like plants in the aster family, have massive fleshy taproots, designed to store water and nutrients. Because of evapotranspiration, the basal leaves of the prairie dock and the compass plant remain cooler than ambient air in hot weather; these leaves also align in a north-south direction, allowing them to catch morning light but avoid the harsh rays of the midday sun. These plants' high stalks keep their flowers above even the tallest grasses.

Some tallgrass forbs have a wide geographic range. Black-eyed susans (*Rudbeckia hirta*) and New England asters (*Symphyotrichum novae-angliae*) can be found growing throughout the eastern half of the United States. They are also important components of tallgrass prairie. Gray-headed coneflowers, round-headed bush clover (*Lespedeza capitata*), and rigid goldenrods

(*Solidago rigida*) grow as well in Indiana as in North Dakota. Between glacial events, numerous species migrated along the edge of the receding glaciers. From the south came many limestone glade species, like the spectacular royal catchfly (*Silene regia*); a native of the dry Missouri prairies, it can be found in isolated populations from southern Illinois to as far north as central Ohio. Sweetfern (*Comptonia peregrina*), mainly a northeastern shrub, grows in the dry oak savannas in Illinois. Many prairie species migrated east, among them leadplant (*Amphora canescens*), prairie ironweed (*Vernonia fasciculata*), and saw-toothed sunflower (*Helianthus grosseserratus*).

By July, the majority of forbs come into bloom. Tall grasses are beginning to compete for sunlight. Purple prairie clover (*Dalea purpurea*), leadplant, and pale purple coneflower (*Echinacea pallida*) brighten hillsides. They are joined by wild quinine (*Parthenium integrifolium*), wild bergamot (*Monarda fistulosa*), black-eyed susan, and gray-headed coneflower. Many species of milkweed (Asclepias spp.) provide an important source of nectar for butterflies, moths, and other insects. Monarch butterfly larvae feed only on milkweeds, thus the gradual decline of milkweed plants has had a negative effect on monarch numbers. Butterfly (*Asclepias tuberosa*), purple (*Asclepias purpurascens*), and Sullivant's milkweeds (*Asclepias sullivantii*), along with many less showy species, add splashes of color to summer landscapes. At this point in the growing season, one still looks down at forbs and grasses. Ranging across the United States as far as Colorado, purple coneflowers (*Echinacea purpurea*) extend farther east than their pale siblings. They are abundant in the southern half of the Prairie Peninsula. In June, many Grand Prairie remnants are blanketed with pale purple coneflowers, but only as far east as western Indiana.

As summer progresses, more composites begin to flower. Imposing and attractive cup-plants (*Silphium perfoliatum*) soar eight feet into the sky. Their fused leaf bases form cups that can hold water used by late-nesting goldfinches and other songbirds. In fall, the birds will return to harvest the seed heads. By late summer it is difficult to see the crowns of many sunflowers and grasses. Saw-toothed sunflowers (*Helianthus grosseserratus*), common in prairie-edge habitats, may reach ten feet in height. By examining distribution maps, we can see that after the retreat of the Wisconsinan Glacier, many plants used the south shores of Lakes Michigan and Erie as migration routes. As one moves west from Lake Michigan, the number and variety of forbs begin to decrease. In Iowa, only about two hundred species can be found in any given remnant; this is 30 percent fewer than in lake plain prairie.

From the end of July through October, the pink flowered wands of blazing stars (Liatris spp.) provide a spectacle not to be missed. Early blooming marsh or slender blazing stars (*Liatris spicata*) can blanket entire meadows. Deeper pink prairie blazing stars (*Liatris pycnostachya*) have dense flower heads and are sometimes common in undisturbed habitats or high-quality prairie. Starting from the top of the stalk, florets gradually bloom downward. Unfortunately, the flowering period for these showy members of the aster family is rather short. Rough blazing stars (*Liatris aspera*) are locally common in dry sand prairies. The large florets begin to bloom in September. Uncommon savanna blazing stars (*Liatris scariosa*) flower in late summer in open oak woodlands.

Gentians, some of the prairie's most beautiful wildflowers, bloom throughout September. Six species of gentians can be found growing just west of Lake Michigan; among these are lesser fringed gentians (*Gentianopsis virgata*), soapwort (*Gentiana saponaria*), and cream gentians (*Gentiana alba*). Delicate fringed gentians wait for the warm rays of the sun to open, and clumps of blue prairie gentians hide in wet grasses. When storms approach, their petals quickly close in a spiral. Goldenrods of many species flower in late summer meadows; fields of Canada goldenrod (*Solidago canadensis*) blanket large open areas. Abundant and weedy, they release allelopathic chemicals through their roots, inhibiting the seed germination and growth of other herbaceous plants. Found in alkaline habitats, Ohio (*Solidago ohioensis*) and Riddell's goldenrod (*Solidago riddellii*) migrated south in front of the advancing ice sheet. When the Wisconsinan Glacier retreated, they remained isolated in alkaline meadows and fens. The rigid goldenrod's (*Solidago rigida*) rough leaves make it ideally suited for dry habitats; this attractive species is especially common in black soil remnants.

Many species of asters, usually white or purple, highlight the late-season landscape. Showy New England asters blanket large areas, becoming quickly established in disturbed margins but seldom dominating original prairie. Their large compound flower clusters vary in color from white and pink to deep purple. When crushed, the purple flower heads of aromatic asters (*Symphyotrichum oblongifolium*) have a balsamlike scent. Beautiful sky blue asters (*Symphyotrichum oolentangiense*) can be found in high-quality habitats. A native of the central prairies, the sky blue aster ranges from eastern Nebraska all the way to New York. The silky aster (*Symphyotrichum sericeum*) is also limited to undisturbed prairie, and dwindling habitat has caused this species to decline throughout its range. Late blooming, asters are an important food source for butterflies, moths, and other beneficial insects.

With the passing of the asters, the growing season ends. By the end of autumn, visitors are left with the dried heads of sunflowers, blazing stars, and asters. Grasses that were once gold have faded. Withered seed heads of Canada wild rye (*Elymus canadensis*) are conspicuous among the giant brown leaves of prairie dock. Many early bloomers have died back, leaving little trace of their existence. They will have to wait until next spring to push up through last year's stems and leaves to begin another growing season.

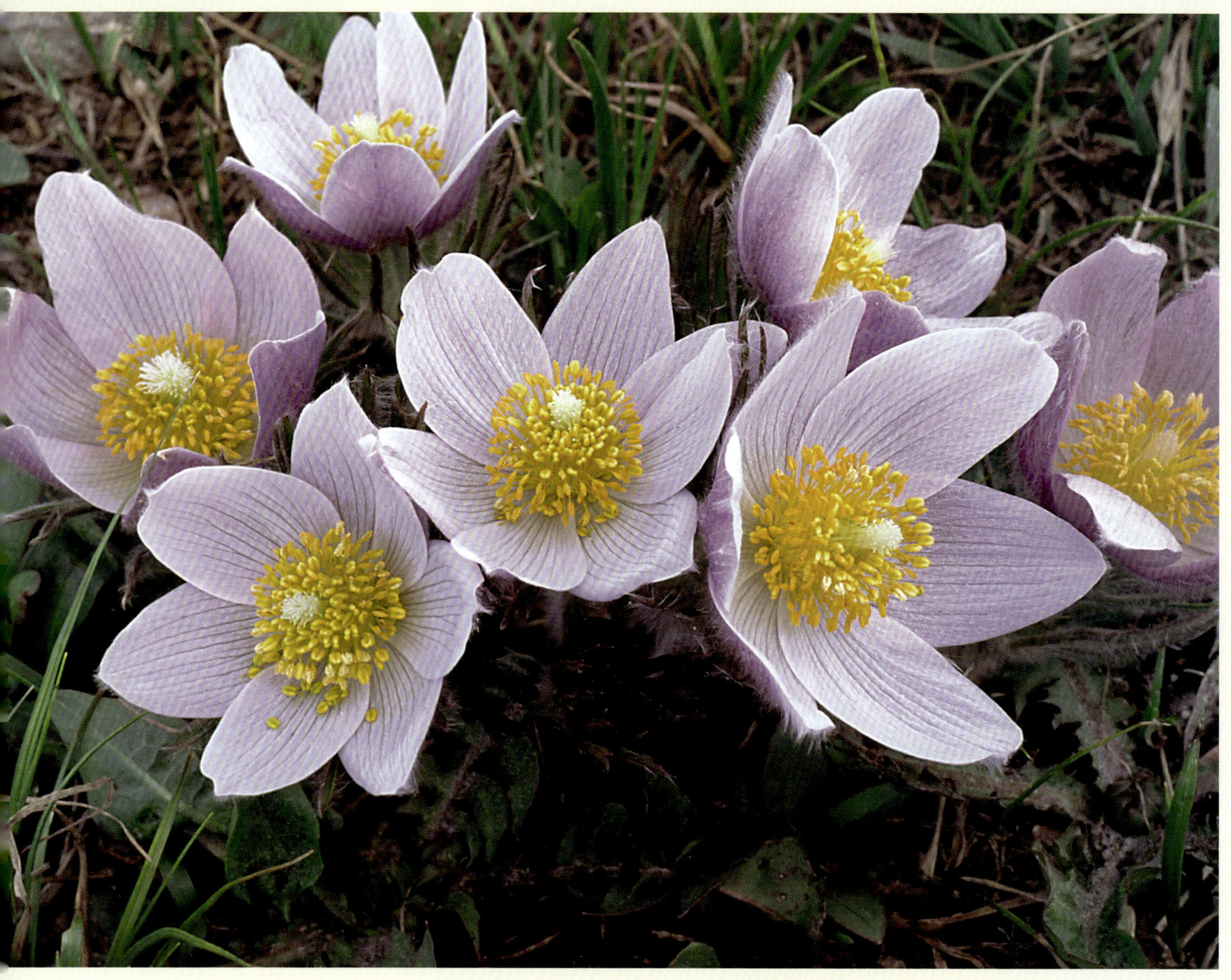

In early May, pasque flowers (*Anemone patens*) begin to push up through last year's stems and leaves to herald another growing season.

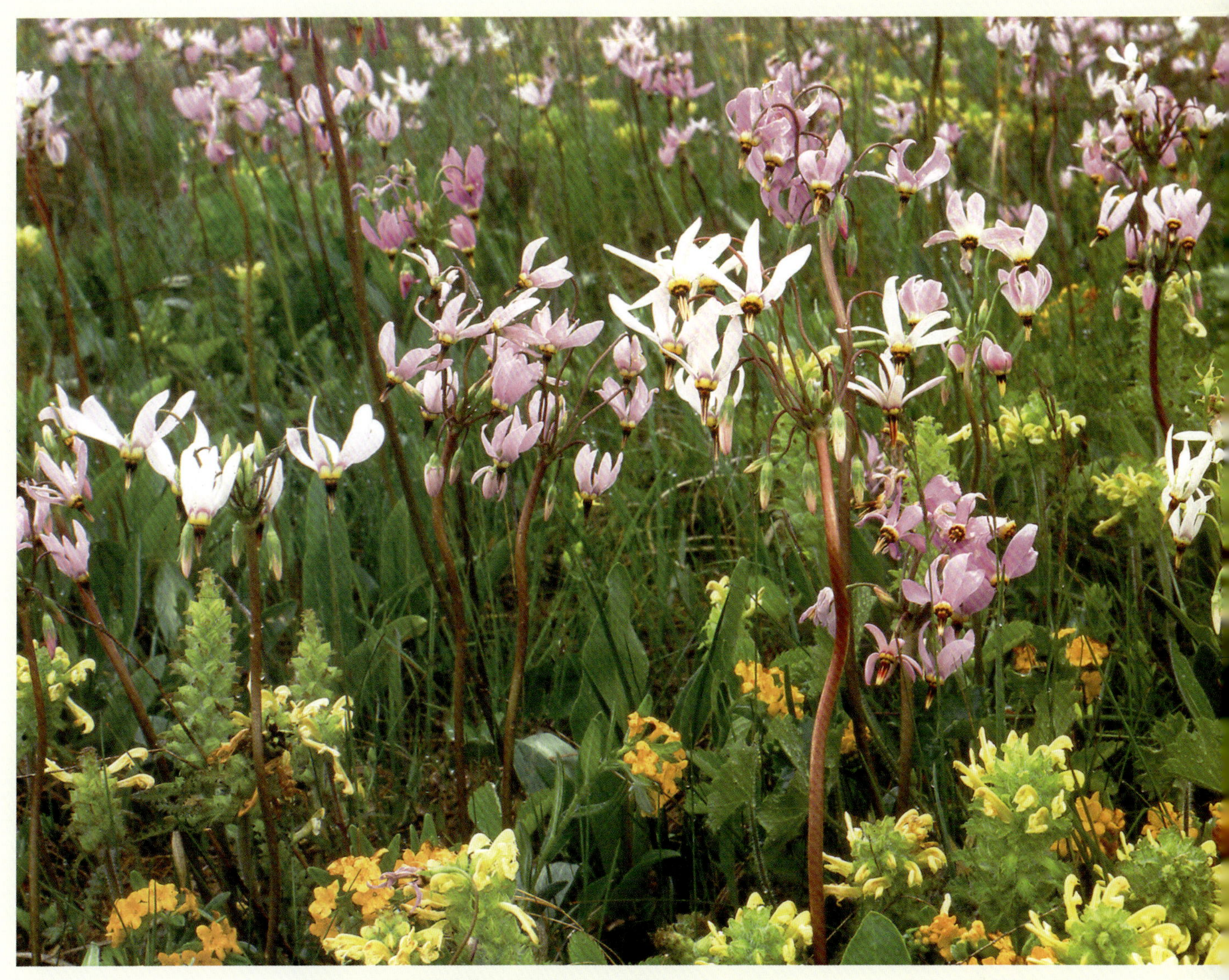

Spring ephemerals, midland shooting stars (*Dodecatheon meadia*) blanket many tallgrass remnants.

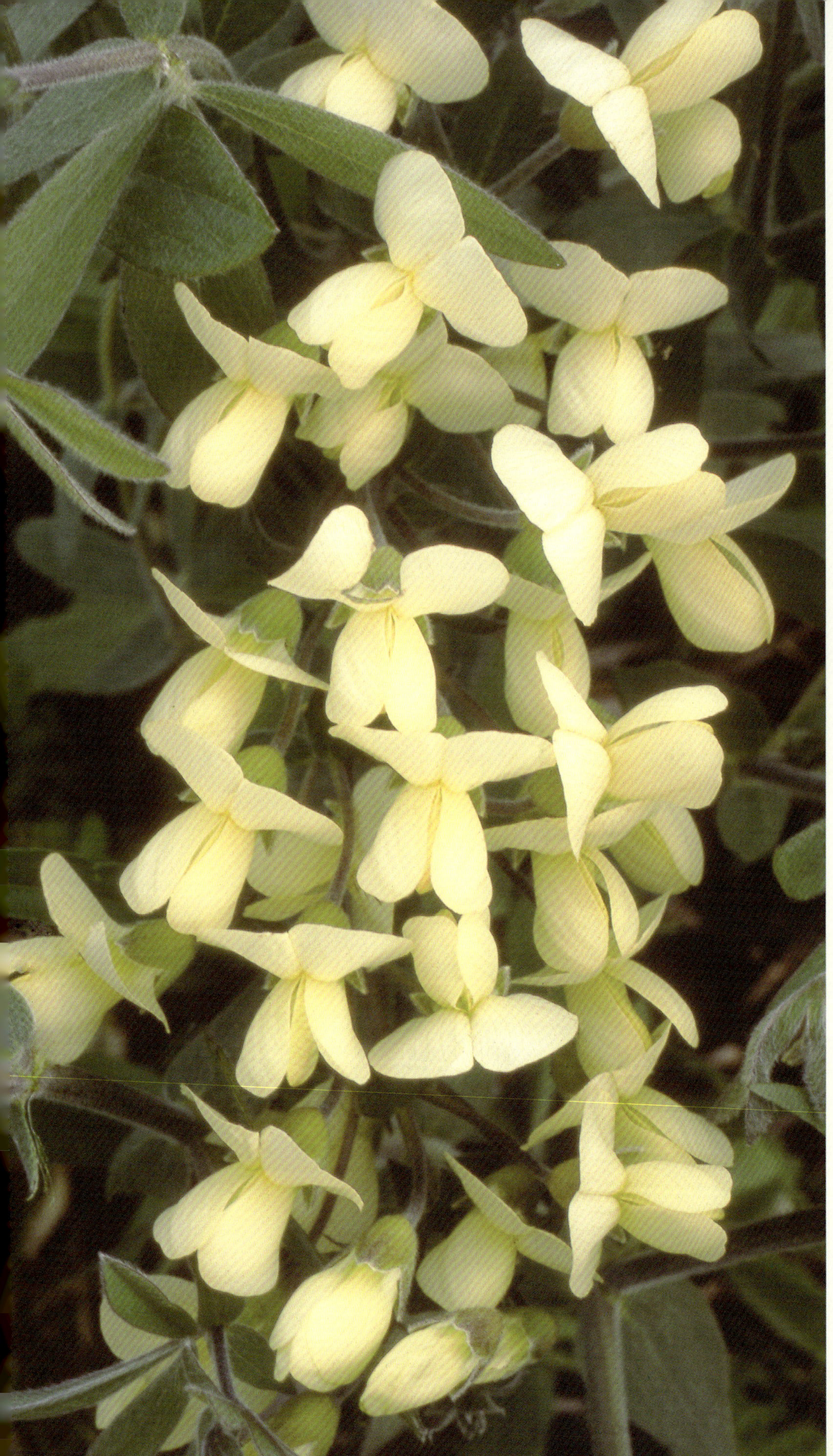

Spikes of uncommon cream false indigo (*Baptisia leucophaea*), an indicator species of undisturbed conditions, bloom in May.

Opposite: In early June, clumps of scarlet Indian paintbrush (*Castilleja coccinea*) brighten prairie meadows. Their roots are partially parasitic on forbs and grasses. Management tools like fire benefit this species.

Opposite: Prairie phlox (*Phlox pilosa*) and Ohio spiderwort (*Tradescantia ohioensis*), two common species, bloom in June at Hoosier Prairie in Lake County, Indiana.

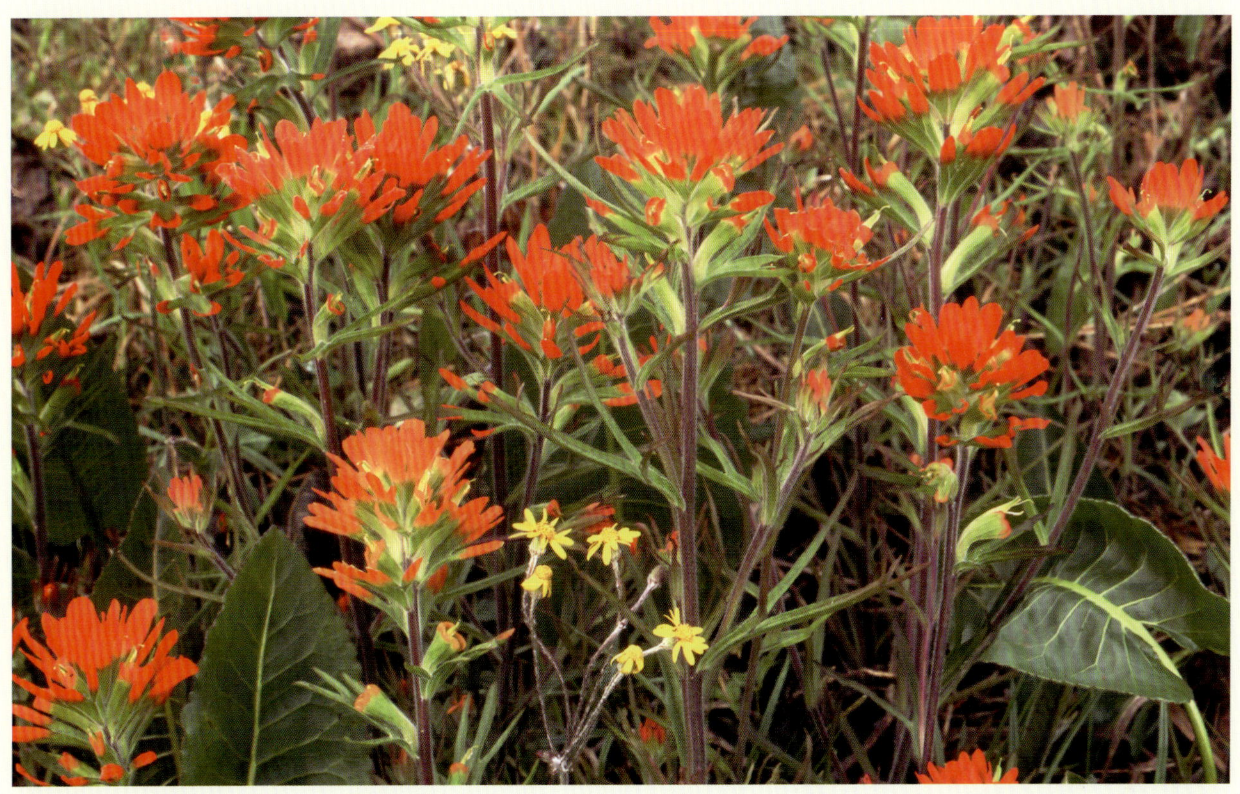

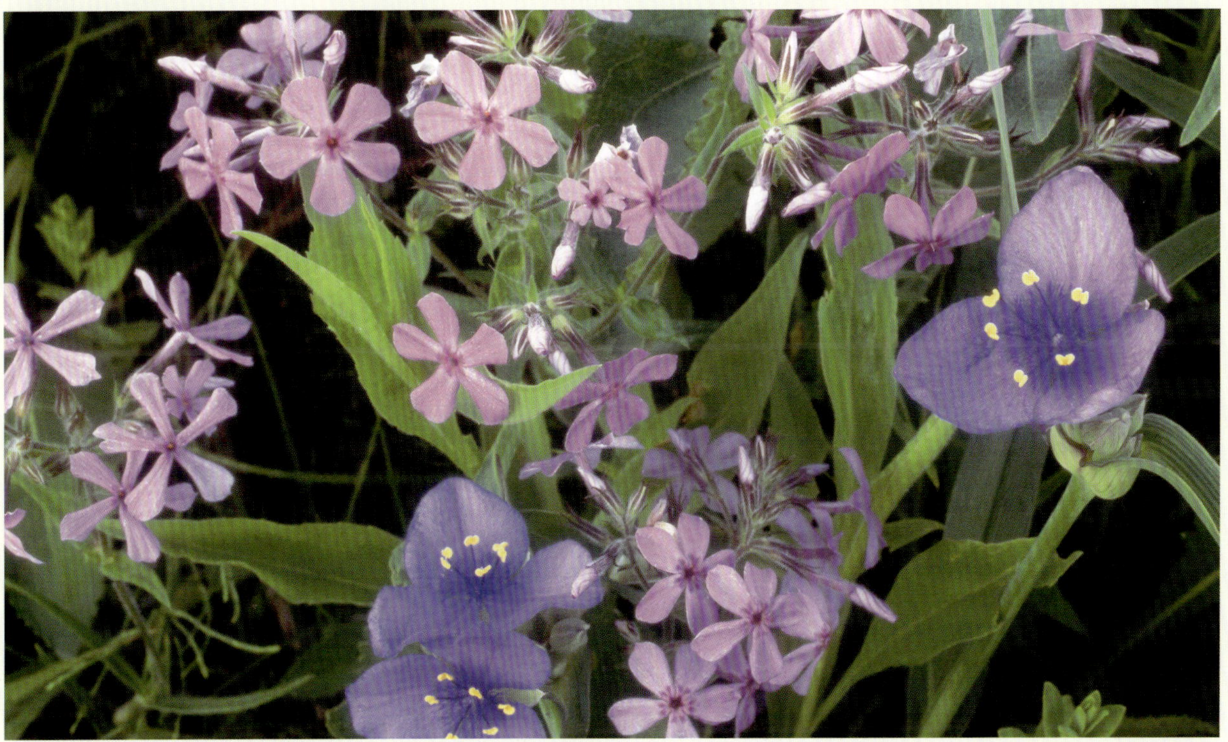

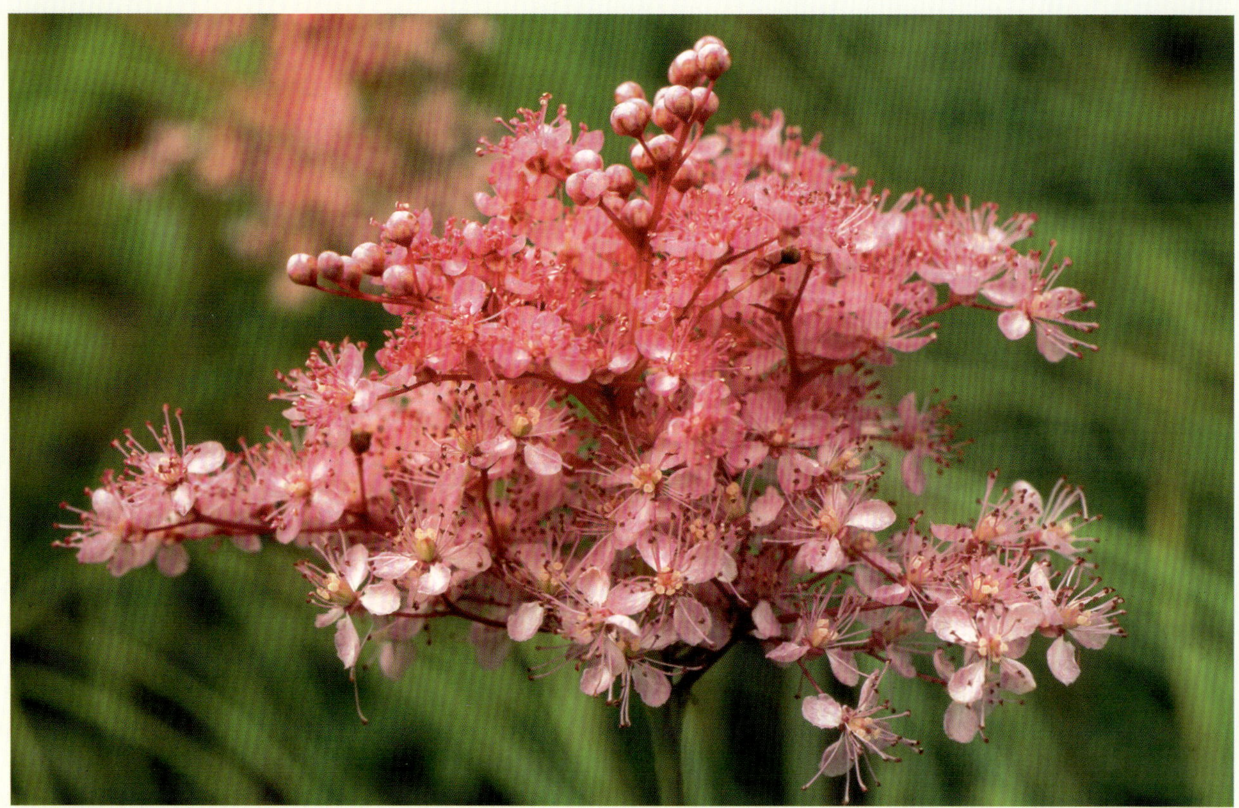

A member of the rose family, queen-of-the-prairie (*Filipendula rubra*) is local in alkaline fens and wet prairie. The long, naked stalks are crowned with small, fluffy pink blossoms.

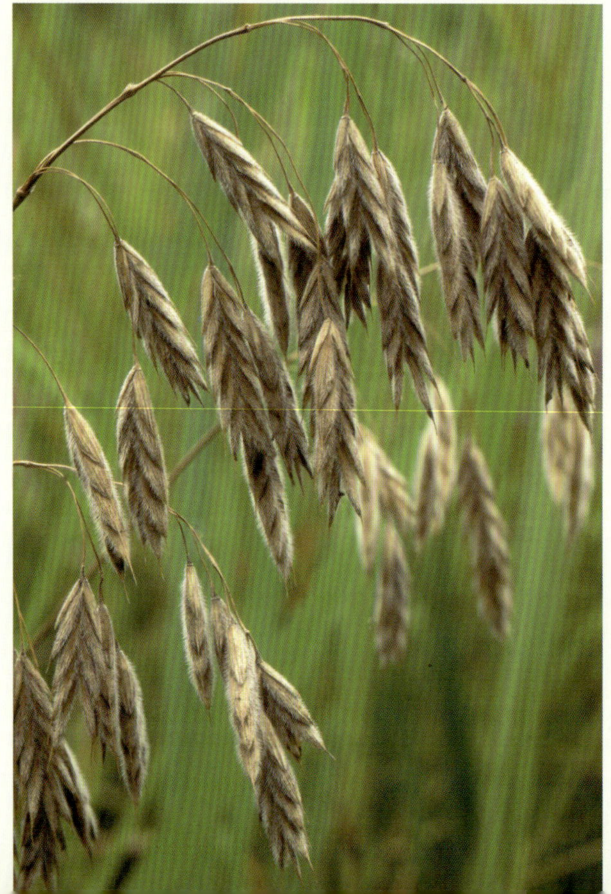

Wind cross-pollinates uncommon prairie brome grass (*Bromus kalmii*). This short-lived perennial is usually found in original prairie.

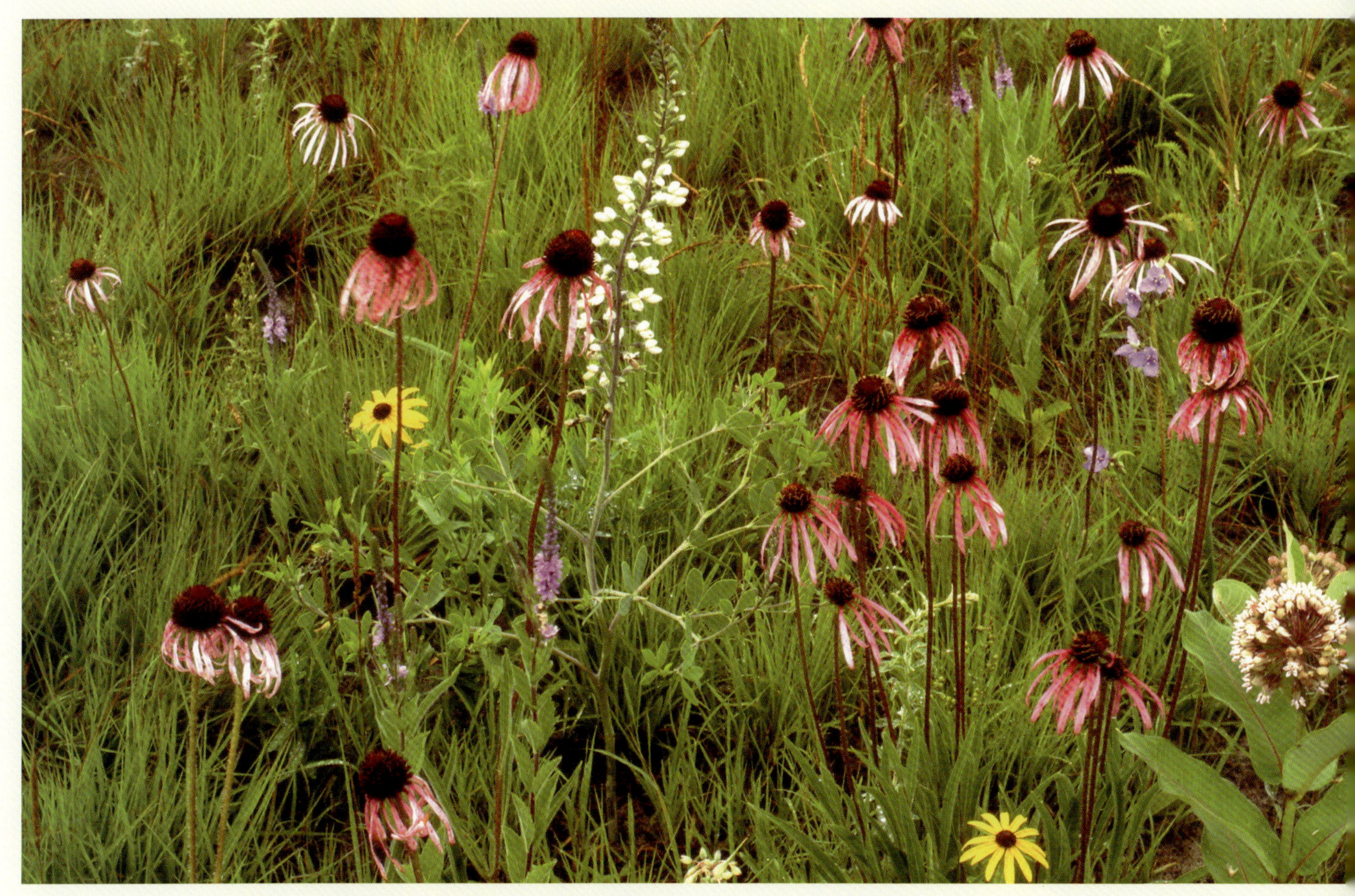

Pale purple coneflowers (*Echinacea pallida*) range as far east as western Indiana. Flowering in late June, they are common in Grand Prairie remnants.

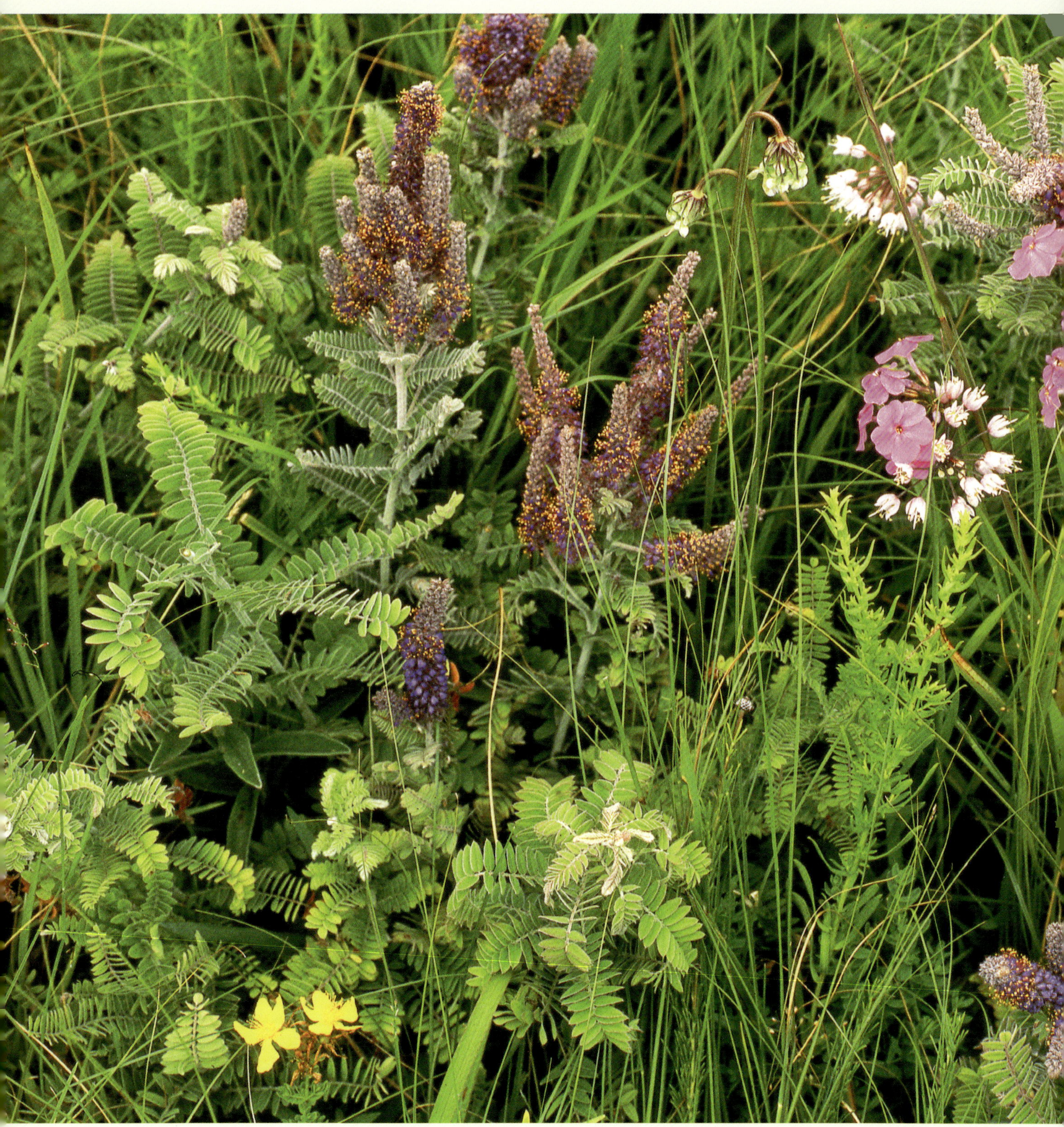

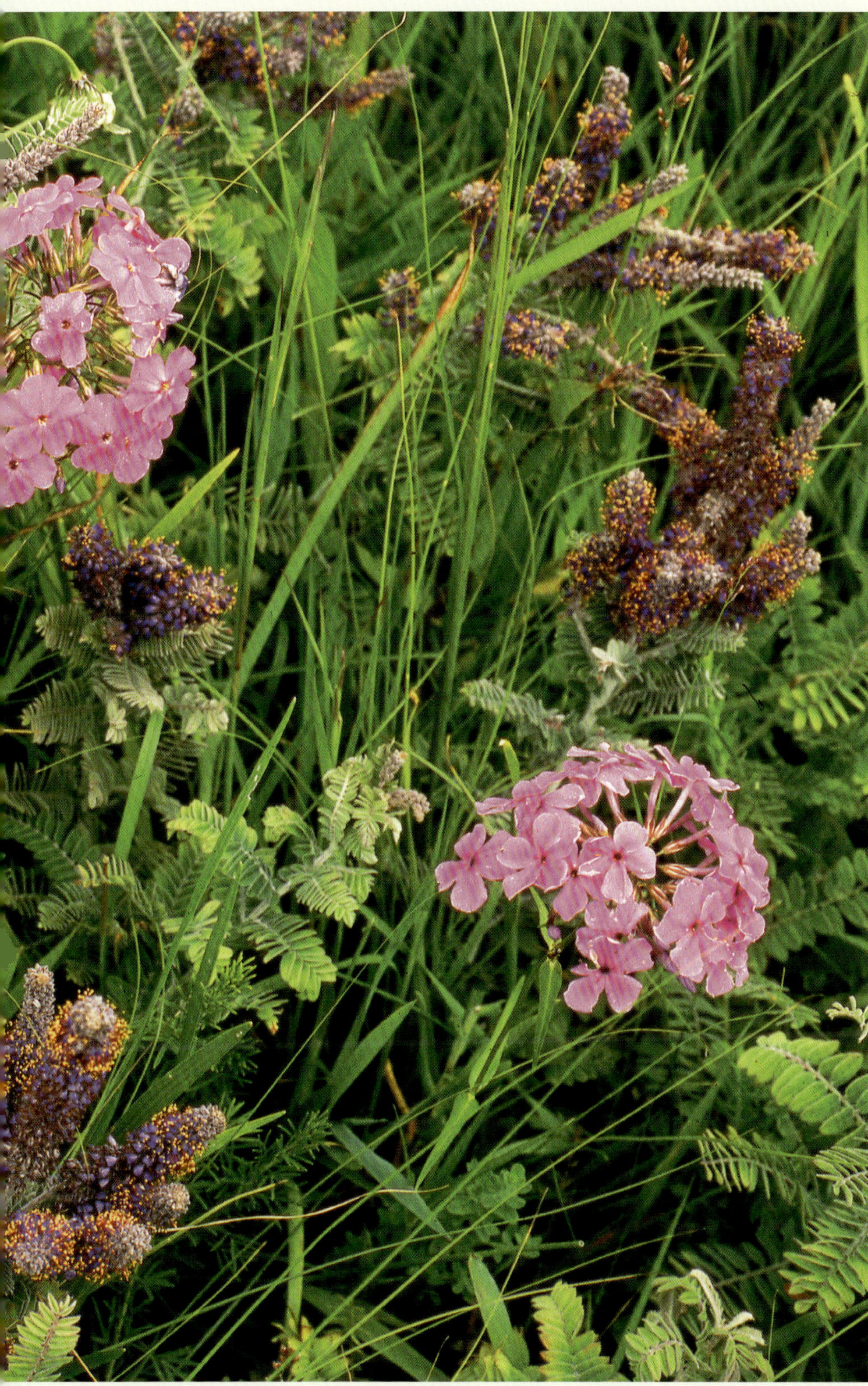

Leadplant (*Amphora canescens*) and smooth phlox (*Phlox glaberrima*) flower in July in Kenosha County, Wisconsin's Chiwaukee Prairie. At this point in the growing season, one still looks down at forbs and grasses.

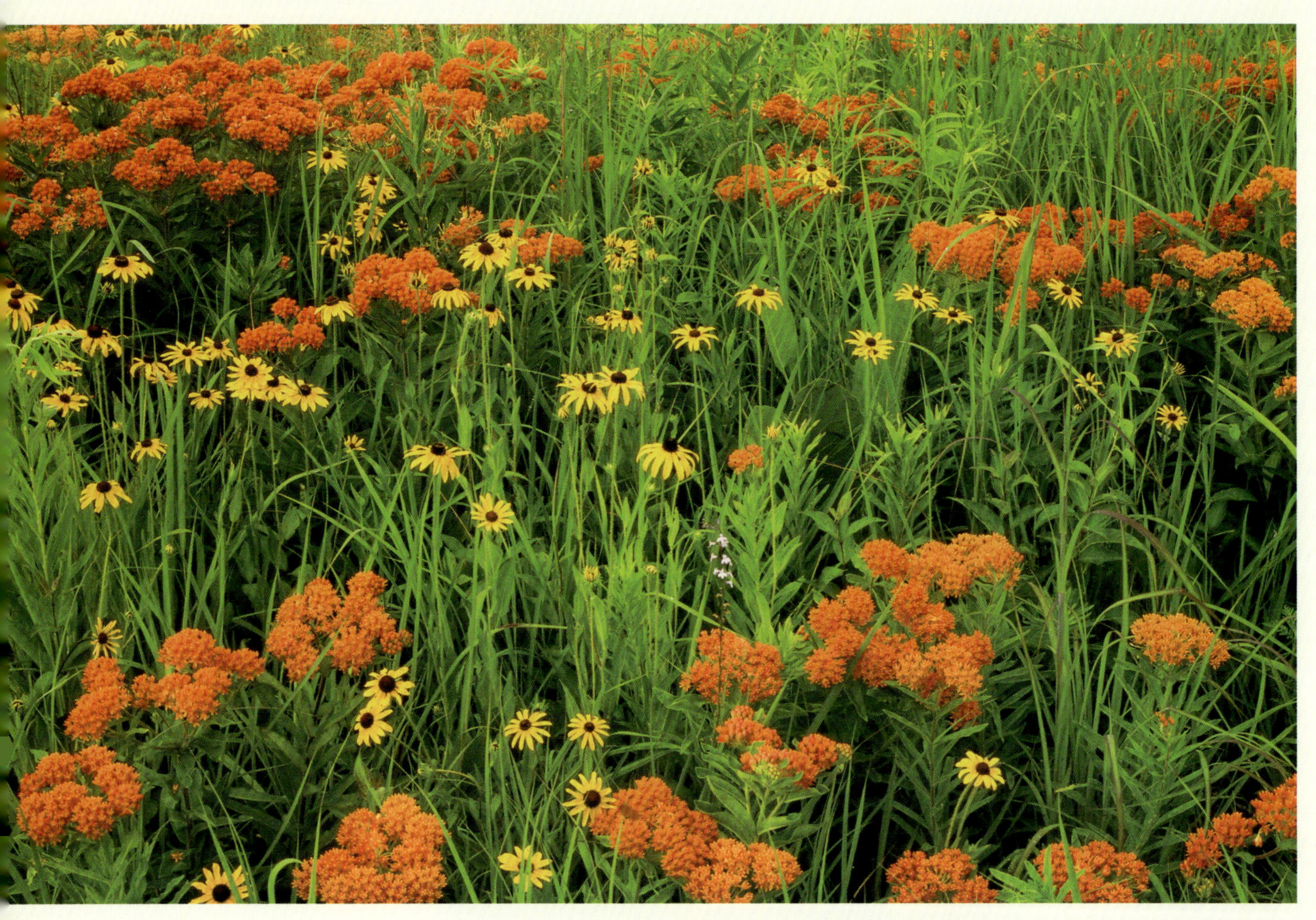

Among the showiest forbs, butterfly milkweed (*Asclepias tuberosa*) lacks the toxic white latex of other milkweeds. Blooming alongside black-eyed susans (*Rudbeckia hirta*), the orange and yellow blossoms attract a host of insect pollinators.

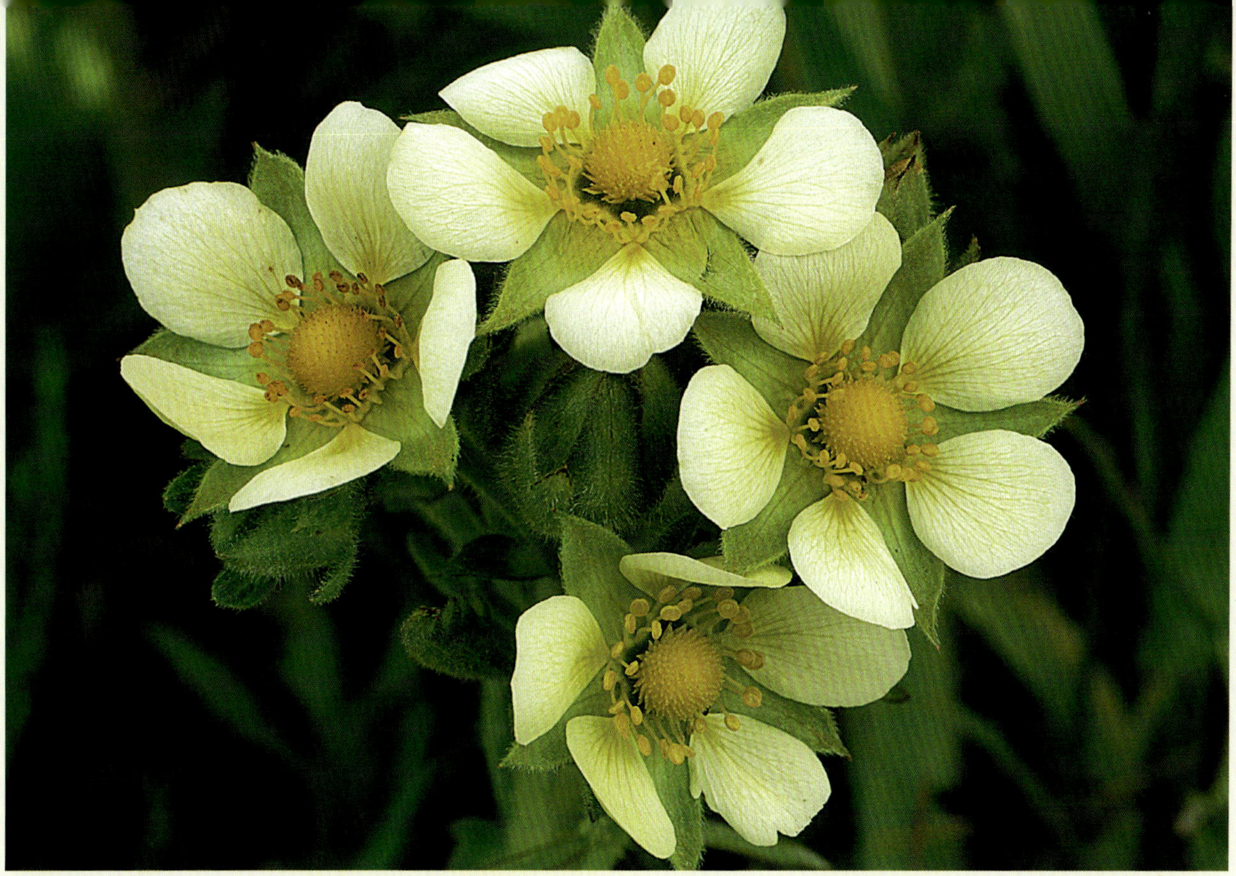

Found in dry grasslands, tall or prairie cinquefoil (*Drymocallis arguta*) ranges west to Colorado.

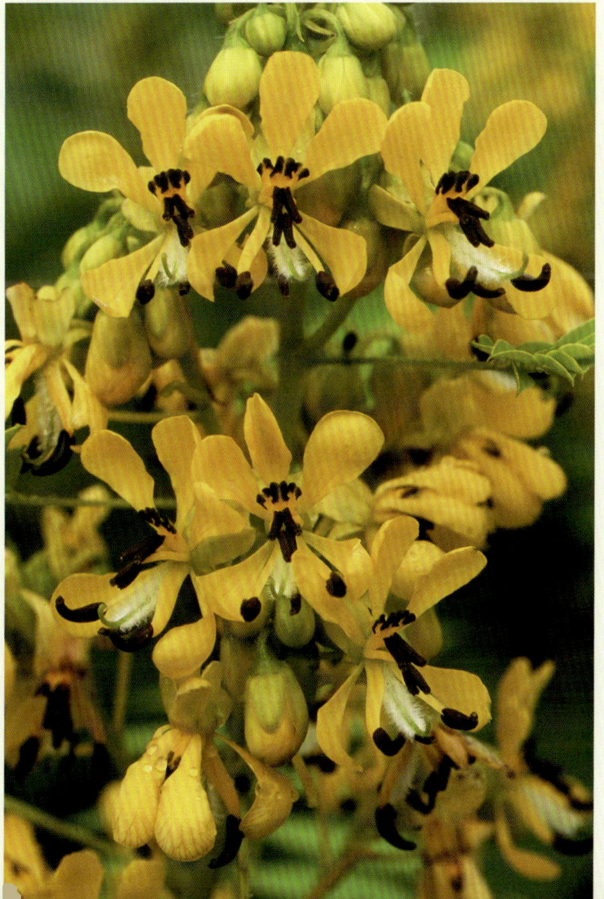

A herbaceous shrub, wild senna (*Senna hebecarpa*) is found in black soil prairie. This member of the legume family is declining throughout its range.

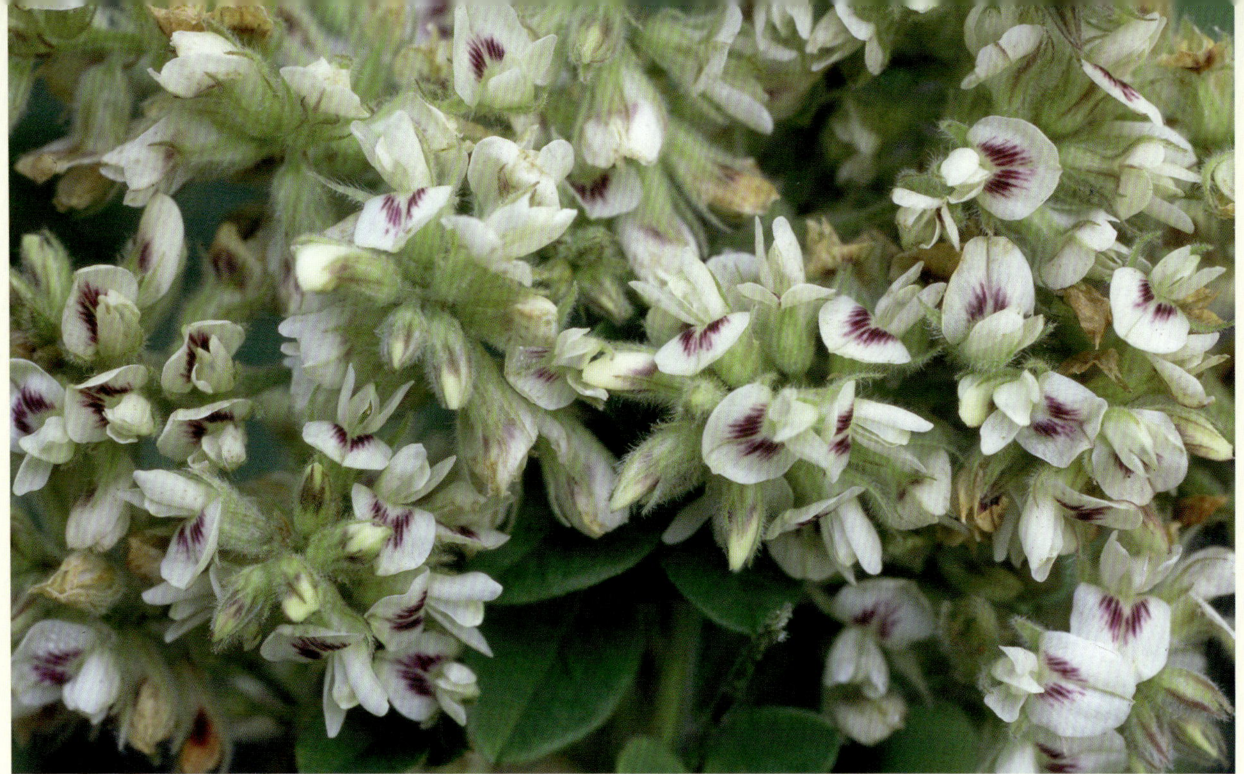

Foliage of the common round-headed bush clover (*Lespedeza capitata*) is high in proteins. Many mammal species eat this palatable plant, and birds consume its seeds.

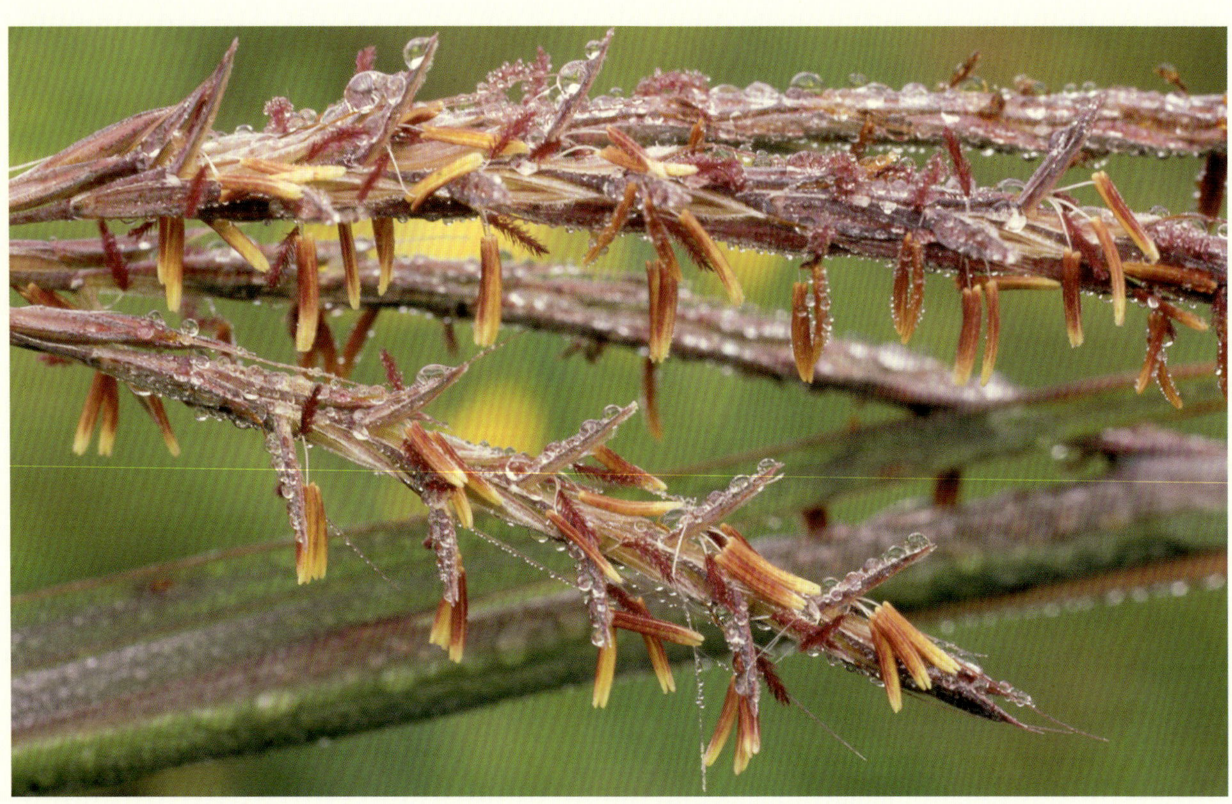

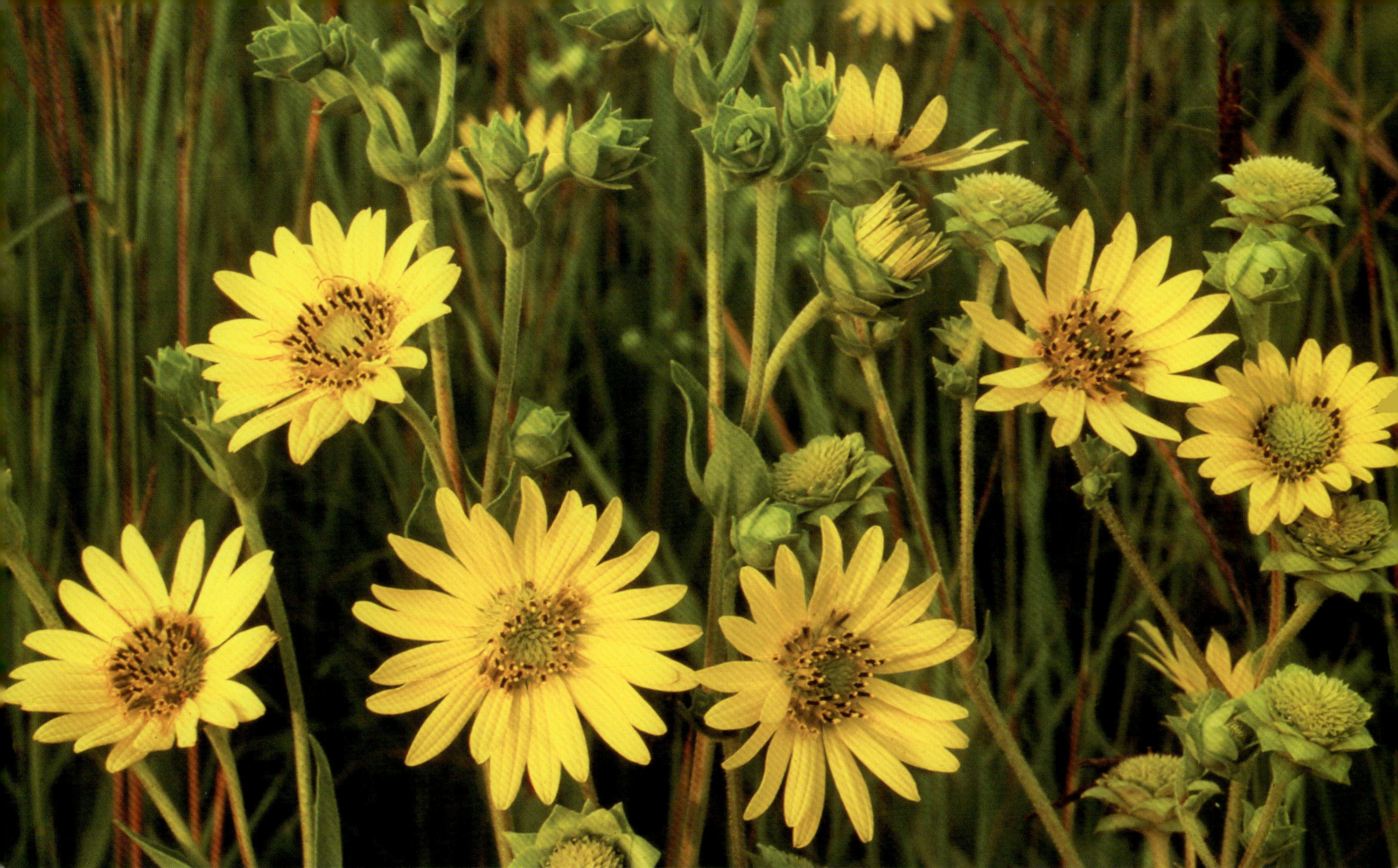

Rosinweed (*Silphium integrifolium*) can be found growing from eastern Indiana westward into Iowa. Resinous sap helps it retain moisture from drying winds.

Opposite: The tops of big bluestem (*Andropogon gerardii*) are usually branched in four parts, giving them a common name: "turkeyfoot" grass. Minute flowers bloom on big bluestem spikes.

In September, lesser fringed gentians (*Gentianopsis virgata*) flower in wet alkaline meadows. This beautiful species favors wet dune-and-swale as well as alkaline seeps.

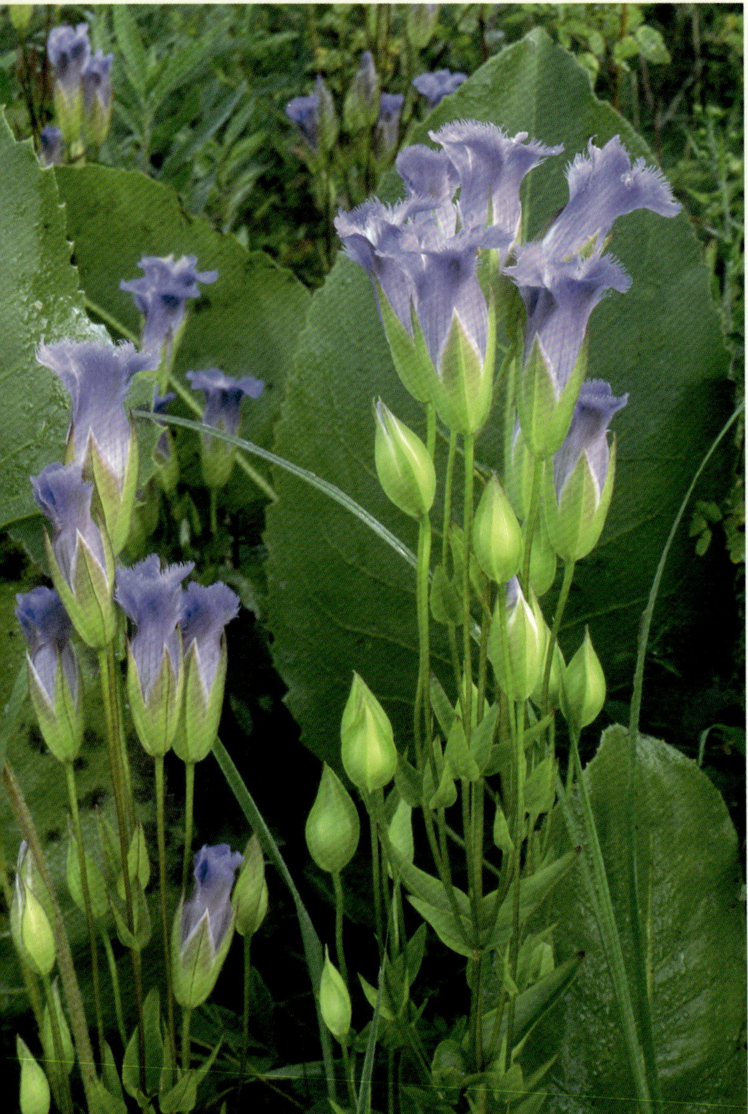

Reaching eight feet into the sky, the stalks of compass plants (*Silphium laciniatum*) stand out in prairie meadows in early summer.

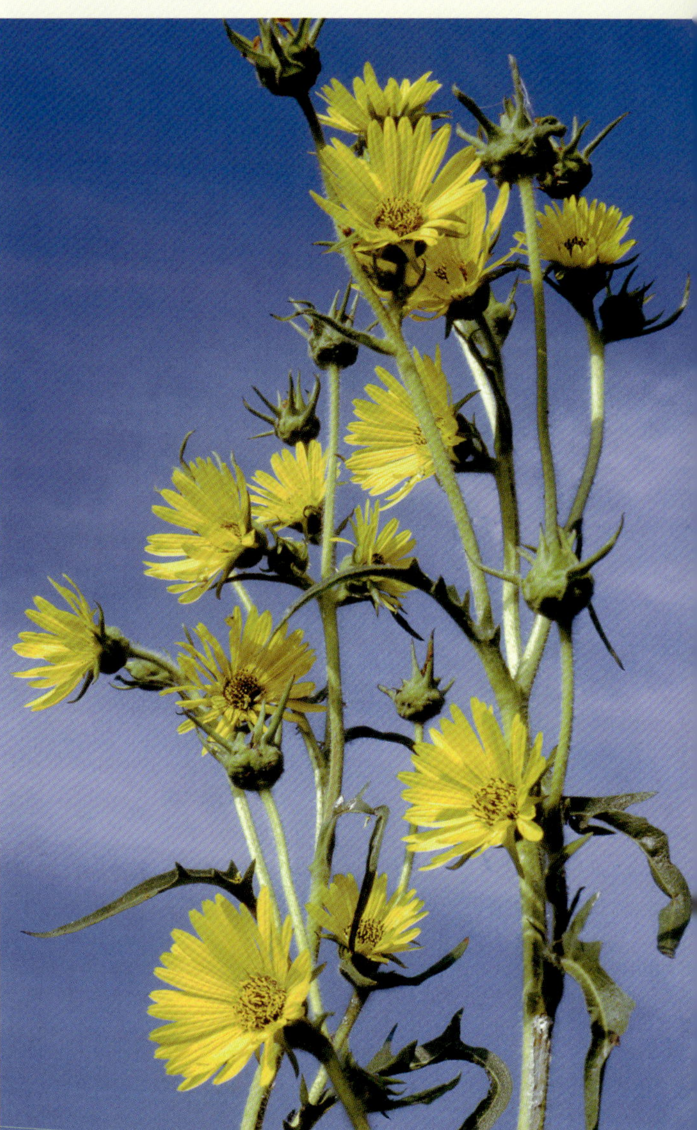

Opposite: Showy prairie lilies (*Lilium philadelphicum*) bloom in June. Slow to mature, they are usually found in high-quality prairie. Loss of habitat is responsible for declining numbers.

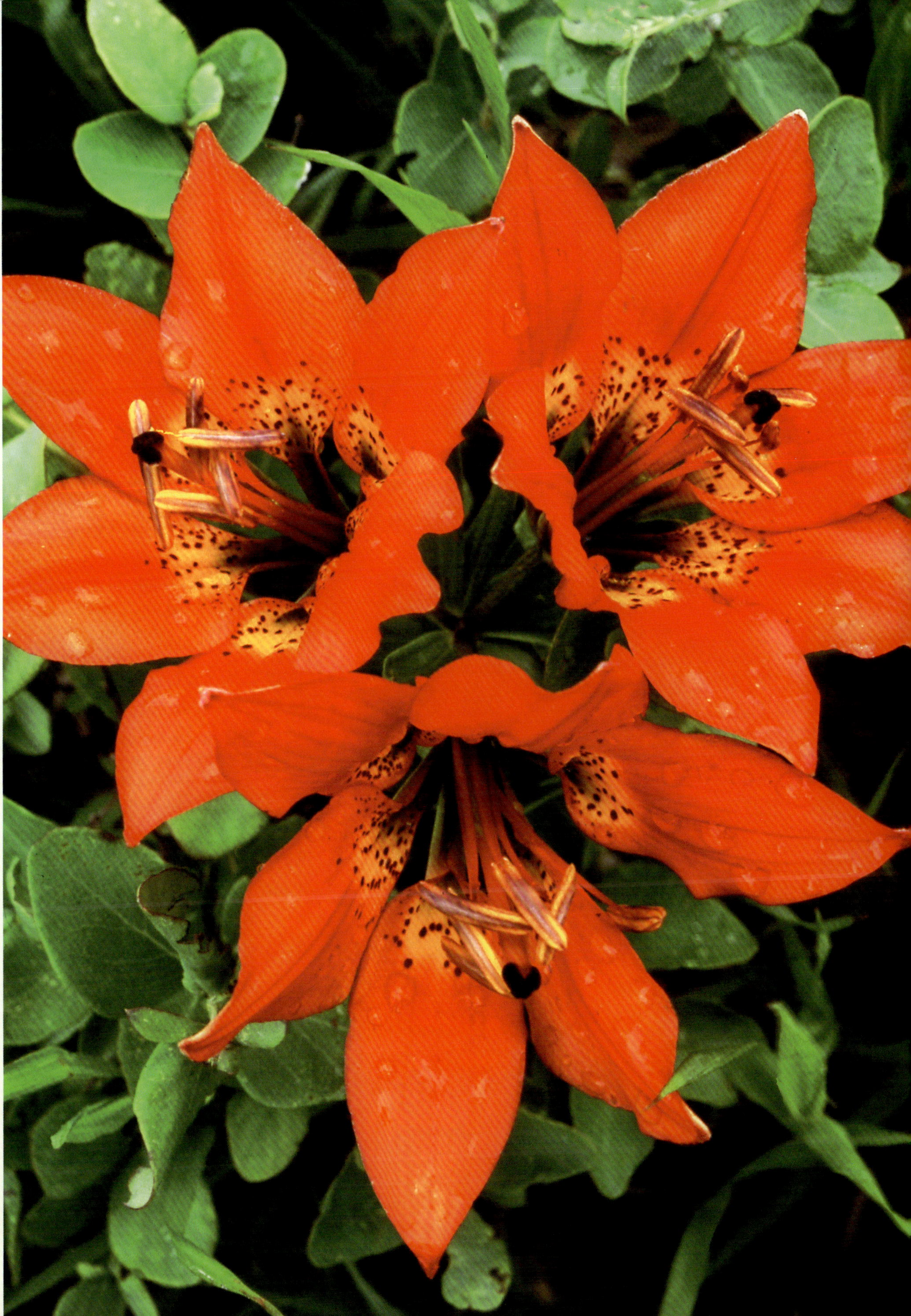

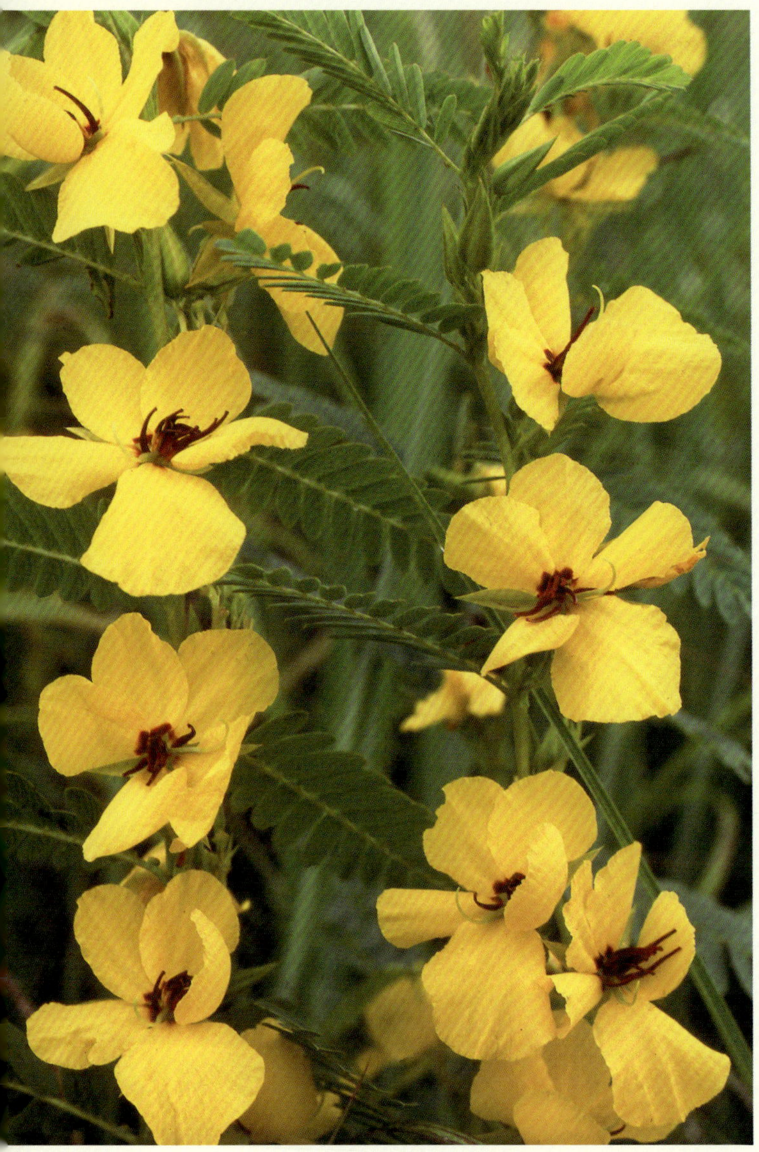

The partridge pea (*Chamaecrista fasciculata*), one of a few annual species that bloom in tallgrass prairie, thrives in sandy soil.

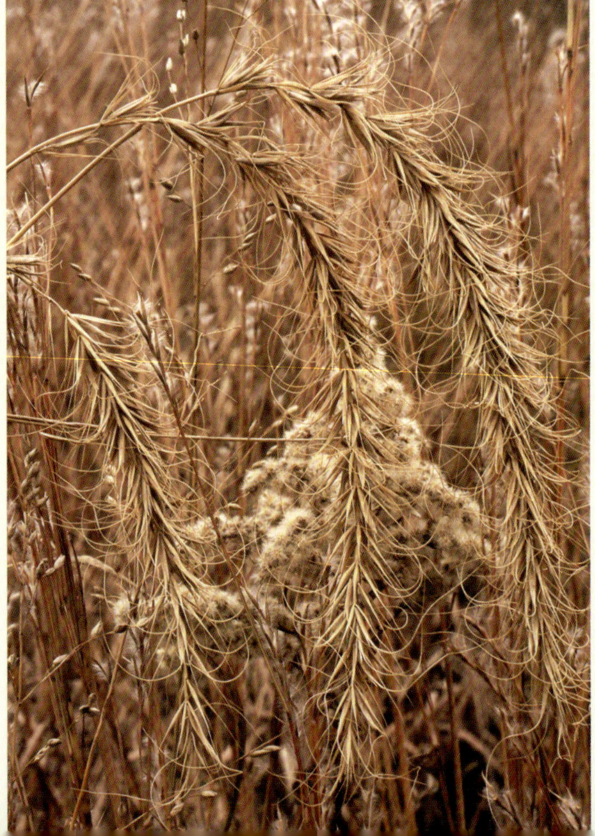

In November, the seed heads of Canada wild rye (*Elymus canadensis*) are conspicuous against the muted browns of forbs and grasses.

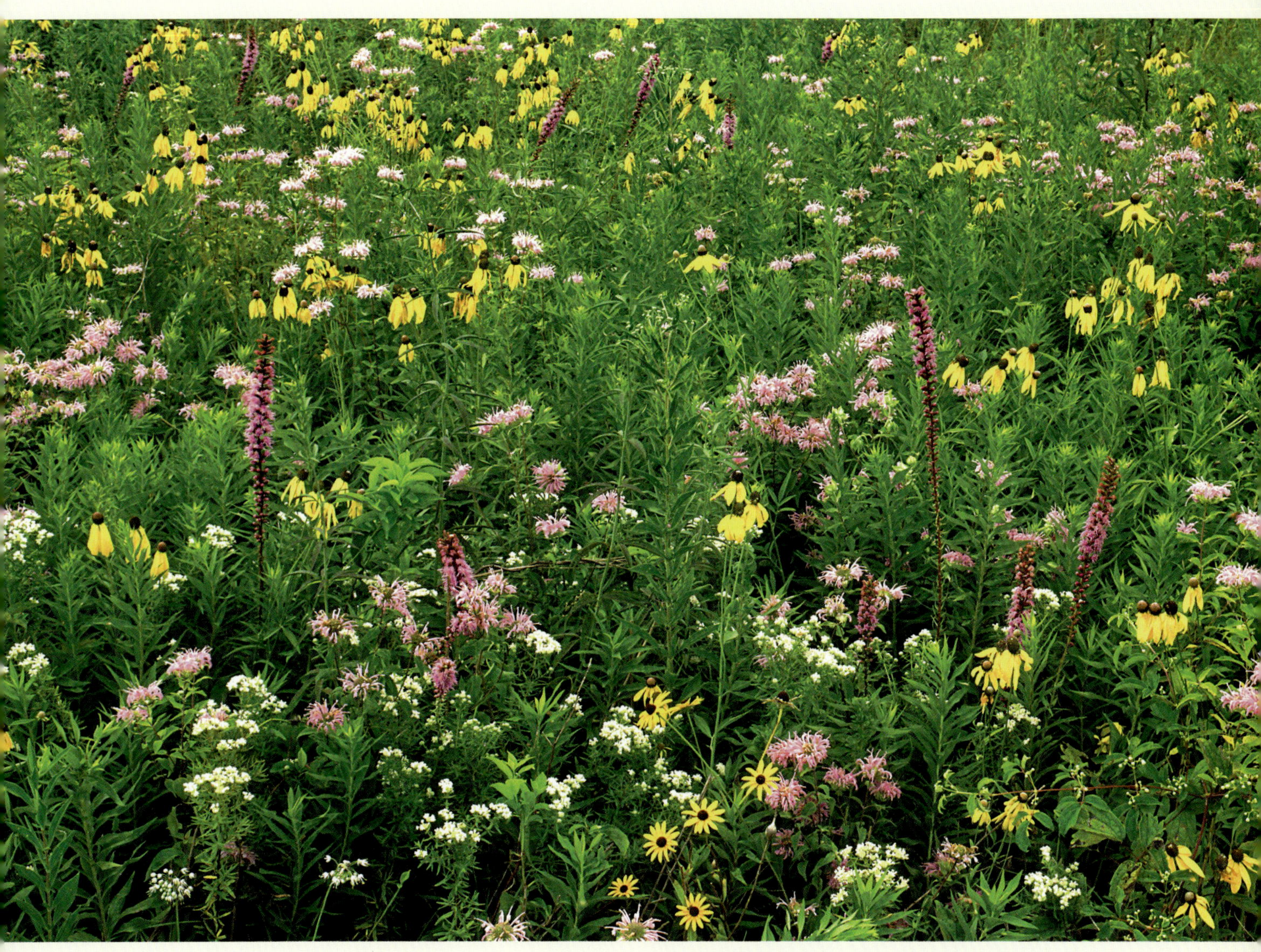

In July, meadows full of colorful flowers brighten the Prairie Peninsula. Early travelers marveled at the sea of billowing grasses and colorful blooms.

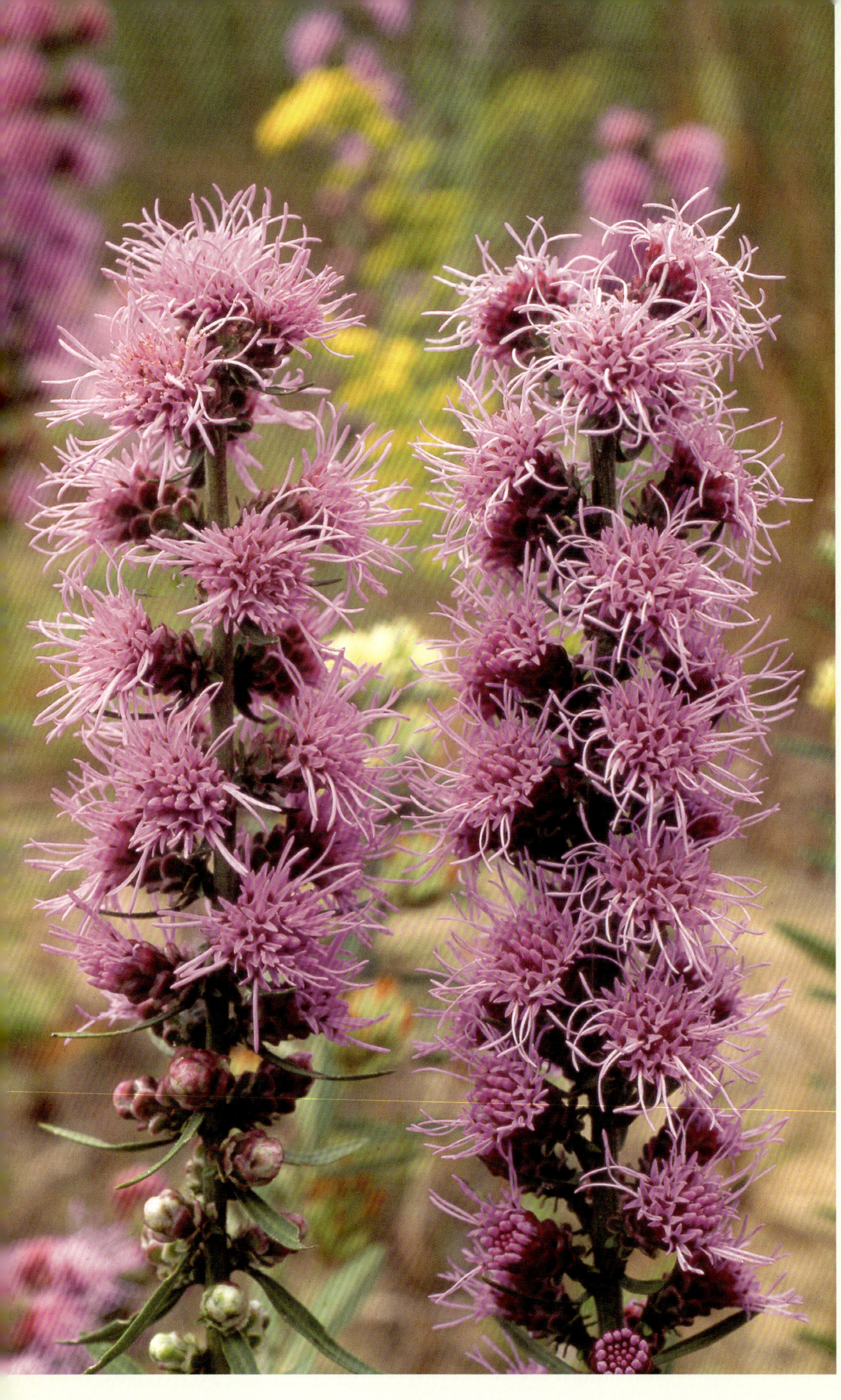

Rough blazing stars (*Liatris aspera*) are common in late summer sand prairies and oak savannas.

CHAPTER 5

The Insects

It is possible that more species of insects live in prairie than in any other North American biome. Clouds of mosquitoes, along with chiggers, no-see-ums, and deerflies can make some prairie experiences memorable. Insects play a critical role in maintaining the fluctuating balance between plants and animals by controlling plant growth, pollinating flowers, and providing a source of food for animals higher up the food chain. In their work in the Chicago region, Ron Panzer and his colleagues found that about 15 percent of all insects could be found only in prairie areas (Panzer et al. 1995).

Among the most important insects in prairies are the grasshoppers, which belong to the Orthoptera, a large family that also includes crickets and katydids. As primary consumers, they feed on the abundance of grasses and forbs throughout the growing season. Although there are numerous grasshopper species, few are widespread or abundant. Two commonly encountered are red-legged (*Melanoplus femurrubrum*) and two-striped grasshoppers (*Melanoplus bivittatus*). Population densities vary from year to year, depending on rainfall and temperature. Dry years tend to have higher numbers. Mortality is also high. About 60 percent of the young orthopterans die during their early stages of metamorphosis (Allen 1967).

Many insects are predators. Perhaps the most voracious are the praying mantids (order Mantodea), which are mainly ambush predators. As small hatchlings they feed on aphids, and as adults they feed on grasshoppers and crickets. Among the robber flies, the red-footed cannibal fly (*Promachus rufipes*) mainly eats bumblebees. A robber fly darts out to grab a passing victim, then carries it to a convenient perch and sucks its body juices. Robber flies belong to the Diptera order, a large and diverse insect order that includes mosquitoes, gnats, and all manner of flies. Most are beneficial pollinators, but a few, like mosquitoes and certain fly species, can carry infectious diseases such as malaria, which affected early pioneers. Tiger beetles (Cicindela spp.) in the order Coleoptera scurry across sandy areas; these have large eyes and long mandibles, which they use to capture slow-moving prey. Tiny black tumbling flower beetle larvae (Rynchites spp.) feed within the stems of many sunflowers, while adults feast on the flower heads (Hamilton 1974). Another species, the silphium weevil (*Haplorhynchites aeneus*, order Curculionidae) enjoys compass plants (*Silphium laciniatum*) as well as other composites. At times, weevils can be destructive, using their long beaks to bore into stems and roots to lay eggs. A few, like the wild indigo weevil (*Apion rostrum*), are specialists, feeding mainly on wild indigo. Still others are beneficial, feeding on plants that are considered weeds.

Male dragonflies (order Odonata) fly back and forth over wetlands trying to defend breeding areas from intruding males. Brightly colored skimmers are the first to get our attention. Common whitetails (*Plathemis lydia*) and twelve-spot (*Libellula pulchella*) and widow skimmers (*Libellula luctuosa*), with their black, white, and blue patterns, are conspicuous. Resting on the ground or favorite perches, they wait patiently for passing meals. Many species of skimmers are on the wing throughout the summer and fall. Less conspicuous are the clubtails (Gomphus spp.), whose yellow and black patterns look similar to the untrained eye. Plains clubtails (*Gomphus externus*) abound along prairie paths in Illinois and western Indiana. Their long legs give them good views of their surroundings. Unlike skimmers, most clubtails breed in the spring. Some are rare, and almost all have short flight seasons. In late summer, large dragonflies, green darners (*Anax junius*), swarm over the prairie. This common species flies to Central and South America but, unlike birds, does not return.

The relationship between plants and insects is a subtle one. We tend to think of insects as takers, nipping away at vegetation or sucking the juices from plant stems, but, for example, the caterpillar that consumes the leaves of a coneflower may return to pollinate it as a butterfly or moth. Flowering plants and their pollinators are interdependent; 85 percent of all plants require pollination by insects. Butterflies and moths (order Lepidoptera) are also important pollinators; most are generalists, their larvae feeding on a wide variety of trees, forbs, and grasses. The larvae of one specialist, the leadplant flower moth (*Schinia lucens*), is restricted to leadplant (*Amphora canescens*). Conversely, leadplants are hosts to many kinds of insects but only a few known moth species; black-spotted prominent (*Dasylophia anguina*), three-staffed underwing (*Catocala amestris*), leadplant flower moth, and two others yet to be described as species. The giant Eucosma, or bird-dropping, moth (*Eucosma giganteana*) is known to feed only on the cup plant (*Silphium perfoliatum*) (Hess and Hatfield 2015). Karner blue butterflies (*Lycaeides melissa samuelis*) are restricted to wild lupine (*Lupinus perennis*). Loss of habitat has put this specialist on the endangered species list; efforts are now underway to plant wild lupine and reintroduce populations that have been previously extirpated.

A small number of insects are prairie obligates, or prairie-dependent species. Ottoe (*Hesperia ottoe*), arogos (*Atrytone arogos*), and byssus skippers (*Problema byssus*) can be found only in original prairie remnants within the prairie province. Nearly a third of butterflies encountered are skippers, and many are found in prairies. These are joined by black swallowtails (*Papilio polyxenes*), common buckeyes (*Junonia coenia*), monarchs (*Danaus plexippus*), painted ladies (*Vanessa cardui*), and viceroys (*Limenitis archippus*), all of which are common species. Once abundant throughout the East and Midwest, regal fritillary (*Speyeria idalia*) populations began a rapid decline in the late 1970s. By the end of the 1980s, they had all but disappeared east of the Mississippi River; today, the few colonies that remain are either isolated or found in high-quality prairie. Through survey work, scientists are beginning to study the ecological connections among prairie-dependent species, their predators, and host plants. New species have been discovered, with many range extensions noted: an excellent example is the rare red-tailed leafhopper (*Aflexia rubranura*). This specialist feeds only on prairie dropseed (*Sporobolus heterolepis*), an uncommon grass found in original prairie. Leafhoppers belong to the order Homoptera, which also includes the true bugs and cicadas. One of three cicada species found in prairies is the inch-long prairie cicada (*Okanagana balli*), best known for the high buzzing sound it emits, usually from the top of some tall plant or grass. Although this cicada appears every year, it cannot complete the egg-to-adult cycle in a single growing season. Population densities can vary from just a few to hundreds in small parcels of original prairie; studies at the James Woodworth Prairie in Illinois suggest a population of about five hundred individuals—a large number for a five-acre site (Popelka 2011).

The order Hymenoptera includes bees, wasps, and ants, some of prairies' most important pollinators. More efficient than honeybees (*Apis mellifera*), bumblebees use buzz pollination, which enables them to gather nectar and pollen at the same time. Bumblebees, unlike honeybees, can still pollinate in cool weather; they also can leave their nests earlier in the day and return later, giving them more time to forage (Hatfield et al. 2012). Since the turn of the twenty-first century, honeybees have experienced serious difficulties from infestations from mites and, more recently, colony-collapse syndrome. This alone is troubling, but some of our native bumblebees have fared even worse: two species that inhabit our prairies—rusty-patched (*Bombus affinis*) and yellow-banded (*Bombus terricola*) bumblebees—have experienced major declines (Hatfield et al. 2012). A 1995 Wisconsin survey reported that yellow-banded bumblebees represented 93 percent of all individuals; by 2015, their numbers had dropped to less than 1 percent. Obviously, the loss of habitat and heavy use of pesticides are factors, but pathogens passed from an unregulated commercial bee industry may play a larger part in the drastic decline of some of our native bees (Platt 2015). Often overlooked, many small species, like mason (Osmis spp.), leaf-cutting (Megachilidae spp.), and sweat bees (Halictidae spp.), are also important pollinators.

Conspicuous mounds can be seen in prairies and savannas; these are homes of mound-builder ants (Formicinae spp.). We hardly think of ants as significant, but they play important roles in loosening soil and bringing up nutrients by continually building and then abandoning nests. Their tunneling action below the root zone improves soil quality by releasing needed minerals, and they help with plant distribution by eating the elaiosomes, oil-rich fleshy structures attached to seeds, then discarding the actual seed. Ants also keep the prairie tidy by disposing of the carcasses of dead animals.

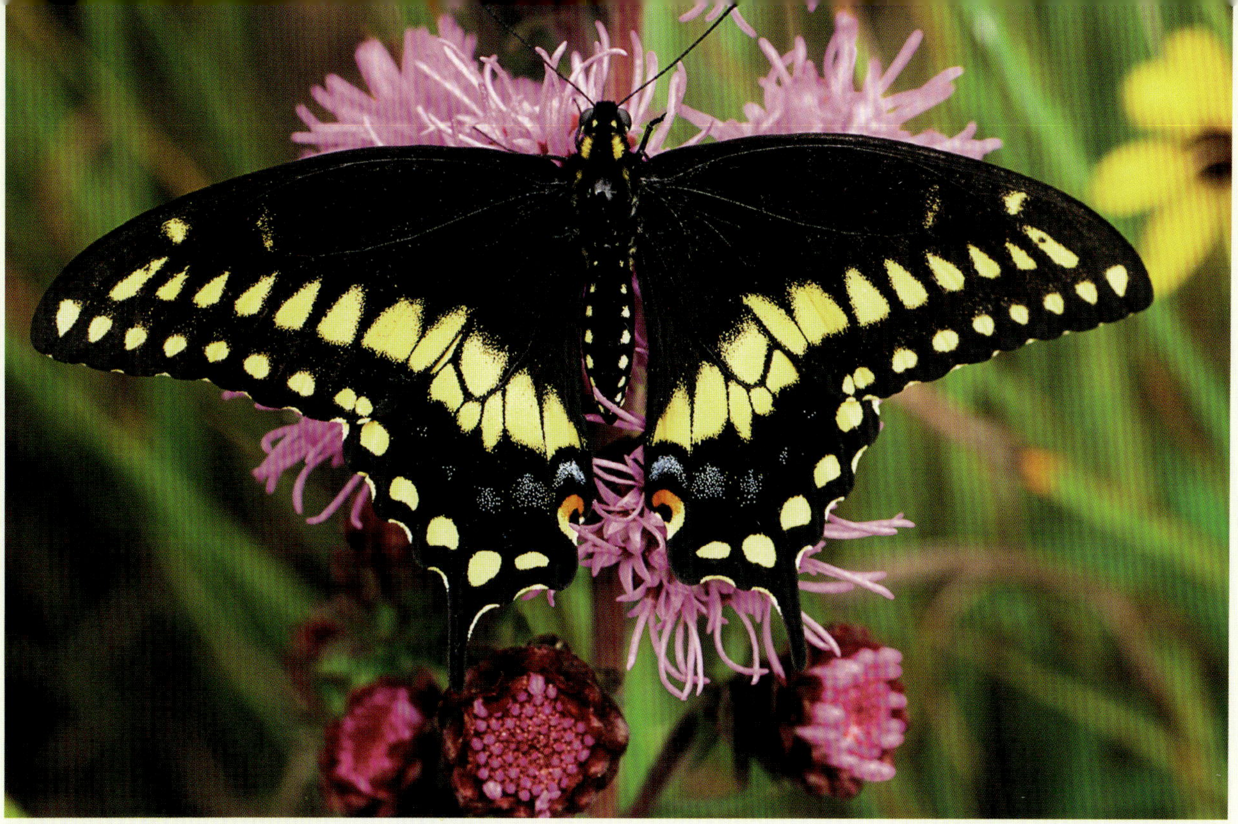

Many colorful butterflies, among them black swallowtails (*Papilio poylexenes*), grace prairie grasslands.

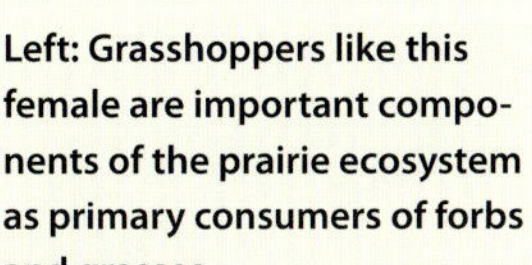

Left: Grasshoppers like this female are important components of the prairie ecosystem as primary consumers of forbs and grasses.

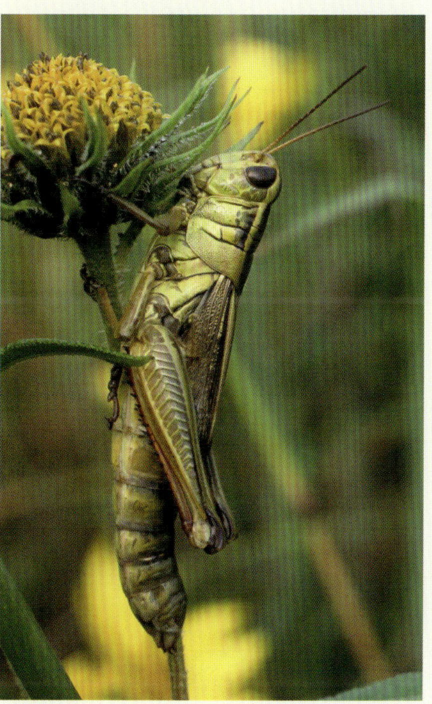

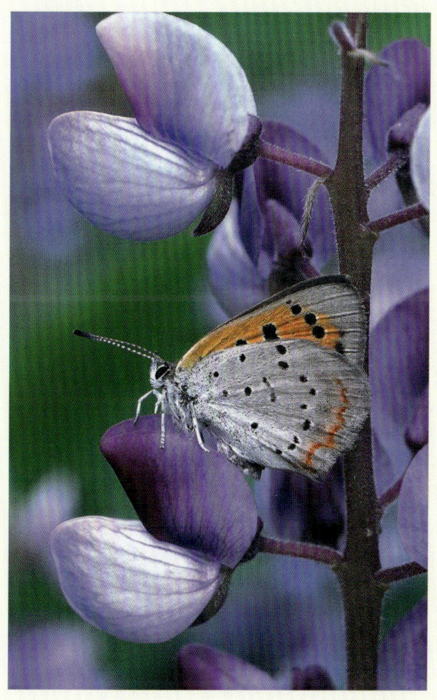

Right: An American copper (*Lycaena phlaeas*) rests on wild lupine. The pugnacious little butterfly attacks anything that enters its range, even large monarchs.

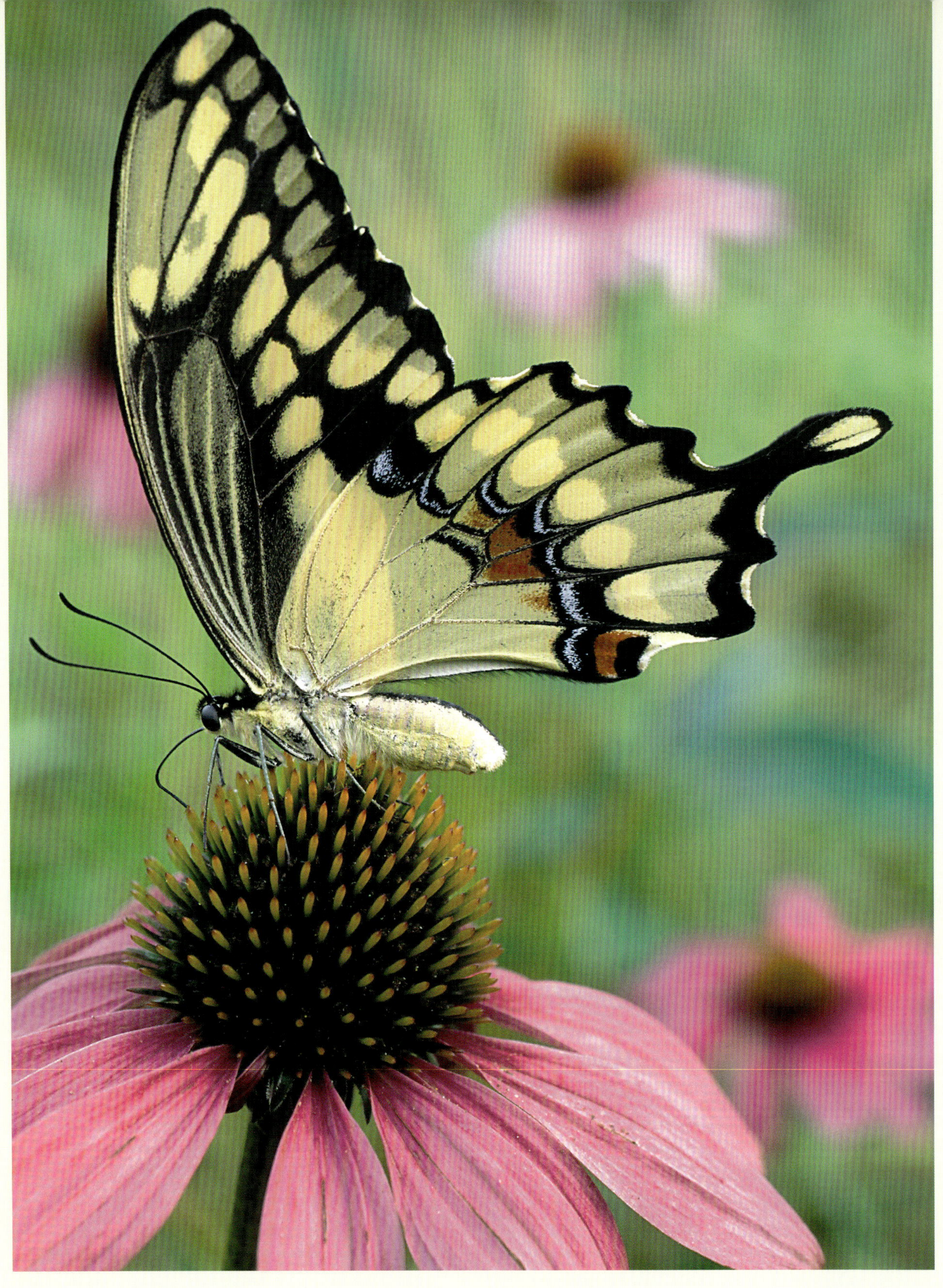

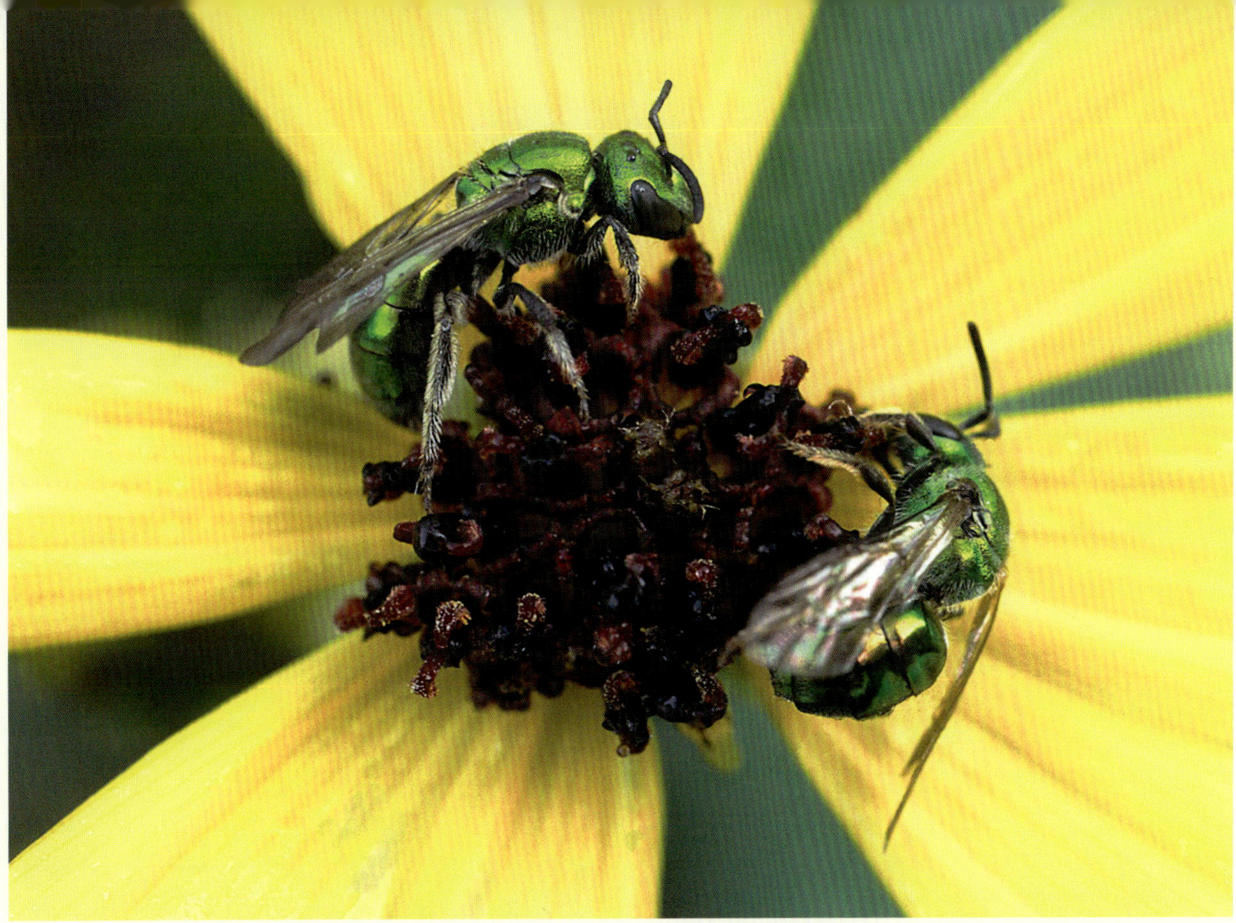

Two metallic sweat bees (Agapostemon spp.) rest on a tall coreopsis. Though often overlooked, small flies and bees are important pollinators.

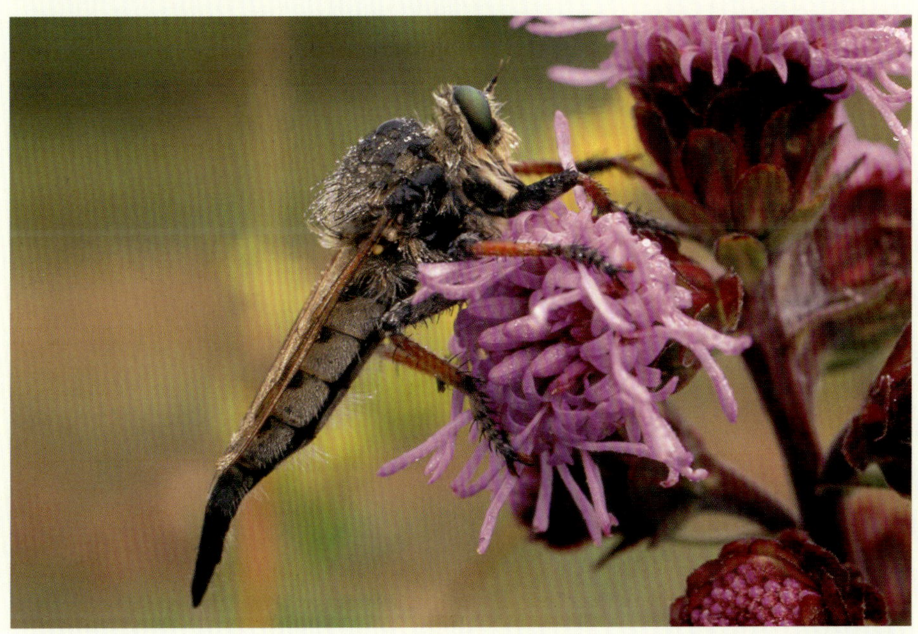

A red-footed cannibal fly (*Promachus rufipes*) rests on a blazing star. This large robber fly preys mainly on bumblebees.

Opposite: One of the Prairie Peninsula's largest native butterflies, the giant swallowtail (*Papilio cresphontes*) can be seen from early July onward. This prairie-edge species feeds on wafer ash.

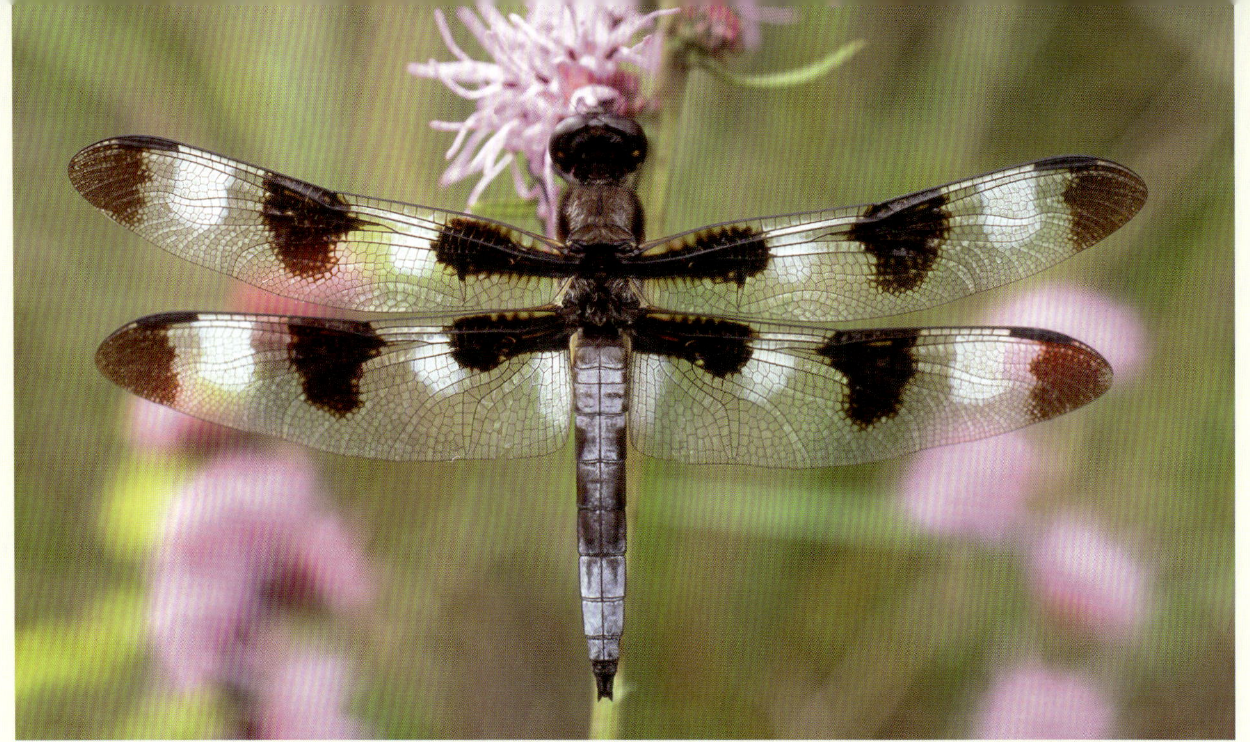

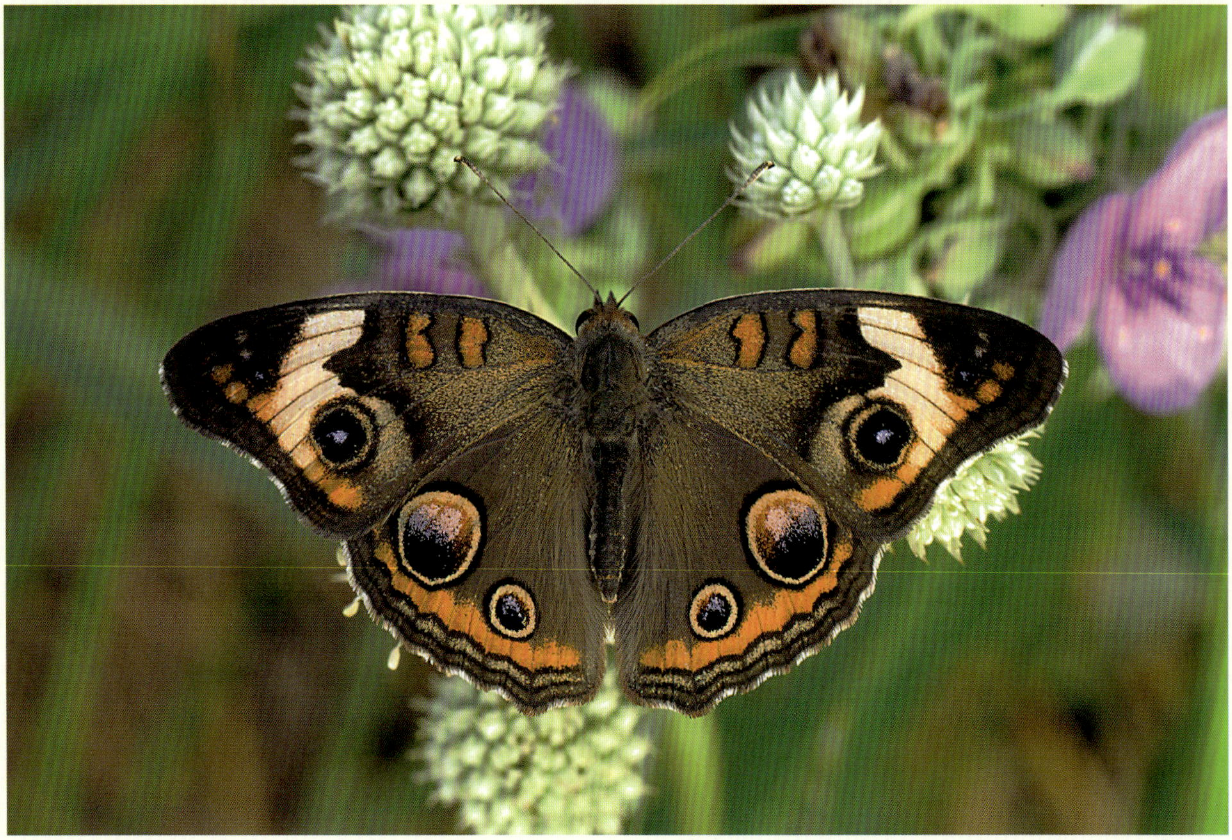

Other pollinators, like this Bembex sand wasp (*Bembex rostrata*), are often overlooked. Fast diggers, they specialize in catching flies to provision their nest burrows. As adults, they feed on nectar.

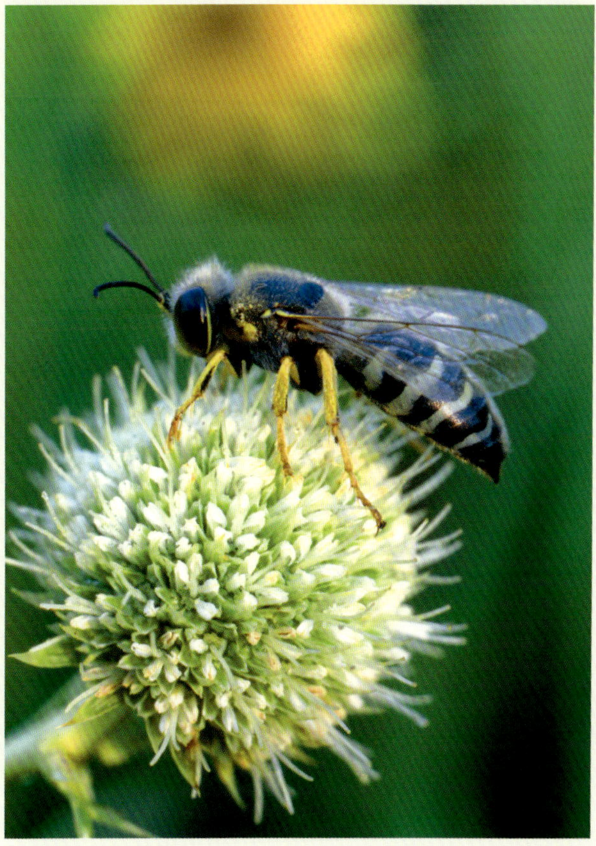

During the day, a pandorus sphinx moth (*Eumorpha pandorus*) rests on a butterfly milkweed. A host of moth species pollinate mainly at night.

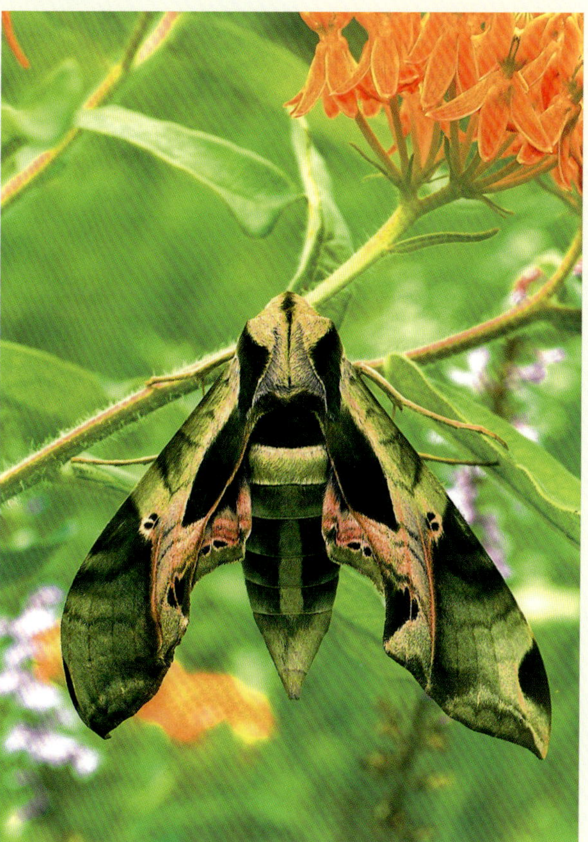

Plains clubtails (*Gomphus externus*) are common in late spring along prairie roads and paths. Black and yellow patterns make different clubtail species hard to identify in the field.

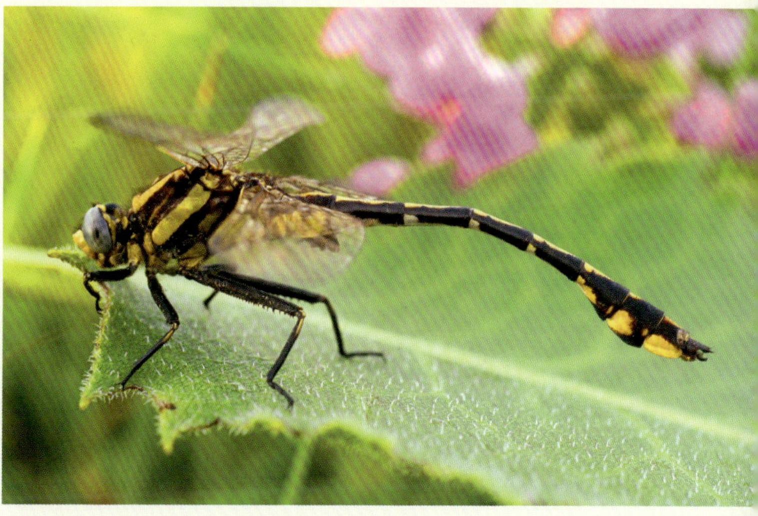

Opposite Top: Many colorful dragonfly species, like common twelve-spot skimmers (*Libellula pulchella*), can be seen hovering or flying over wet prairie meadows. Most skimmers have long flight seasons.

Opposite Bottom: A common buckeye (*Junonia coenia*) pollinates a rattlesnake master; these butterflies experience cycles of abundance.

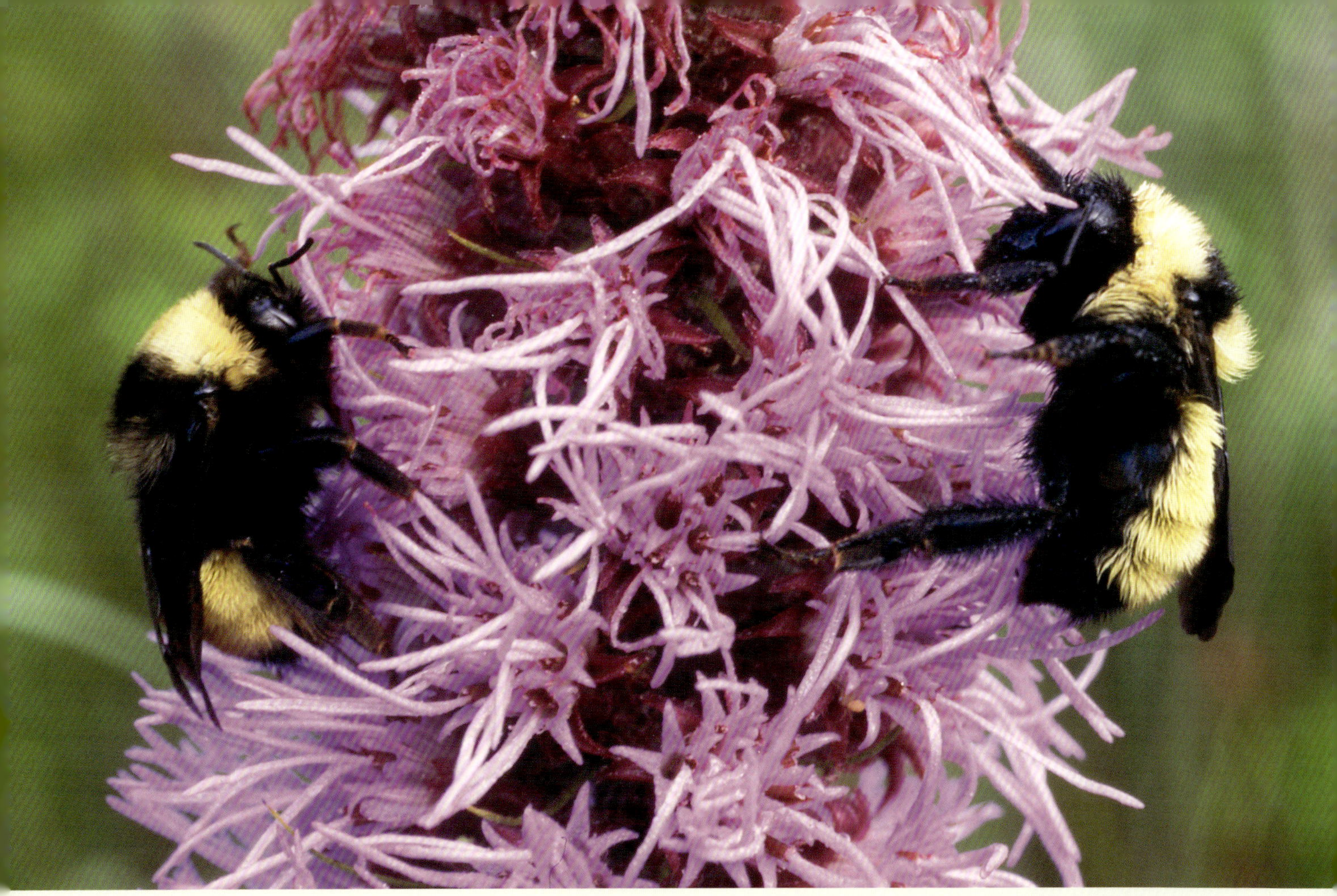

These bumblebees have spent the night on a prairie blazing star (*Liatris pycnostachya*). Some bumblebee species, as well as the common honeybee (*Apis mellifera*), have experienced large population declines.

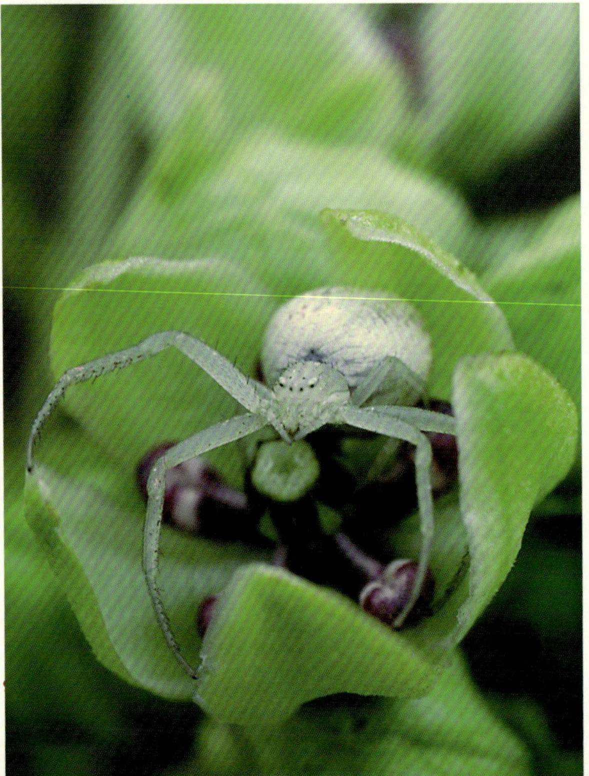

A crab spider (*Misumena vatia*) waits in a spider milkweed blossom for incoming insects, using camouflage and long legs to slowly surround a hapless victim.

A common species, the tiger swallowtail (*Papilio glaucus*), gathers nectar on a marsh blazing star.

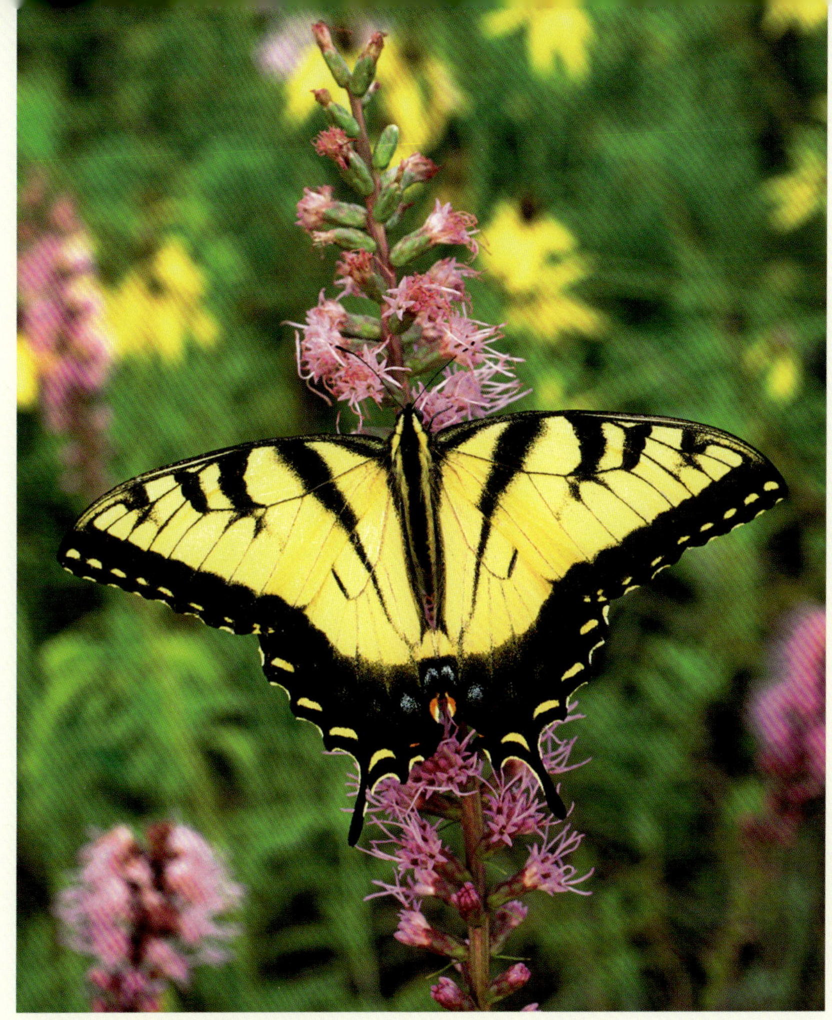

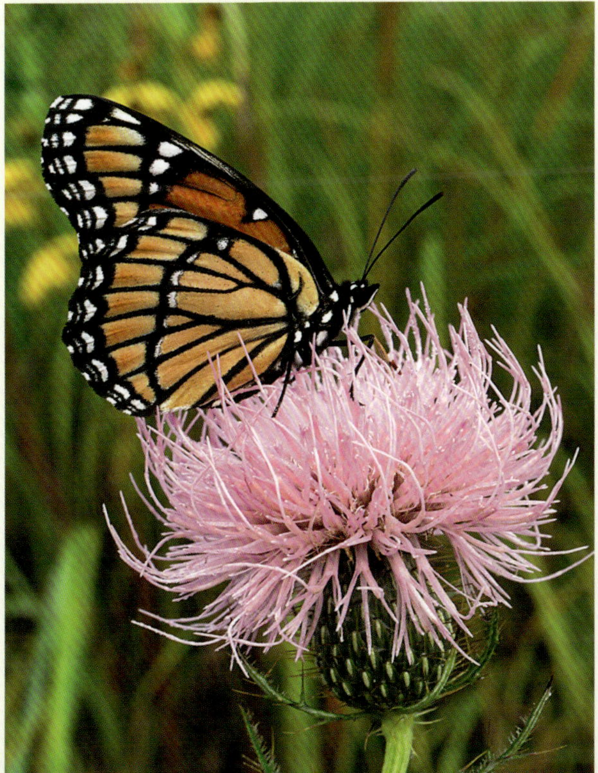

Looking similar to the monarch butterfly, this viceroy (*Limenitis archippus*) lands on a pasture thistle. The ubiquitous thistle can be found growing in pristine tallgrass remnants as well as vacant urban lots.

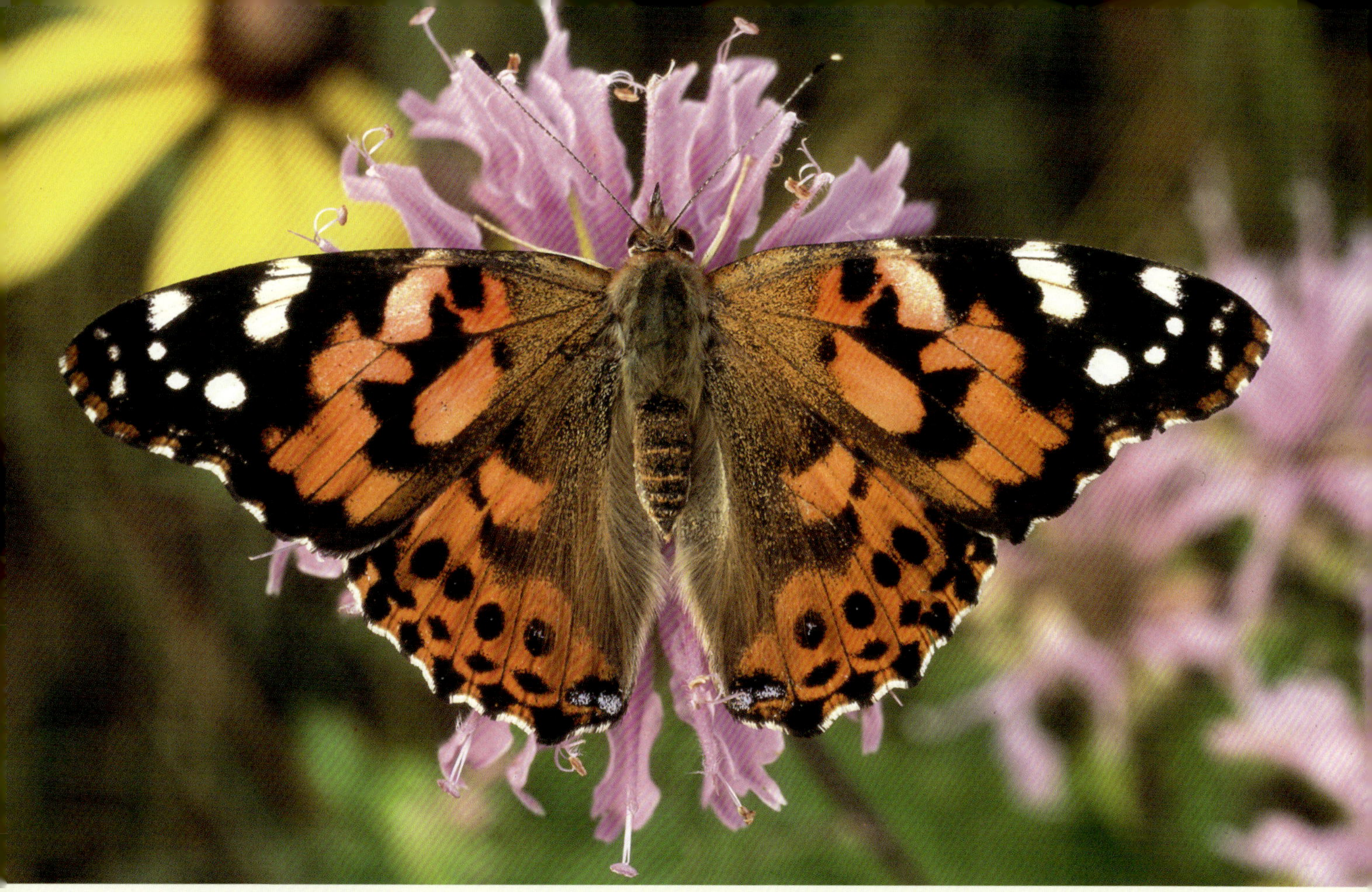

Feeding on wild bergamot (*Monarda fistulosa*), painted lady butterflies (*Vanessa cardui*) can be abundant some years and scarce in others. Lepidopterists believe that wet and dry cycles influence butterfly numbers.

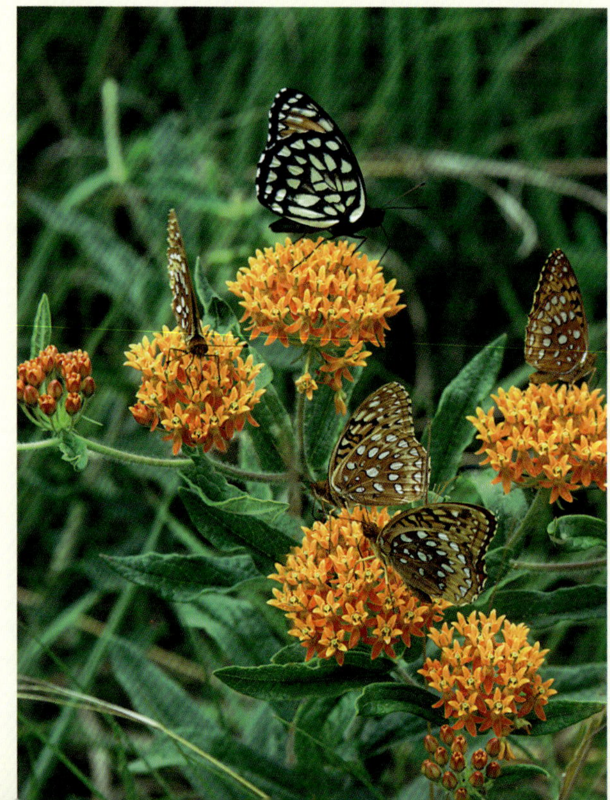

Fritillaries (Speyeria spp.) swarm on butterfly milkweed in early summer.

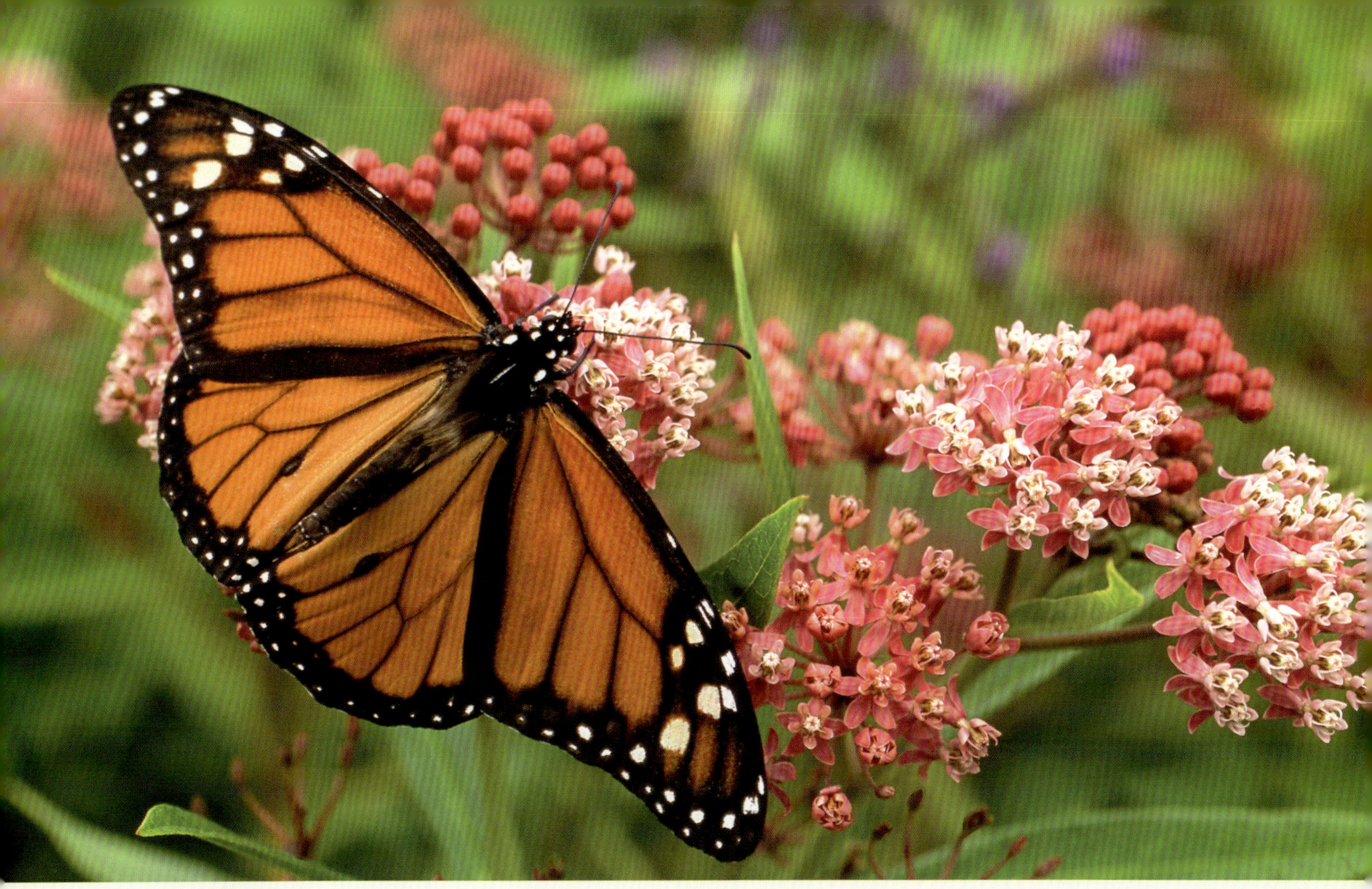

The destruction of most of their wintering grounds in Mexico and dwindling milkweed plants are major factors in the recent decline of monarch butterflies (*Danaus plexippus*).

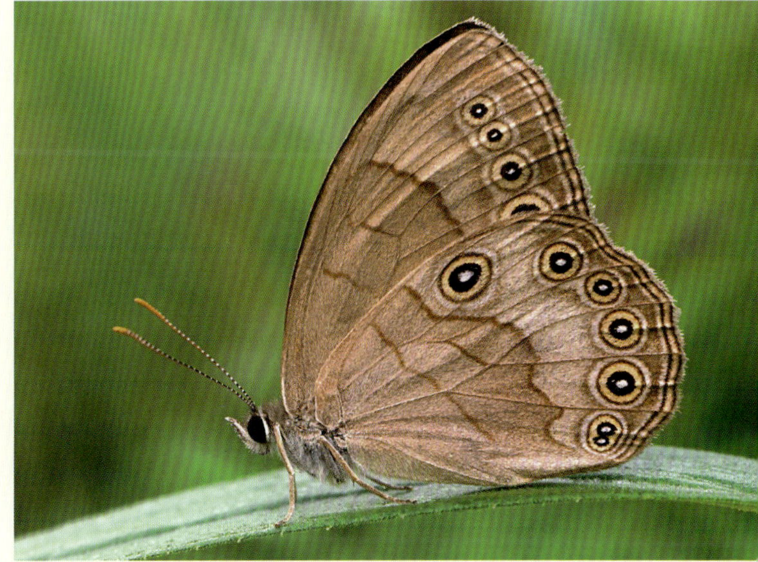

Uncommon eyed brown butterflies (*Satyrodes eurydice*), which fly slowly and erratically, are local in wet prairie meadows.

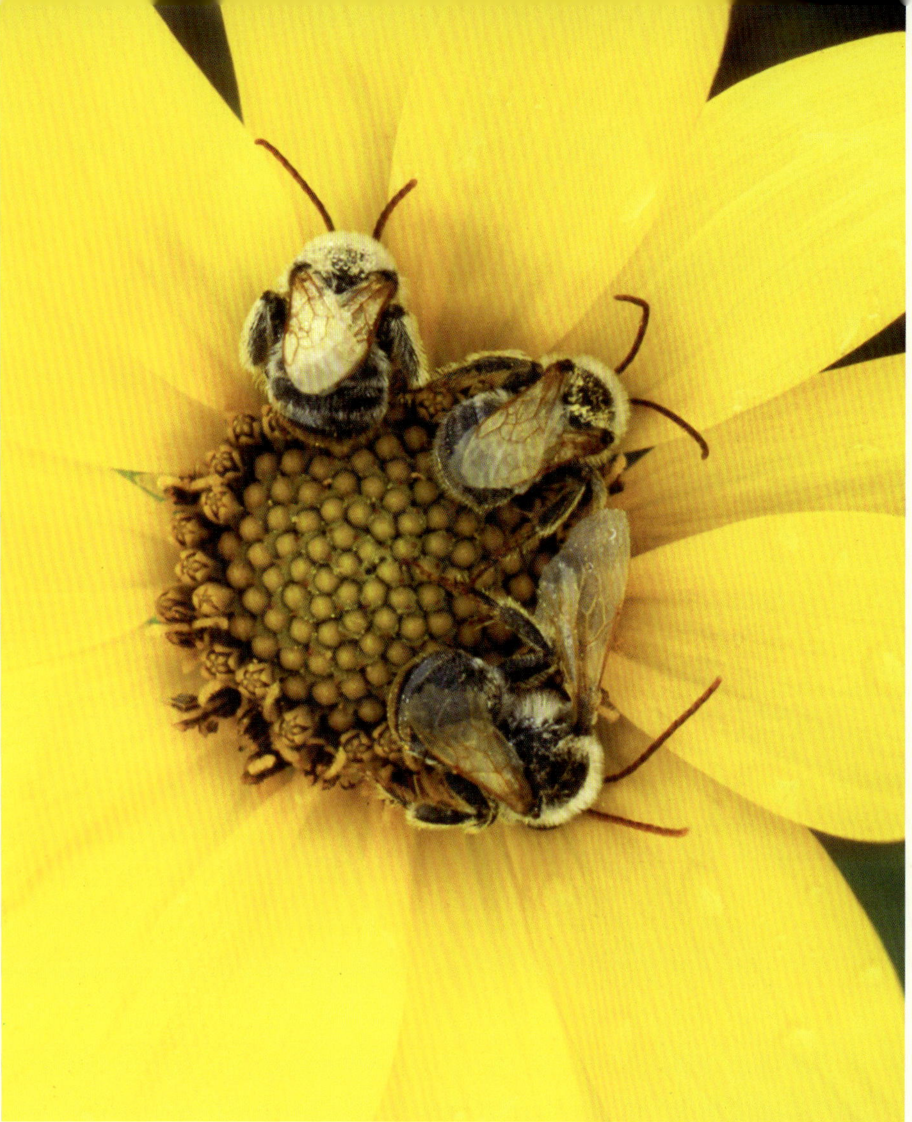

Important pollinators, these leaf-cutting bees (Megachilidae spp.) spend the night on a rosinweed flower. Unlike other bee species that carry pollen on their hind legs, these bees pick up pollen with hairs on the undersides of their bodies.

Associated with hackberry woodlands, hackberry butterflies (*Asterocampa celtis*) are common in prairie-edge habitat. They are double-brooded and sometimes experience cycles of abundance.

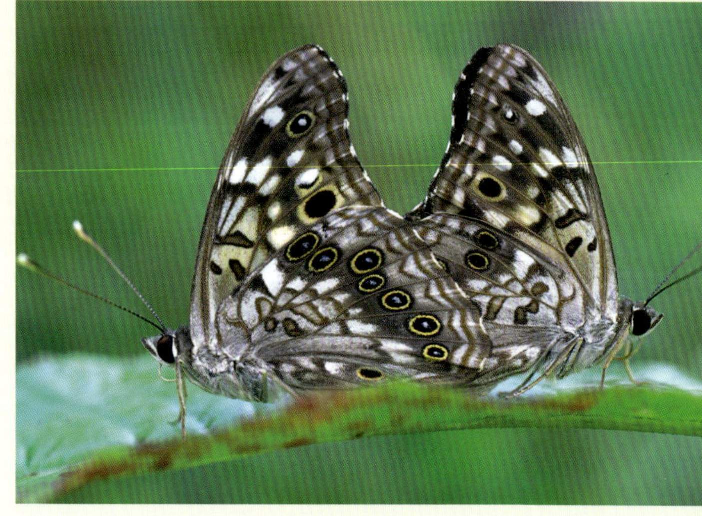

CHAPTER 6

Remnants

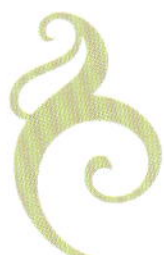

Early settlers saw the prairie as a source of disease and fires. The fires were so feared many called them the "messengers of death"—black clouds of smoke and flames rose across the horizon as it swept across the prairie, engulfing everything in their path. The invention of the self-scouring steel moldboard plow sealed the prairie's fate. Rich, black soil could now be turned into cropland and dry hillsides into pasture. By the beginning of the twentieth century, more than 20 million acres of Illinois Grand Prairie had vanished from the American landscape. Similar losses had occurred throughout the Prairie Peninsula: in Iowa, less than one tenth of 1 percent of original prairie remains, about five thousand acres, and only twenty-three hundred acres survive in Illinois. Formerly large openings covering thousands of acres are now fragmented ecosystems reduced to small parcels in pioneer cemeteries and along railroad lines, high bluffs, and sandy areas of Lakes Michigan and Erie. A majority of these sites are sand prairies with poor soil quality, too arid to farm. Only a few examples of mesic black soil prairie survive. Because of urban development, the use of management tools like fire is limited. Many of these small parcels lie next to fields of corn and soybeans, where nitrogen-rich fertilizers leaching into the ground affect species composition and ambient soil fertility, favoring some species while limiting the growth of others. Invasions of alien plants and insecticides drifting over from nearby farms pose the greatest threat to these surviving fragments. In some cases, buffer zones have been added to protect significant remnants.

Before 1960, twentieth-century Illinoisans were unaware of their prairie heritage. No one realized what was locked away in the state's pioneer cemeteries. Robert Betz and Herbert F. Lamp of Northeastern Illinois University, opened the door by discovering forty-five pioneer cemeteries in northern Illinois that still had prairie vegetation (1992). Finished in 1978, a complete inventory of Illinois cemeteries listed twenty-four untouched remnants. Stephen Ambrose recounts Robert Betz finding his first cemetery. "Early in 1960, I was looking for prairie in Will County . . . I looked down the railroad tracks and I saw an old cemetery with an iron fence around it. I could see there were prairie plants there" (Ambrose 2007). Neighboring states would also benefit from his pioneering work and make their own discoveries.

A number of ongoing large restorations have been initiated in Illinois and Indiana. Notable among these are the Midewin National Tallgrass Prairie and Goose Lake State Park in Illinois and Kankakee Sands in Indiana. Though these sites give the visitor a view of endless prairie, they are usually low in quality. Even the best restorations can never approach the floristic composition or biodiversity accumulated over thousands of years in original prairie. Much time and energy are spent on creating these mega-preserves, with little emphasis on the long-term viability of original remnants. The tremendous value of these sites cannot be understated; a list of outstanding remnants follows.

Illinois

Bluff Spring Fen, Cook County

Once a gravel quarry and dumping site, the ninety-acre fen has been restored by an army of volunteers. The preserve is a patchwork of wetlands, wet prairie, and forest. More than four hundred species of native plants have been recorded at this site. Alkaline water seeps from kames, creating a large fen meadow. Many rare calciphiles grow here. Grass pink orchids (*Calopogon tuberosus*) as well as small white lady's slippers (*Cypripedium candidum*) are a treat. Rare butterflies include mulberry wing skippers (*Poanes massasoit*) and Baltimore checkerspots (*Euphydryas phaeton*); the latter is at the western edge of its breeding range.

Gensburg-Markham Prairie, Cook County

This National Natural Landmark just south of Chicago preserves an outstanding example of sandy loam and black soil prairies. It is one of a cluster of four units—Gensburg-Markham, Dropseed, Sundrop, and Indian Paintbrush Prairies—that make up the Indian Boundary Prairies, a shared total of over 435 acres. More than one hundred acres, this lake plain prairie is one of the finest examples of tallgrass prairie remnants in the Midwest. Its rare insects include the regal fritillary butterflies (*Speyeria idalia*) and Ottoe (*Hesperia ottoe*) and bunchgrass skippers (*Euphyes bayensis*) and leadplant flower moths (*Schinia lucens*). Henslow's sparrows (*Ammodramus henslowii*) and sedge wrens (*Cistothorus platensis*) are summer residents. Eastern prairie white-fringed orchids (*Platanthera leucophaea*) as well as six species of gentian occur here. Intensively managed, parts of the site are burned annually with invasive species eliminated by hand picking.

Harlem Hills, Winnebago County

In the month of June each year this 95-acre preserve is blanketed with pale purple coneflowers (*Echinacea pallida*). Harlem Hills is Illinois's largest and finest remaining example of gravel hill prairie. Rare plants found growing on the steep hillsides include the downy yellow paintbrush (*Castilleja sessiliflora*), Hill's thistle (*Cirsium pumlum hillii*), pasque flower (*Anemone patens*), and pink milkwort (*Polygala incarnata*).

Illinois Beach State Park, Lake County

The park encompasses the only surviving natural shoreline in the state. Two units comprise 4,160 acres. Extensive dune-and-swale topography grades into black oak savanna. Vast expanses of marsh support dense stands of cattails, bluejoint (*Calamagrostis canadensis*), switchgrass (*Panicum virgatum*), big bluestem (*Andropogon gerardii*), and sedges (Carex spp.). Large areas of native prickly-pear cactus (*Opuntia humifusa*) add interest. Bearberry (*Arctostaphylos uva-ursi*) and Waukegan juniper (*Juniperus horizontalis*), both northern species, grow on the dunes. More than 650 species of plants have been observed in this largest prairie remnant in Illinois. The shoreline is an important migration corridor for songbirds and raptors.

James Woodworth Prairie, Cook County

In sharp contrast to surrounding urban development, this five-acre remnant of virgin black soil prairie is the largest and finest remaining example of its type in Illinois. Soil analysis shows the prairie to be about five thousand years old. It has never been plowed or mowed. A large population of prairie cicadas (*Okanagana balli*) can be found here as well as small white lady's slippers and cream false indigo (*Baptisia leucophaea*). Michigan (*Lilium michiganense*) and prairie lilies (*Lilium philadelphicum*) bloom in midsummer. The site is used as a standard for evaluating floristic components in original black soil remnants and ecological restorations.

Lockport Dolomite Prairie, Will County

Located next to the Des Plaines River, this 254-acre strip of almost pristine dolomite prairie survives. Too rocky to plow, the varied habitats include mesic prairie, sedge meadows, and calcareous fens. Many rare species, among them the federally listed Hine's Emerald dragonflies (*Somatochlora hineana*), leafy prairie clover (*Dalea foliosa*), and lakeside daisies (*Hymenoxys herbacea*), as well as the state-listed spotted turtle (*Clemmys gutta*), inhabit the site. More than four hundred species of plants have been recorded; at least nine are considered threatened.

Loda Cemetery Prairie Nature Preserve, Iroquois County

At just four acres, this preserve is an outstanding example of black soil prairie. One of the few intact remnants within the Grand Prairie region, it hosts prairie cicadas (*Okanagana balli*), eastern prairie-fringed orchids (*Platanthera leucophaea*), and prairie gentians (*Gentiana puberulenta*). A high percentage of forbs, including leadplant (*Amphora canescens*) and wild quinine (*Parthenium integrifolium*), cover the ground. A large buffer zone adjacent to the prairie has been planted in forbs and grasses.

Nachusa Grasslands, Lee and Ogle Counties

Large prairie preserves like Nachusa Grasslands can sustain healthy ecosystems. Its three-thousand-acre rolling landscape is a mosaic of eleven natural communities, including sand prairie, oak savanna, sedge meadow, and dry hillsides—the last being the most significant. Sandstone outcrops saved much of Nachusa from the plow. Low areas have been seeded with forbs and grasses; alien clover still grows there. A dedicated work force of volunteers who gather and sow seed into degraded areas do ecological restoration work. The Nature Conservancy has introduced a small herd of bison. The largest stand of the federally threatened prairie bush clover (*Lespedeza leptostachya*) grows here. Other candidates for the "threatened" list are fame flower (*Talinum calycinum*), forked aster (*Eurybia furcata*), Hill's thistle (*Cirsium pumlum hillii*), and kittentails (*Besseya bullii*). Northern harriers (*Cicrus cyaneus*), upland sandpipers (*Bartramia longicauda*), bobolinks, dickcissels (*Spiza americanus*), lark (*Chondestes grammacus*), grasshoppers (*Ammodramus savannarum*), and Henslow's sparrows (*Ammodramus henslowii*) perch on tall prairie grasses.

Revis Hill Prairie, Mason County

Lying high above the Sangamon River, the 412-acre prairie preserves the finest loess deposits in the state. Typical dry prairie species—like compass plant (*Silphium laciniatum*), pale purple coneflower (*Echinacea pallida*), and purple prairie clover (*Dalea purpurea*)—bloom in June and July. Rare Ottoe skippers (*Hesperia ottoe*) and a population of western hognose snakes (*Heterodon nasicus*) inhabit the preserve.

Prospect Cemetery Prairie Nature Preserve, Ford County

This five-acre cemetery remnant has many rare plants. Eighty species, including cream wild indigo (*Baptisia leucophaea*), prairie blazing star (*Liatris pycnostachya*), and prairie gentians (*Gentiana puberulenta*), grow among the gravestones. Prairie dropseed (*Sporobolus heterolepis*), an indicator of undisturbed conditions, is also present; one third of the cemetery has not been disturbed.

Shoe Factory Road Prairie, Cook County

Walk across the site, and step back in time in this outstanding, nine-acre example of hill prairie, perched on a glacial deposit of sand and gravel. Well-drained, it is hot and dry in the summer. Grasses include little bluestem (*Schizachyrium scoparium*), side-oats grama (*Bouteloua curtipendula*), and porcupine grass (*Hesperostipa spartea*). In June leadplants (*Amphora canescens*), prairie coreopsis (*Coreopsis palmata*), and purple prairie clover (*Dalea purpurea*) adorn the hillside. Rare prairie bush-clover (*Lespedeza leptostachya*) and wooly milkweed (*Asclepias lanuginosa*) are also found here.

West Chicago Prairie Forest Preserve, DuPage County

This 358-acre preserve features sedge meadows, oak savanna, and swampy glacial potholes. More than four hundred species of plants, along with a small population of prairie cicadas (*Hymenoxys herbacea*), have been recorded. Wet areas have large stands of Indian grass (*Sorghastrum nutans*). A third of the preserve has never been plowed.

Weston Cemetery Prairie, McLean County

This five-acre fragment of black soil prairie is a remnant of the Grand Prairie that once covered 13 million acres of Illinois. Grasses include big bluestem (*Andropogon gerardii*), Indian grass (*Sorghastrum nutans*), and prairie dropseed (*Sporobolus heterolepis*). Prairie gentians (*Gentiana puberulenta*) bloom in September.

Wolf Road Prairie, Cook County

Wolf Road Prairie ranks as one of the finest black soil remnants in the prairie peninsula. The stands of prairie dropseed (*Sporobolus heterolepis*) indicate undisturbed conditions in this fifty-acre preserve. Over 370 species of native plants have been documented. In spring a blanket of wild hyacinths (*Camassia scilloides*) covers the oak savanna. The north end of the preserve is enhanced with many colorful forbs. Rare prairie crayfish (*Procambarus gracilis*) live here as well. To protect this important remnant, better management is needed.

Iowa

Cedar Hills Sand Prairie, Black Hawk County

The ninety-acre Cedar Hills Sand Prairie is one of the largest surviving examples of sand prairie in Iowa. The preserve lies on a ridge of aeolian, or wind-deposited, sand. Over three hundred species of plants have been seen here, among them the hairy puccoon (*Lithospermum caroliniense*), pink milkwort (*Polygala incarnata*), rough blazing star (*Liatris aspera*), and silky prairie clover (*Dalea villosa*). Bobolinks (*Dolichonyx oryzivorus*), grasshopper sparrows (*Ammodramus savannarum*) and savanna sparrows (*Passerculus sandwichensis*) inhabit the site.

Hayden Prairie State Preserve, Howard County

Hayden Prairie, home to more than two hundred species, is located on the northeastern border between Iowa and Minnesota. At over 240 acres, this National Natural Landmark is the largest parcel of original mesic black soil prairie remaining in Iowa. Pale purple coneflowers (*Echinacea pallida*), Michigan lilies (*Lilium michiganense*), and prairie smoke (*Geum triflorum*) bloom in spring. The display of midland shooting stars (*Dodecatheon meadia*) is especially noteworthy. Butterflies include regal fritillaries (*Speyeria idalia*) and two-spotted skippers (*Euphyes bimacula*). Henslow's sparrows (*Ammodramus henslowii*) and bobolinks (*Dolichonyx oryzivorus*) breed here. The prairie is named after early conservationist Ada Hayden, a leader in the preservation of Iowa's prairies. Hayden Prairie is one of only a few high-quality sites remaining east of the loess hills.

Loess Hills Corridor, Plymouth County

Lying along the western edge of the Prairie Peninsula, the Loess Hills rise two hundred feet above the Missouri River Valley. Some of the deepest loess deposits in North America can be found on the Iowa side of the Missouri

River. At seven thousand acres, the chain of hills is the largest contiguous original prairie in the state, with the Nature Conservancy's Broken Kettle grasslands forming its core. Plants typical of the western Great Plains include the ten-petal blazing star (*Mentzelia decapetala*), prairie moonwort (*Botrychium campestre*), and yucca (*Yucca glauca*). A herd of more than a hundred bison live on the preserve, as do upland sandpipers (*Bartramia longicauda*), plains spadefoot toads (*Spea bombifrons*), and prairie rattlesnakes (*Crotalus viridis*).

Ohio

Bigelow and Smith Cemetery State Nature Preserves, Madison County

Bigelow and its neighbor Smith Cemetery together occupy less than two acres. Both are superb examples of prairie cemeteries, especially for being so far east. The only unplowed prairie in the Darby Plains, Bigelow is important for its stand of royal catchfly (*Silene regia*), which blooms here at the eastern end of its natural range.

Daughmer Prairie Savannah State Nature Preserve, Crawford County

Formerly in sheep pasture, this thirty-five-acre remnant of the Sandusky plains features trees up to three hundred years old. The lower limbs of the large oaks have not been pruned, giving the visitor an idea of how undisturbed oak savanna looked two hundred years ago.

Kitty Todd Nature Preserve, Lucas County

Lying in the oak openings region of Ohio, the thousand-acre preserve is a complex of oak savanna and wet sand prairie. The Nature Conservancy has played a critical role in restoring the landscape. The largest stand of wild lupine (*Lupinus perennis*) in the state grows here, with the Karner blue butterfly (*Lycaeides melissa samuelis*), which was successfully reintroduced. At the eastern end of their range, rare lark sparrows (*Chondestes grammacus*) nest in the sand prairie. Interesting plants include cross-leaved milkwort (*Polygala cruciata*), prickly-pear cactus (*Opuntia humifusa*), skinner's foxglove (*Agalinis skinneriana*), and yellow-fringed orchids (*Platanthera ciliaris*).

Resthaven Wildlife Area (Castalia Prairie), Erie County

Sears (1967) recounts the history from its past use as a marl and peat strip mine to its present status as a wildlife area. The vegetation varies from marl fens to wet prairie. Over one hundred acres are kept in prairie meadow. Rare plants include small white lady's slippers (*Cyripedium candidum*),

New England blazing stars (*Liatris novae-angliae*), and Great Plains ladies' tresses (*Spiranthes magnicamporum*). In summer, the yellow blooms of prairie dock (*Silphium terebinthinaceum*) blanket large portions of the wildlife area. Another hundred acres to the north and east has many interesting forbs; unfortunately, this area has been neglected, and woody vegetation is taking over. Even with disturbances, however, Resthaven remains one of the best examples of marl prairie in the Midwest.

Indiana

Hoosier Prairie State Nature Preserve, Lake County

Hosting over 350 native plants, Hoosier Prairie is one of the finest natural areas in Indiana. A National Natural Landmark, it is part of the Indiana Dunes National Lakeshore. The 548-acre site hosts a variety of natural communities, from marshes and wet prairie to oak savanna. The lake plain oak savanna is the most significant part of the preserve. A large stand of white false indigo (*Baptisia leucantha*) grows under the oaks.

Clark and Pine Nature Preserve, Lake County

Clark and Pine protects one of the best lake plain dune-and-swale habitats remaining in the Midwest. At just forty acres, this high-quality preserve has perhaps the highest diversity of plants in Indiana. Wet meadows contain rarities like Baltic rush (*Juncus balticus*), low nutrush (*Scleria verticillata*), golden-seeded (*Eleocharis elliptica*) and hairbeak spikerush (*Eleocharis rostellata*), purple bladderworts (*Utricularia purpurea*), and rare bluehearts (*Buchnera americana*) can also be found here. In August, cylindric blazing stars (*Liatris cylindracea*) cover the dunes. A population of six-lined racerunner lizards (*Aspidoscelis sexlineata*) inhabits the site.

Gibson Woods Nature Preserve, Lake County

This 131-acre preserve is an excellent example of lake plain dune-and-swale left by the gradual retreat of ancient Lake Chicago. A black oak (*Quercus velutina*) savanna dominates the ridges. Its notable mammals include plains pocket gopher (*Geomys bursarius*) and Franklin's ground squirrel (*Poliocitellus franklinii*). Rare Karner blue butterflies (*Lycaeides melissa samuelis*) have been recently introduced. Three hundred species of plants—including Indian paintbrush (*Castilleja coccinea*) and lesser fringed gentians (*Gentianopsis virgata*)—inhabit the preserve.

Wisconsin

Chiwaukee Prairie, Kenosha County

Lying within the Prairie Peninsula, this 477-acre lake plain prairie is situated on gently undulating dune-and-swale left by the lowering level of Lake Michigan. One of the largest prairie complexes in the state, the site contains an exceptional diversity of plants and animals. More than four hundred species of vascular plants and animals can be found here. Plant communities range from wet prairie, sedge meadow, dry mesic prairie, to calcareous fen. Oak savanna occupies the higher ground. In spring, many acres are blanketed with midland shooting stars (*Dodecatheon meadia*). In late summer, the display of rough blazing stars (*Liatris aspera*) is also significant. The many habitats and locations on the southern shore of Lake Michigan give this site great biodiversity. Prairie white-fringed orchids (*Platanthera leucophaea*) are among twenty-six rare plant species seen here. Its many rare animals include Franklin's ground squirrels (*Poliocitellus franklinii*), upland sandpipers (*Bartrami longicauda*), Blanding's turtles (*Emys blandingii*) and red-tailed leafhoppers (*Aflexia rubranura*). The preserve is recognized as a National Natural Landmark, state nature preserve, and globally rare wetland.

Ontario

Walpole Island, Lambton County

At twenty-four thousand hectares (about fifty-seven thousand acres), Walpole Island is a large delta complex at the mouth of the St. Claire River. Its pristine sand prairies and black oak savanna are virtually devoid of alien plants. The island preserves four thousand hectares of some of the finest tallgrass remnants in the Prairie Peninsula. A large number of the seven hundred described species are found here at their only stations in Canada. The island's marshes, about sixteen thousand hectares (almost forty thousand acres) have breeding redhead (*Aythya americana*) and canvasback ducks (*Aythya valisineria*), and king rails (*Rallus elegans*). Rare Henslow's sparrows (*Ammodramus henslowii*) nest in the sand prairies. Rare plants include goats-rue (*Tephrosia virginiana*), small white lady's slipper (*Cypripedium candidum*), and white gentian (*Gentiana alba*). The private island is owned by the Ojibwe, Potawatomi, and Odawa peoples of Walpole Island. A ferry to the island from Algonac, Michigan, operates year-round.

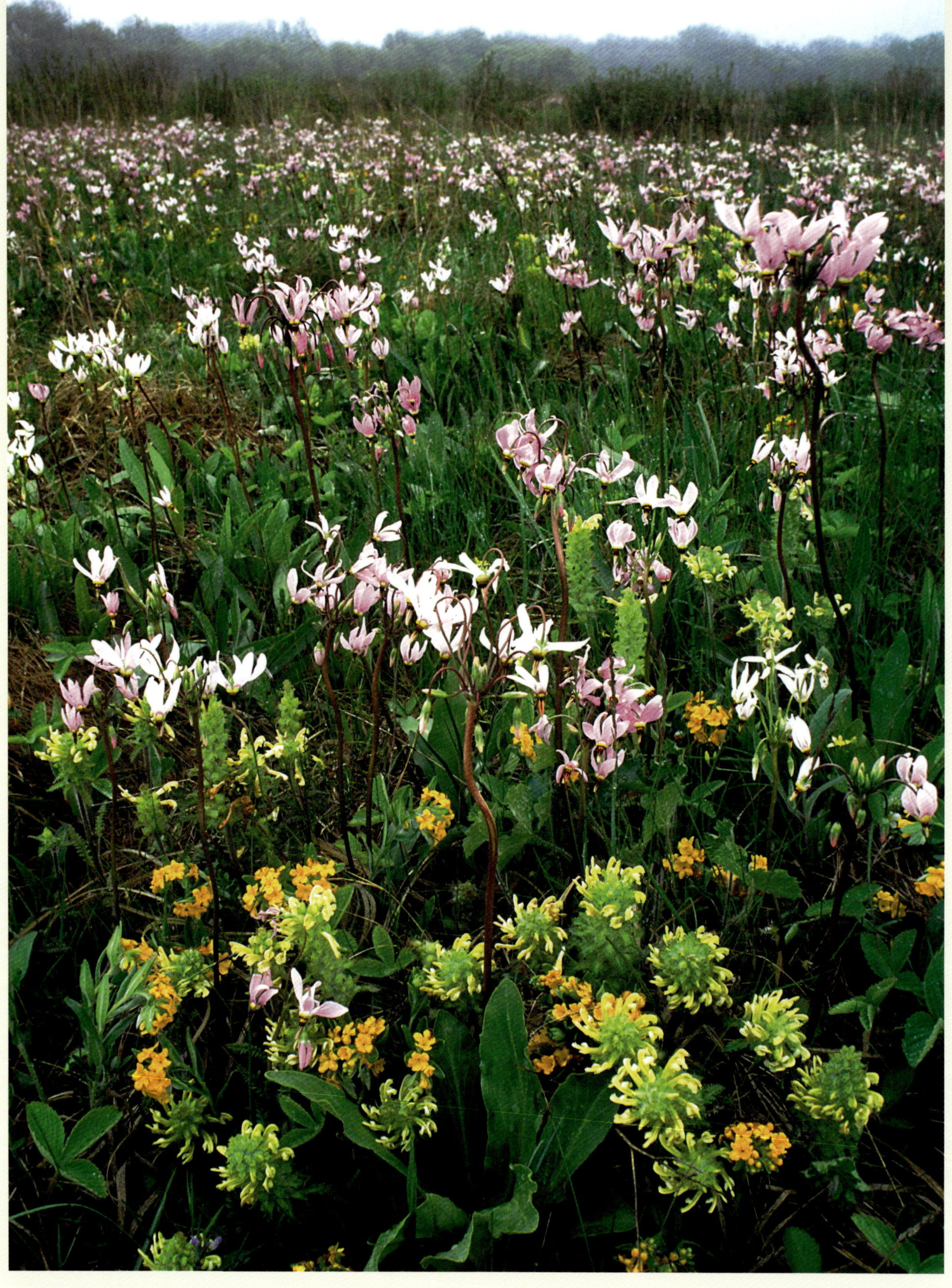

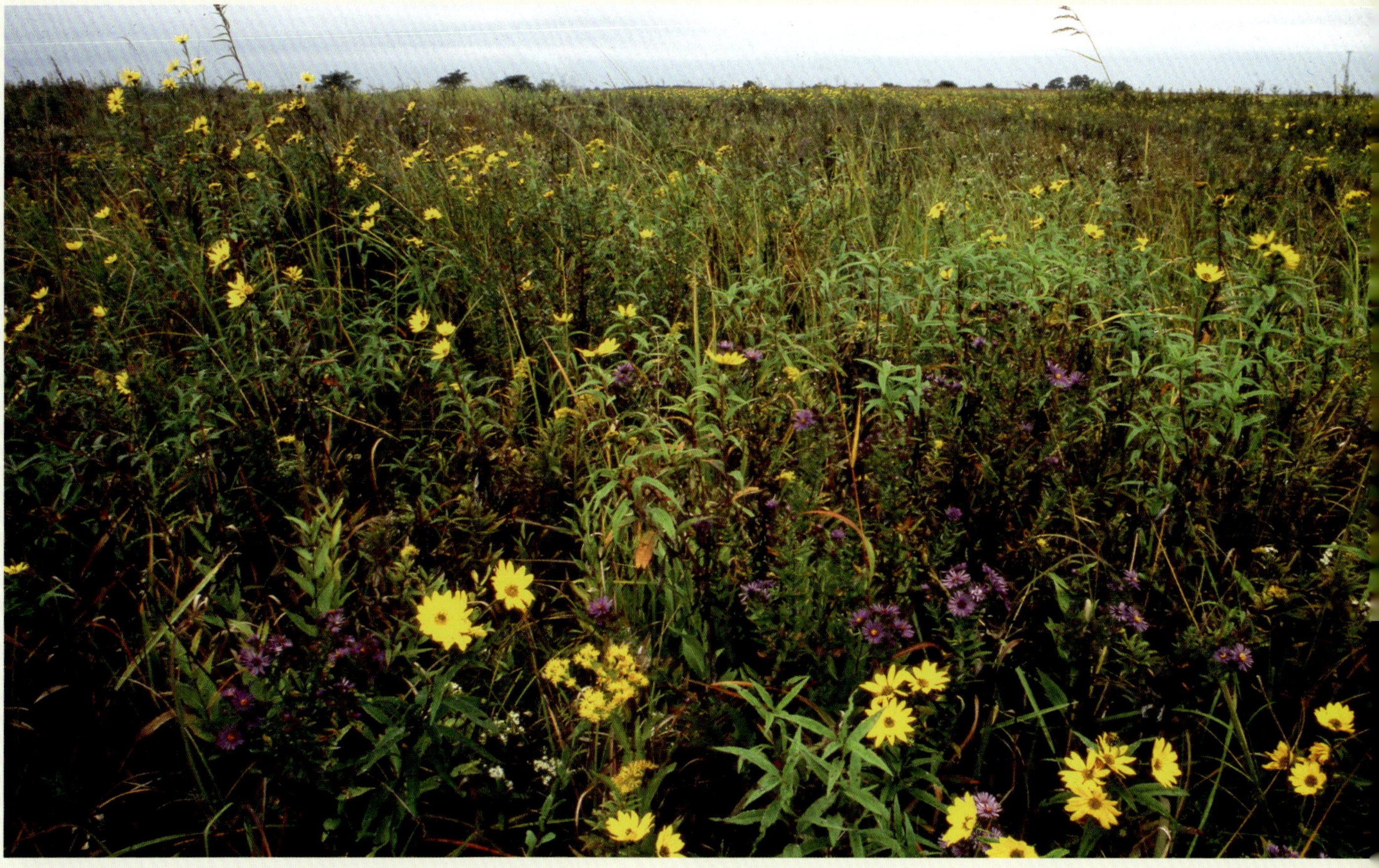

Like most black soil remnants, Loda Cemetery Prairie, Iroquois County, Illinois, has a large number of plant species. It is one of the few surviving sites within the Grand Prairie region.

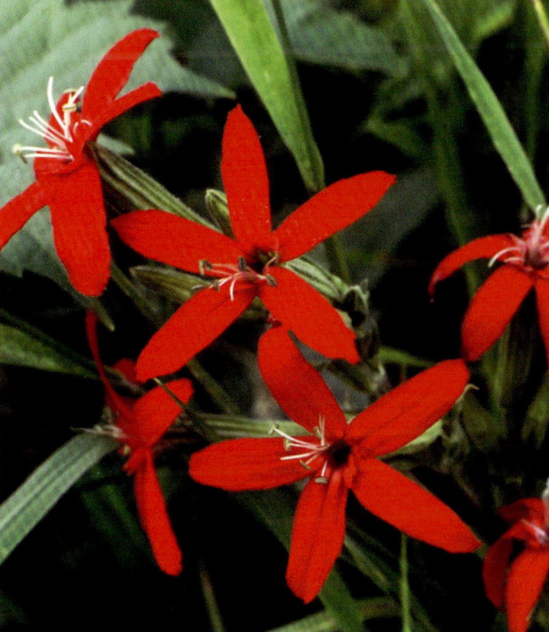

Royal catchfly (*Silene regia*) blooms at the eastern end of its range at Bigelow Cemetery in Madison County, Ohio.

Opposite: In May, midland shooting stars (*Dodecatheon meadia*) blanket many acres of Chiwaukee Prairie in Kenosha County, Wisconsin.

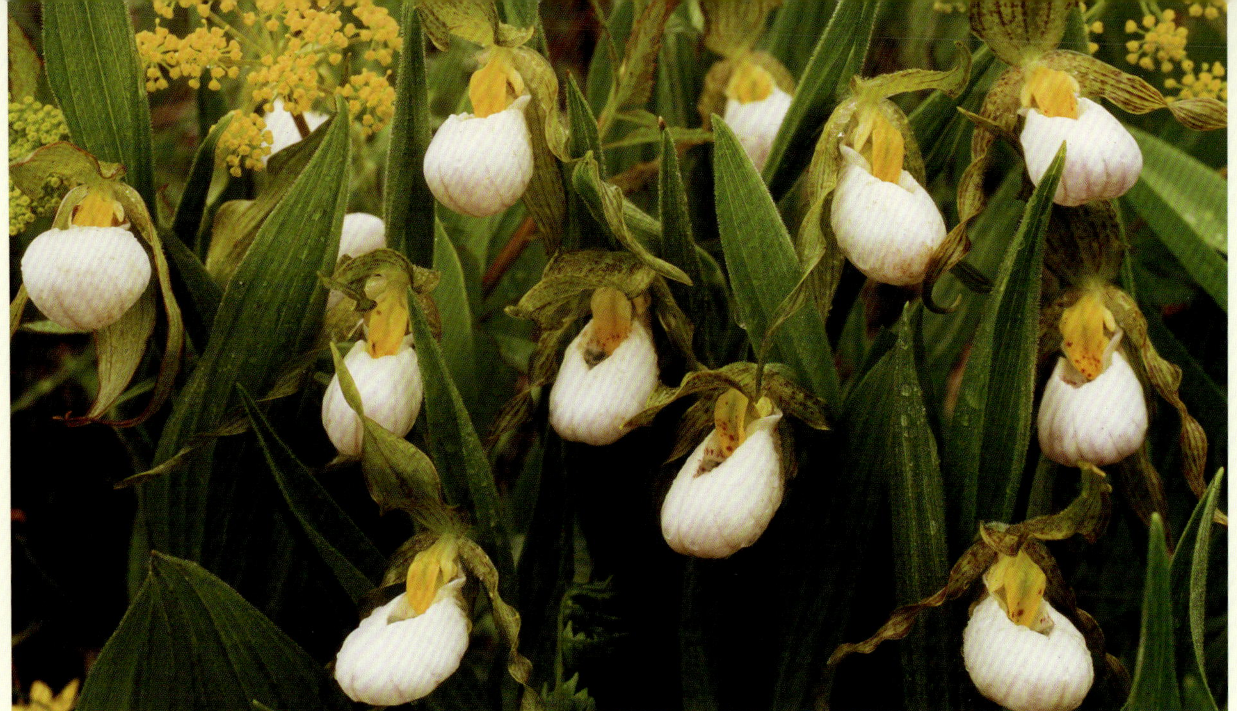

An army of volunteers restored Bluff Spring Fen in Cook County, Illinois. Many rare calciphiles, like small white lady's slippers (*Cypripedium candidum*), can be found here.

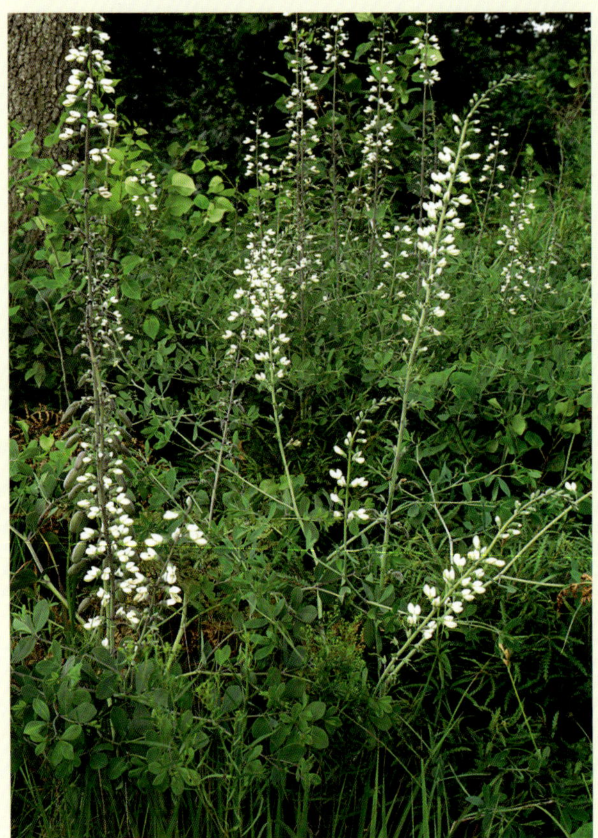

Hoosier Prairie, in Lake County, is Indiana's best surviving remnant. The floor of the oak savanna is blanketed with bracken fern (*Pteridium aquilinum*) and sweetfern (*Comptonia peregrina*). A spectacular stand of white false indigo (*Baptisia leucantha*), shown here, grows under the oaks.

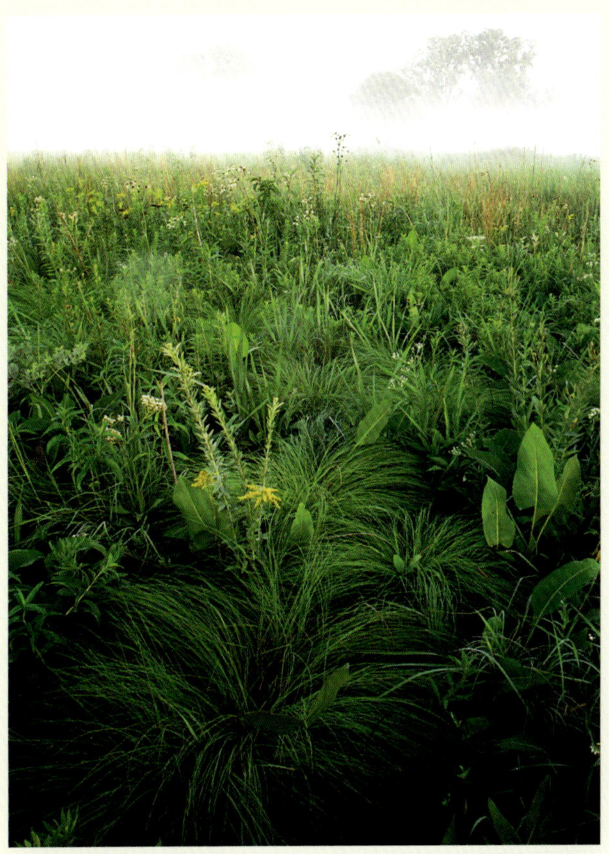

Wolf Road Prairie, in Cook County, Illinois, was miraculously saved from becoming a housing development. Sprays of prairie dropseed (*Sporobolus heterolepis*) indicate undisturbed conditions in this fifty-acre black soil remnant.

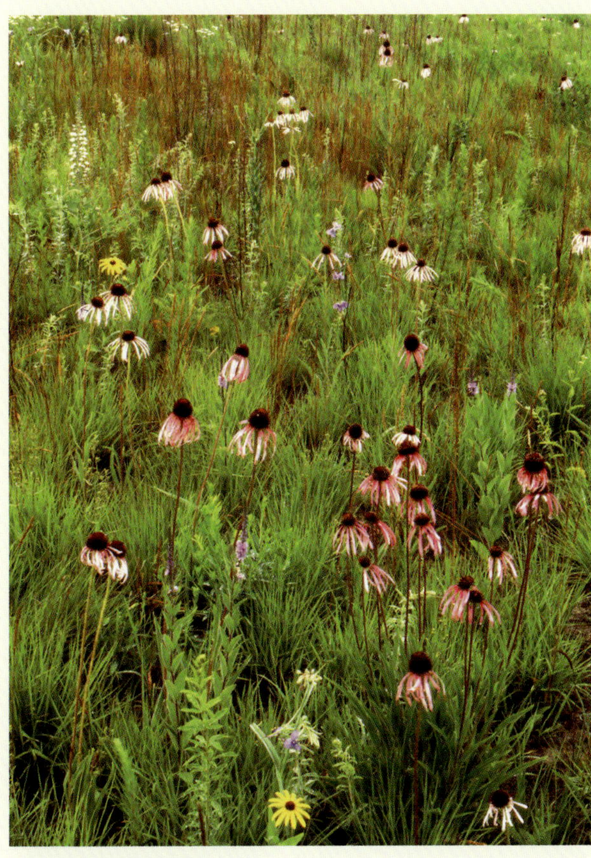

The Nachusa grasslands preserve three thousand acres of original Illinois prairie. In 1986, The Nature Conservancy thought Nachusa provided the best opportunity to restore a large and diverse prairie in Illinois.

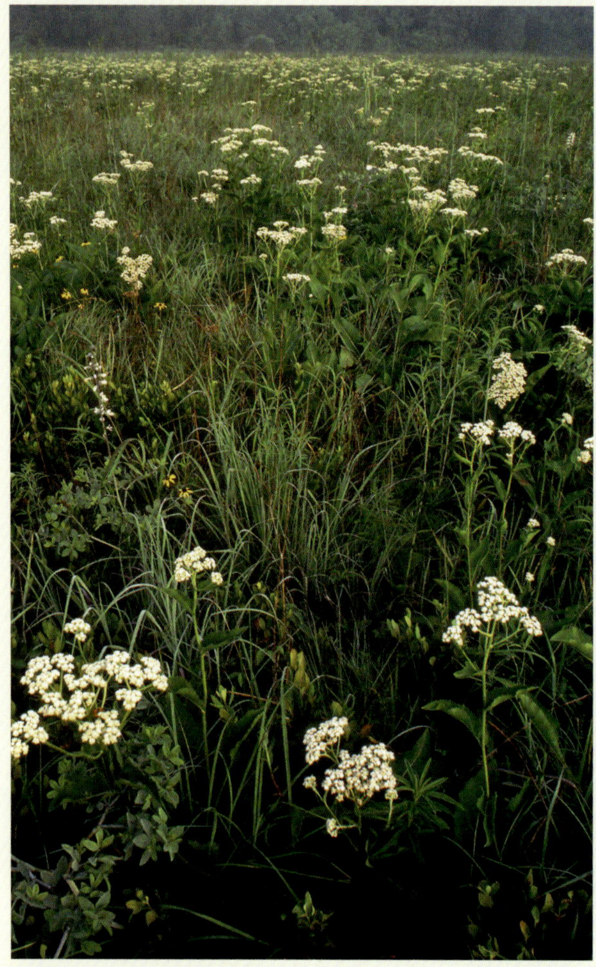

In late July, wild quinine (*Parthenium integrifolium*) flowers in Gensberg-Markham Prairie of Cook County, Illinois. One of the old Indian boundary prairies, the site is now surrounded on all sides by freeway and urban development.

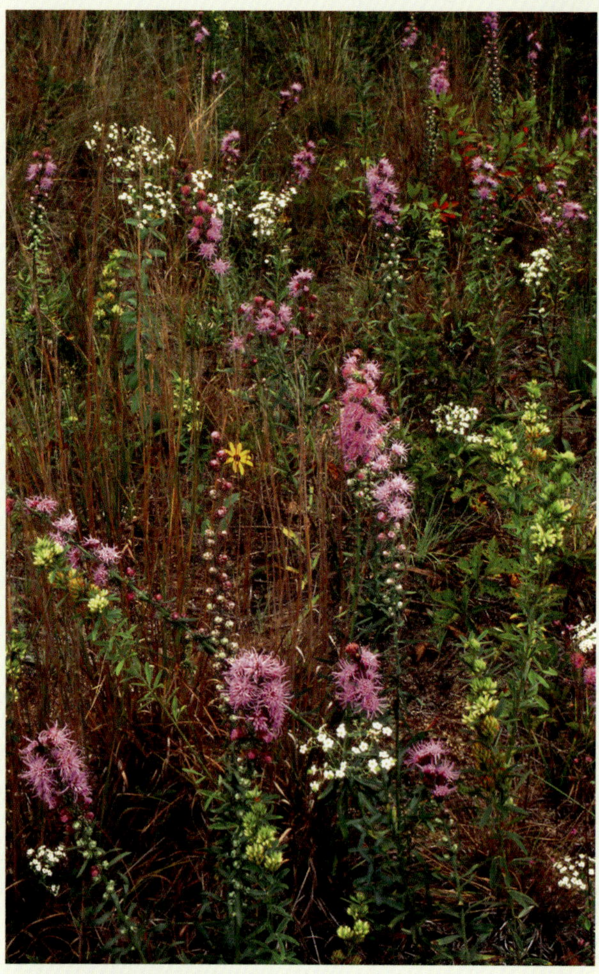

Rough blazing stars (*Liatris aspera*) and bush clover (*Lespedeza capitata*) bloom in late summer in lake plain sand prairies.

Opposite: Large stands of Indian grass (*Sorghastrum nutans*) can be seen at West Chicago Prairie, where more than four hundred species have been recorded.

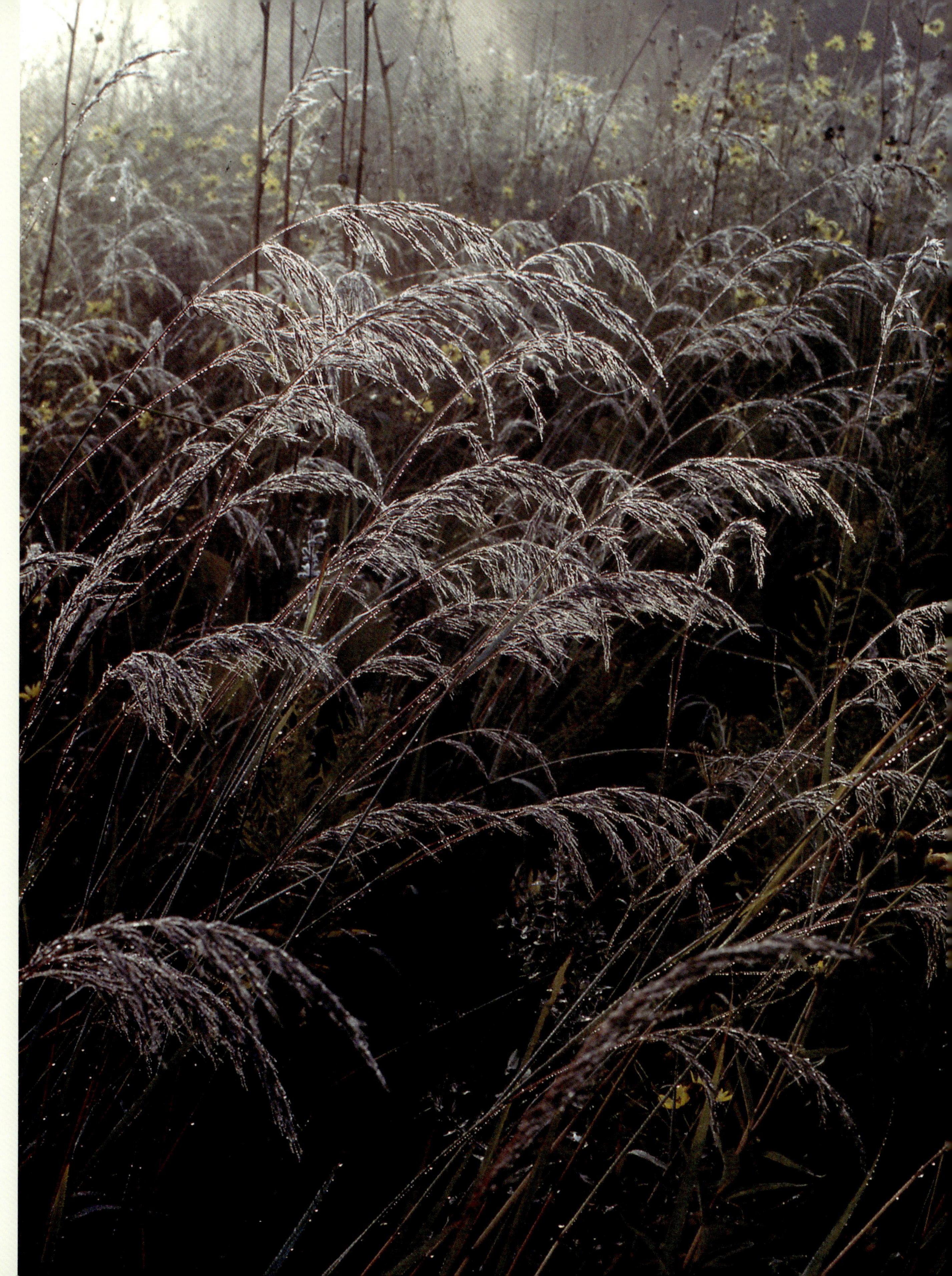

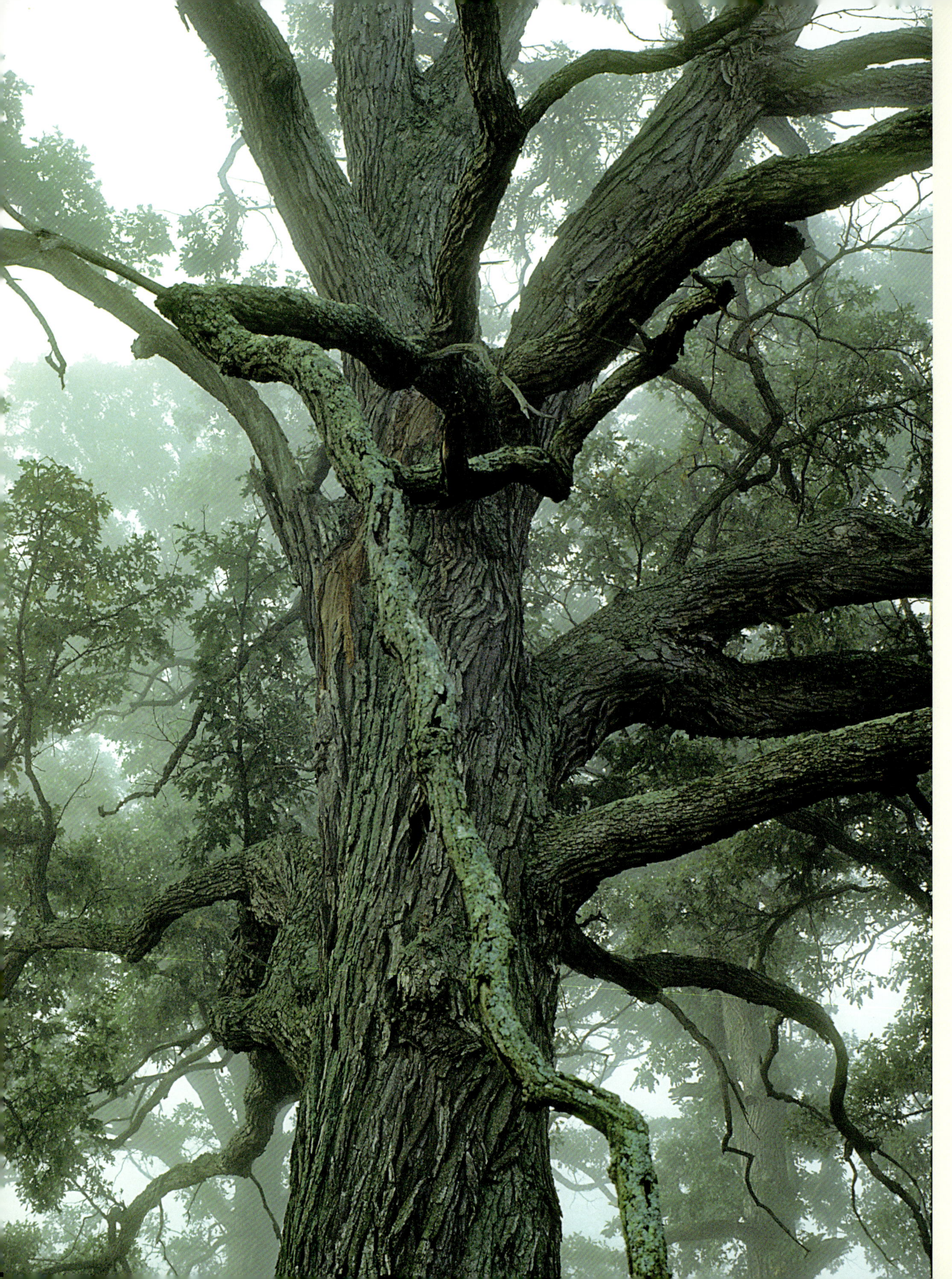

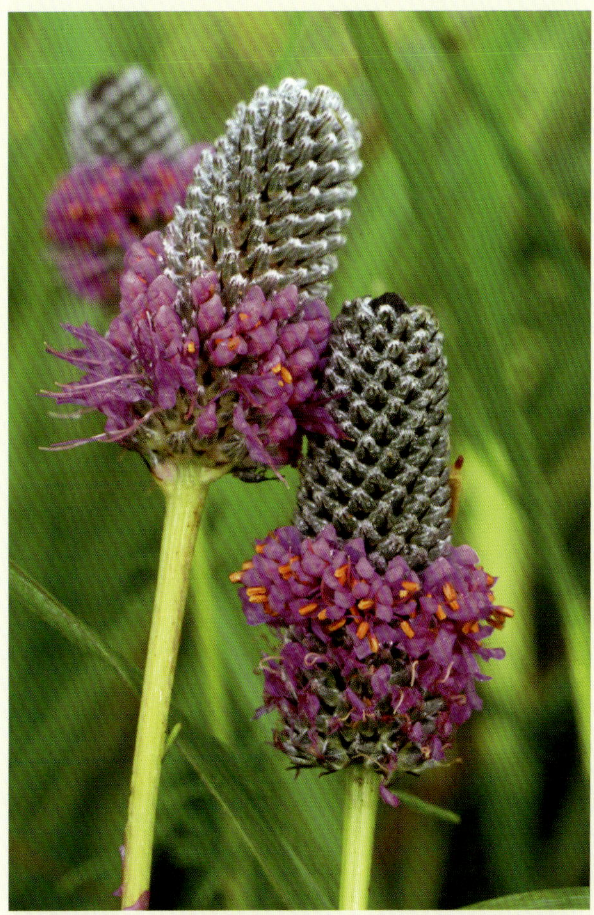

Prospect Cemetery, in Ford County, Illinois, is a fragment of original Grand Prairie. Many plants, such as the purple prairie clover (*Dalea purpurea*) pictured here, bloom in this black soil remnant. It is ironic that early pioneers lay buried in the prairie they tried to conquer.

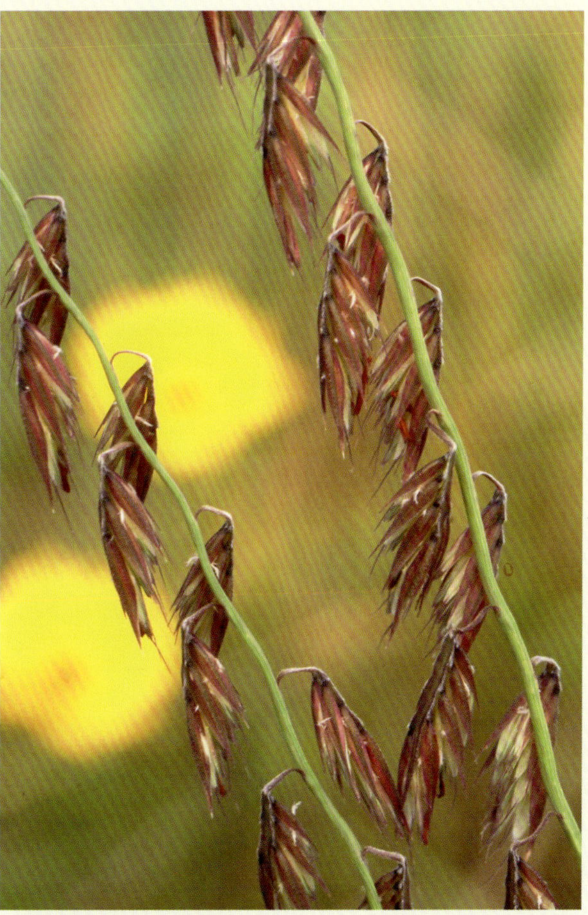

Side-oats grama (*Bouteloua curtipendula*) blooms at Shoe Factory Road Prairie. Located not far from downtown Chicago, it is an outstanding example of hill prairie.

Opposite: Mature oaks like this old bur oak (*Quercus macrocarpa*) were once common across the Prairie Peninsula.

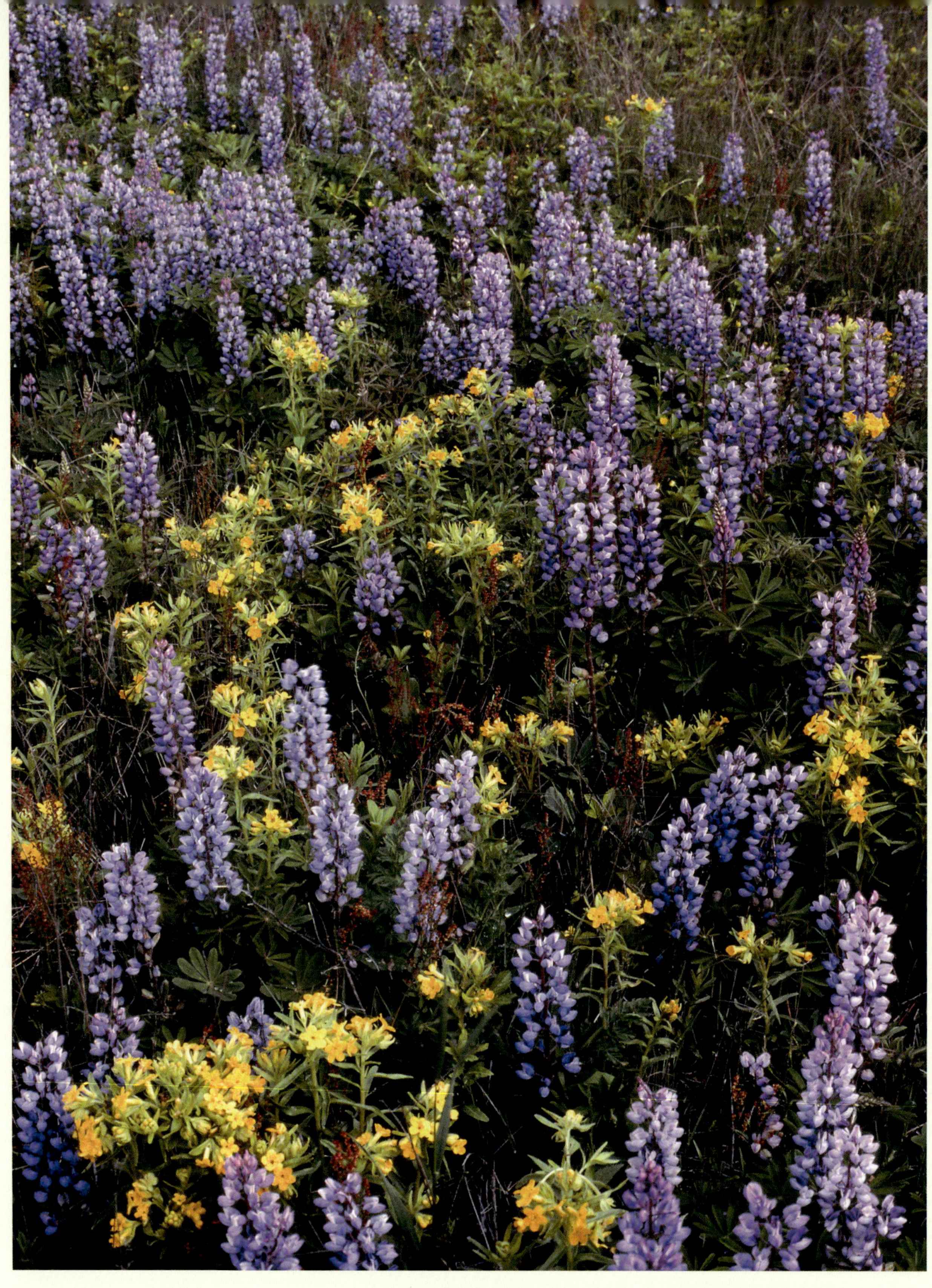

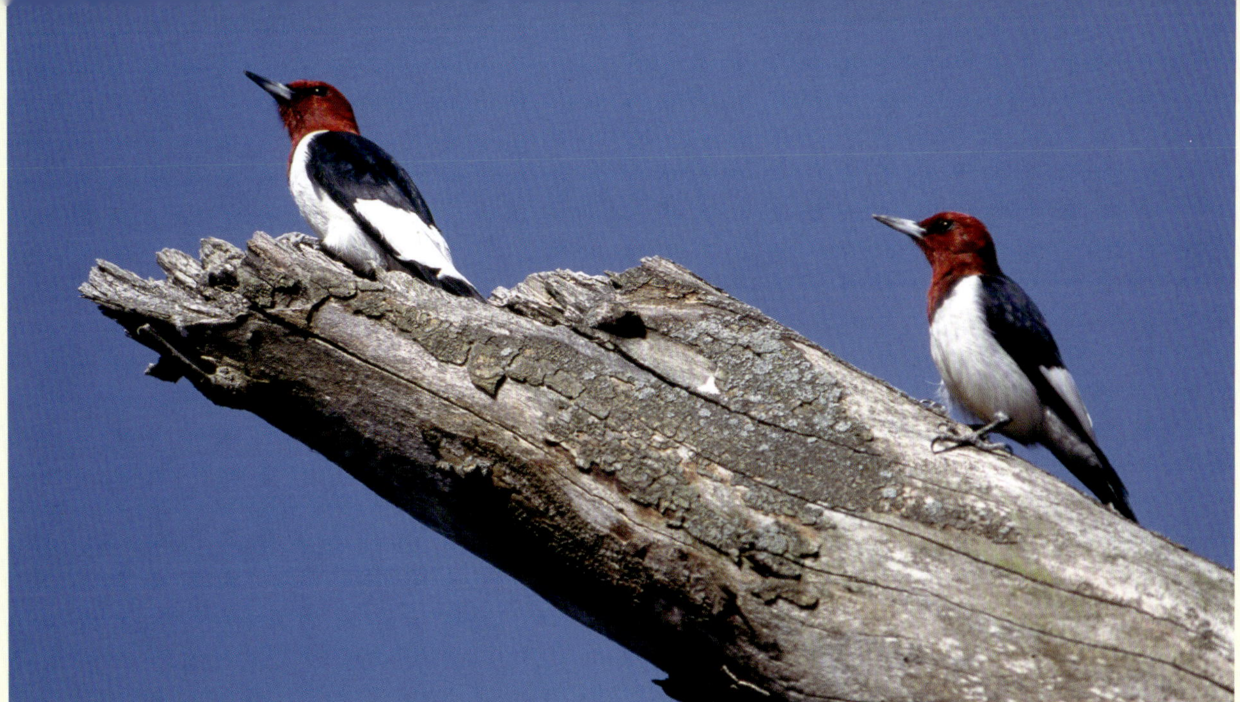

Red-headed woodpeckers (*Melanerpes erythrocephalus*) are common inhabitants of oak savannas.

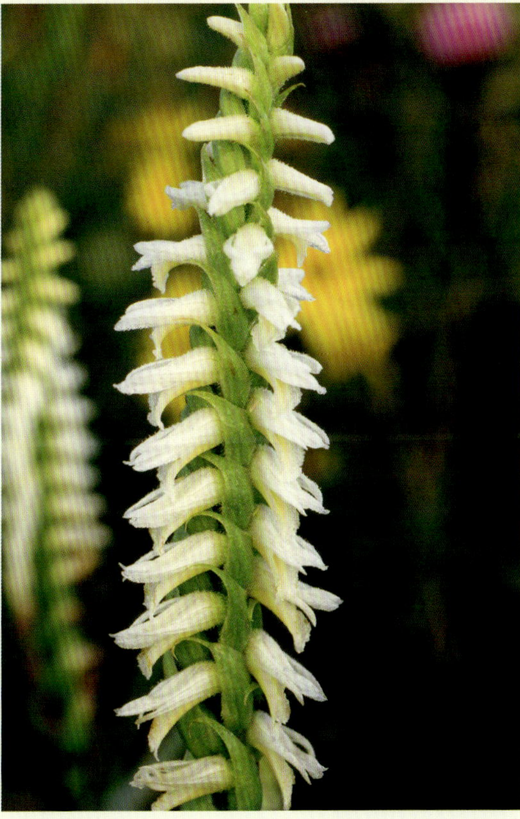

High above the Sangamon River, Revis Hill Prairie is Illinois's best example of loess prairie. Interesting species like Great Plains ladies' tresses (*Spiranthes magnicamporum*) flower in September.

In May, wild lupine (*Lupinus perennis*) and puccoons (Lithospermum spp.) bloom at Kitty Todd Nature Preserve. The Nature Conservancy owns and manages this Lucas County, Ohio, sand prairie and oak savanna.

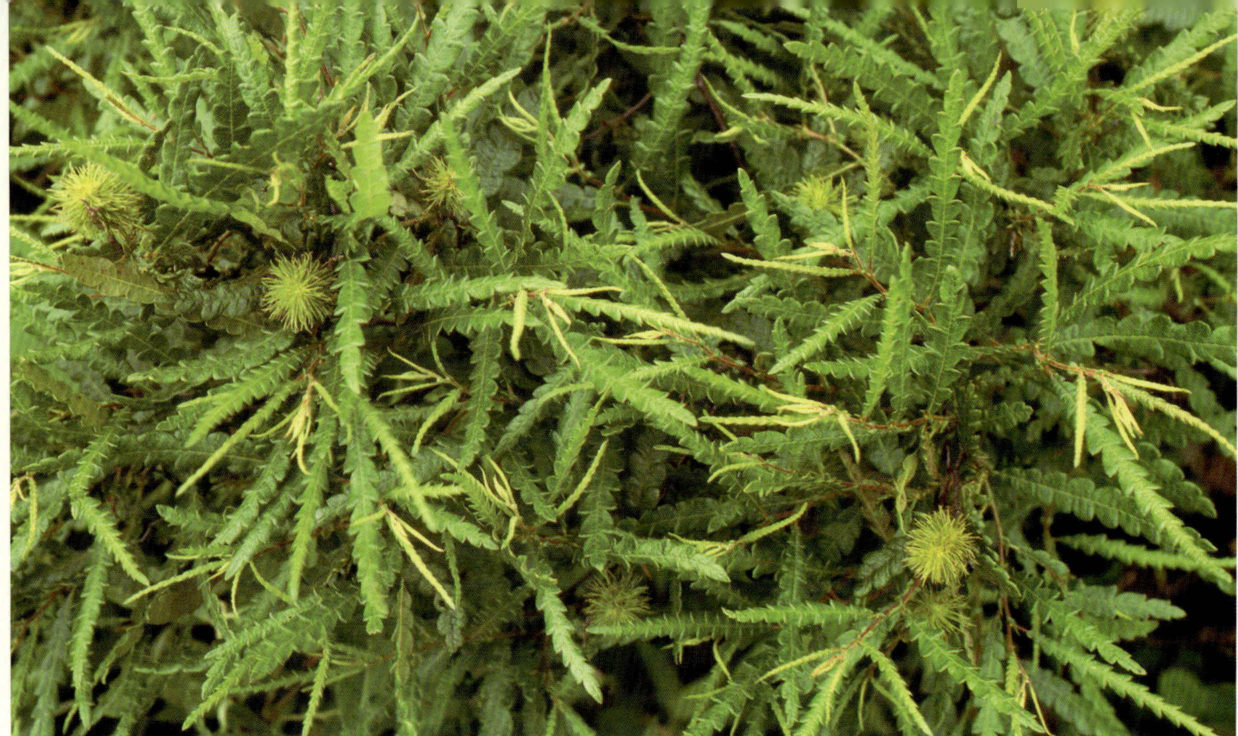

Sweetfern (*Comptonia peregrina*) blankets the understory of the oak savanna at Hoosier Prairie in Lake County, Indiana. This northeastern shrub, which can be found growing in lake plain sand prairies as far west as Illinois, probably migrated westward along the retreating glacial boundary.

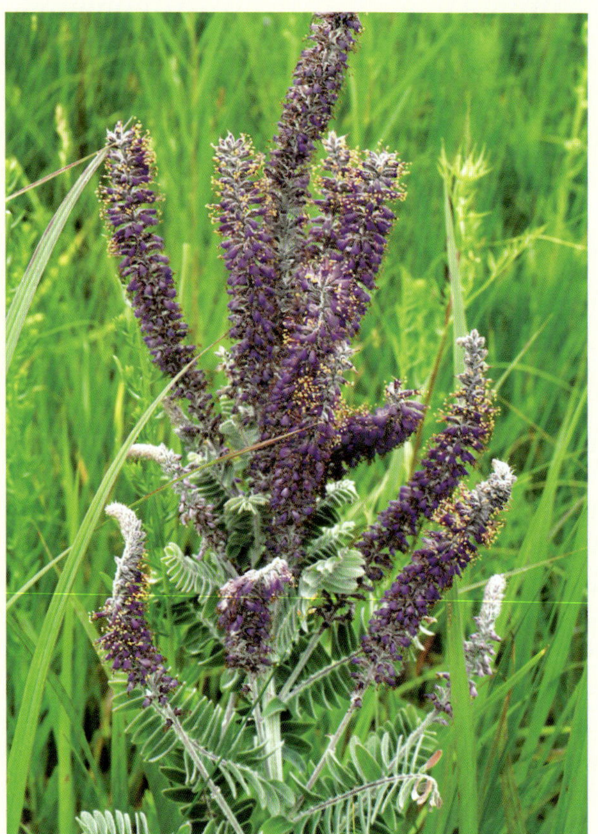

The most abundant prairie forb, the leadplant flowers (*Amphora canescens*) in Weston cemetery, a fragment of the Grand Prairie. Even when properly managed, these small sites gradually become degraded with alien species.

Harlem Hills, in Winnebago County, Illinois, is an excellent example of gravel hill prairie. Clumps of little bluestem (*Schizachyrium scoparium*) grow in this arid environment.

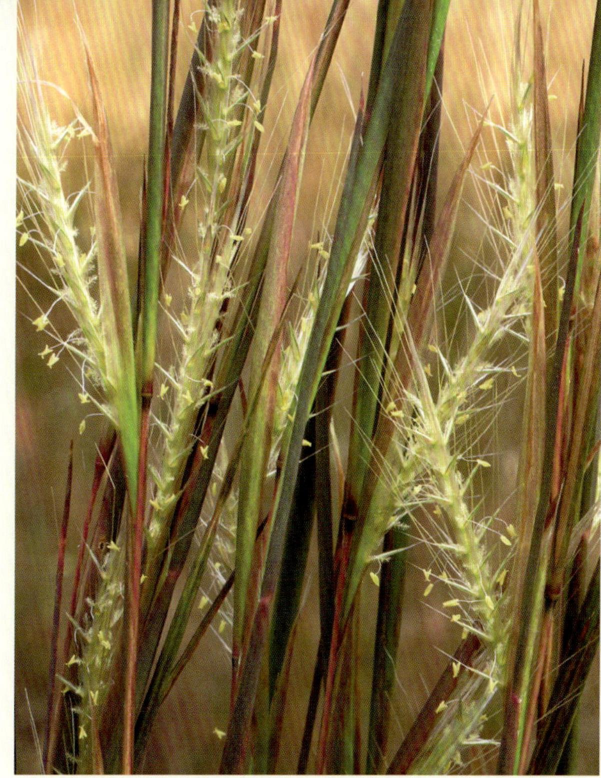

Small flocks of bright yellow American goldfinches (*Spinus tristis*) are common sights in tallgrass prairie. Here one rests among Ohio spiderworts (*Tradescantia ohioensis*) at Hoosier Prairie in Lake County, Indiana.

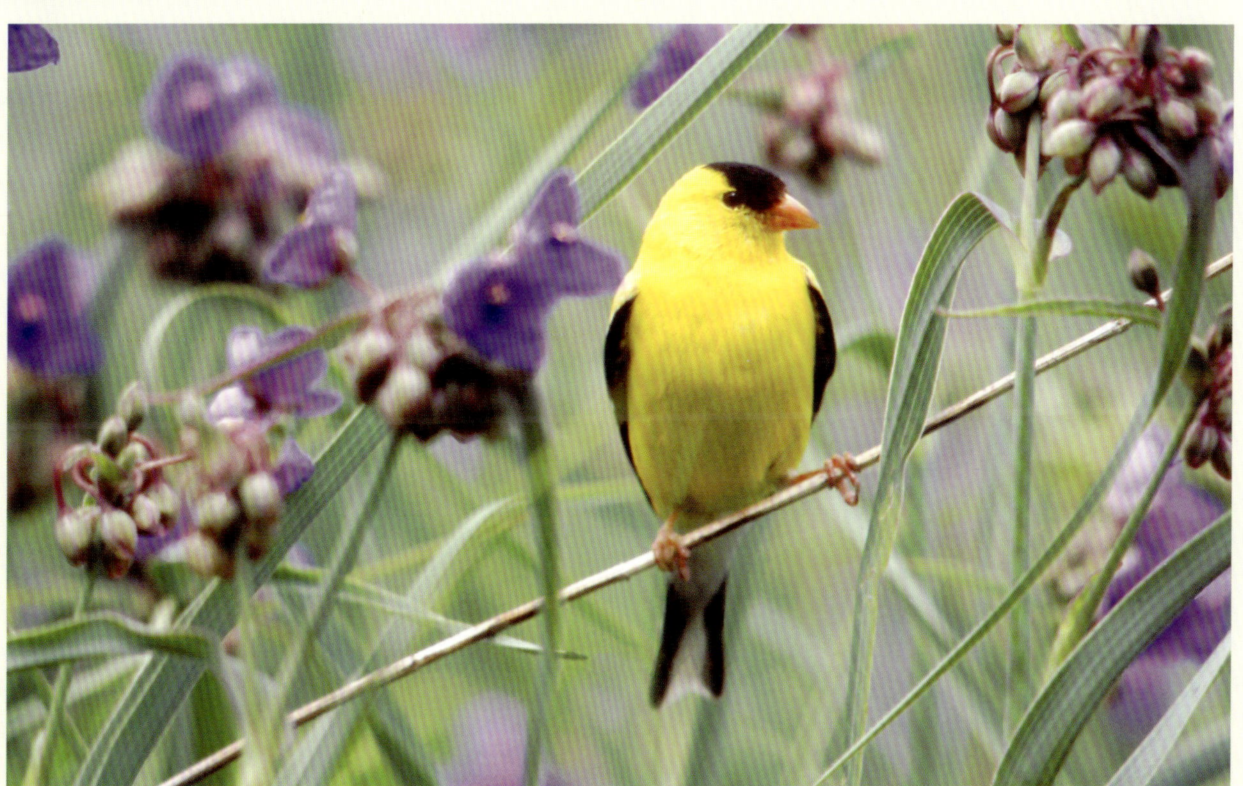

Bibliography

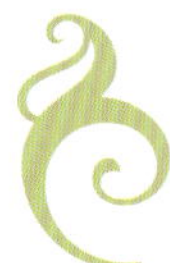

Abner, J. S. 1991. "Glaciation of Kansas." *Boreas* 20 (4): 297–314.

Adams, Charles C. 1920. "Postglacial Origins and Migrations of the Life of the Northeastern United States." *Journal of Geography* 1:303–10, 352–57.

Allen, Durward L. 1967. *Our Living World of Nature: The Life of Plains and Prairies.* New York: McGraw-Hill.

Ambrose, Dave. 2007. "Tombstones and Tallgrass." http://www.rootsweb.ancestry.com/~ilmoult2/Cemeteries/tombstones.html. Article originally appeared in *Outdoor Illinois.*

Anderson, R. C. 1991. "Illinois Prairies: A Historical Perspective." *Illinois Natural History Survey Bulletin* 34 (4): 384–91.

Anderson, W. A. 1943. "A Fen in Northwestern Iowa." *American Midland Naturalist* 29 (3): 787–91.

Bakowsky, Wasyl, and John L. Riley. 1992. "A Survey of the Prairies and Savannas of Southern Ontario." *Proceedings of the Thirteenth North American Prairie Conference: Spirit of the Land Our Prairie Legacy.* Ed. Robert G. Wickett, Patricia Dolan Lewis, Allen Woodliffe, and Paul Pratt, 7–16. Windsor, Ont.: Department of Parks and Recreation, Canada.

Betz, Robert F. 1976. "The Prairies of Indiana," In *Proceedings of the Fifth Midwest Prairie Conference.* Ed. D. C. Glen-Lewin and R. Q. Landers, 79–87. Ames: Iowa State University Press.

Betz, Robert F., and Herbert F. Lamp. 1992. "Species Composition of Old Settler and Sand Prairie Cemeteries in Northern Illinois and Northwestern Indiana." *Proceedings of the Twelfth North American Prairie Conference: Recapturing a Vanishing Heritage.* Ed. D. D. Smith and C. Jacobs. 79–87. Cedar Falls: University of Northern Iowa.

Black, Merel R., and Emmet J. Judziewicz. 2009. *Wildflowers of Wisconsin and the Great Lakes Region: A Comprehensive Field Guide.* 2d. ed. Madison: University of Wisconsin Press.

Boellstorff, J. 1978. "North American Pleistocene Stages Reconsidered in Light of Probable Pliocene-Pleistocene Continental Glaciation." *Science* 202 (4365): 305–7.

Brandenburg, David M. 2010. *National Wildlife Federation Field Guide to Wildflowers of North America.* New York: Sterling.

Braun, E. Lucy. 1928. "Glacial and Postglacial Plant Migrations Indicated by Relic Colonies of Southern Ohio." *Ecology* 9:284–302.

Chapman, K. A., M. A. White, M. R. Hoffman, and D. Faber-Langendoen. 1995. "Ecology and Stewardship Guidelines for Oak Barren Landscapes in the Upper Midwest." *Proceedings of the Midwest Oak Savanna Conference.* Ed. Victor Guarino and Jean Guarino, 129. Chicago: Northeastern Illinois University.

Camp, Mark J. 2006. *Roadside Geology of Ohio.* Missoula, Montana: Mountain Press.

Campbell, Lou. 1968. *Birds of the Toledo Area.* Toledo, Ohio: Toledo Blade Company.

Cavender, Nicole D. 2001. "Genetic Variation of Big Bluestem (*Andropogon gerardii*) and Its Association with Arbuscular Mycorrhizal Fungi: Implications for Prairie Restoration." PhD diss., Ohio State University.

Cochrane, Theodore S., Kandis Elliot, and Claudia S. Lipke. 2006. *Prairie Plants of the University of*

Wisconsin–Madison Arboretum. Madison: University of Wisconsin Press.

Cohen, Dan 2003. *Iowa Prairies* (IAN-203). Iowa State University Extension Service. Ames: Iowa State University.

Cohen, Joshua G., Michael A. Kost, Bradford S. Slaughter, and Dennis Albert. 2015. *A Field Guide to the Natural Communities of Michigan.* East Lansing: Michigan State University Press.

Corbett, Erica, and Roger Anderson. 2004. "A Comparison of Illinois Remnant Prairies, 1976–1988." *Proceedings of the North American Prairie Conference.* Ed. D. Egan and J. Harrington, 36–43. Madison: University of Wisconsin.

———. 2006. "Landscape Analysis of Illinois and Wisconsin Remnant Prairies." *Journal of the Torrey Botanical Society* 133 (2): 267–79.

Curtis, John T. 1959. *The Vegetation of Wisconsin: An Ordination of Plant Communities.* Madison: University of Wisconsin Press.

Eaton, Eric R., and Kenn Kaufman. 2007. *Kaufman Field Guide to Insects of North America.* New York: Houghton Mifflin.

Elias, Thomas S. 1980. *The Complete Trees of North America: Field Guide and Natural History.* New York: Book Division, Times Mirror Magazines.

English, Joseph M., and Stephen T. Johnston. 2004. "The Laramide Orogeny: What Were the Driving Forces?" *International Geology Review* 46:833–38.

Forsberg, Michael, with Dan O'Brien, D. Wishart, and T. Kosher. 2009. *America's Lingering Wild Great Plains.* Chicago: University of Chicago Press.

Gleason, Henry Allen. 1923. "The Vegetational History of the Middle West." *Annals of the Association of American Geographers* 12:39–85.

Haddock, Michael John. 2005. *Wildflowers and Grasses of Kansas: A Field Guide.* Lawrence: University Press of Kansas.

Hamilton, R. W. 1974. "The Genus Haplorhynchites (Coleoptera: Rhynchitidea) in America North of Mexico." *Annals of the Entomological Society of America* 67 (5): 787–94.

Harding, James H. 1997. *Amphibians and Reptiles of the Great Lakes Region.* Ann Arbor: University of Michigan Press.

Hatfield, R. J., S. Jepsen, E. Mader, and S. H. Black. 2012. *Conserving Bumble Bees: Guidelines for Creating and Managing Habitat for America's Declining Pollinators.* Portland, Oregon: Xerces Society for Invertebrate Conservation.

Helzer, Chris J. 1986. "The Effects of Landscape Structure on Grassland Breeding Birds." In Springer 1999, 133–35.

Herzberg, Ruth, and John Pearson, 2001. *The Guide to Iowa's State Preserves.* Iowa City: University of Iowa Press.

Hess, Marci, and M. J. Hatfield. 2015. "Are Our Prairie Plantings Working?" *Prairie Promoter* 28 (3): 4–5.

Illinois State Museum. 2012. "Illinois Prairie Communities." *Prairies in the Prairie State: Midewin National Tallgrass Prairie.* Springfield: State of Illinois Department of Natural Resources. http://exhibits.museum.state.il.us/exhibits/midewin/prcommunities.html.

Jason, Marion T., ed. 1997. *The Natural Heritage of Indiana.* Bloomington: Indiana University Press.

Ladd, Doug M. 1995. *Tallgrass Prairie Wildflowers: A Field Guide.* Helena, Montana: The Nature Conservancy and Falcon Press.

Lata, Mary, and Frank Weirich. 1999. "Fire Temperature Dynamics in Grasslands of the Eastern Great Plains." In Springer 1999, 95–105.

Leopold, Aldo. 1966. *A Sand County Almanac: With Other Essays on Conservation from Round River.* New York: Oxford University Press.

Lindsay, Alton A., ed. 1966. *Natural Features of Indiana.* Indianapolis: Indiana Academy of Science.

Longwell, Chester R., Richard Foster Flint, and J. Sanders. 1969. *Physical Geology.* New York: Wiley.

Lyle, Shane A. 2008. "Glaciers in Kansas." *Kansas Geological Survey, Public Information Circular* 28. http://www.kgs.ku.edu/Publications/PIC/pic28.html.

Mack, John J. 2002. *At the Tip of the Prairie Peninsula: Flora and Natural History of Prairie Remnants in the Sandusky Plains of Crawford, Marion, and Wyandot Counties, Ohio:* PhD diss., Ohio State University.

Milton, Sherman A. Jr. 2001. *Amphibians and Reptiles of Indiana.* 2d ed. Indianapolis: Indiana Academy of Science.

Nelson, Paul W. 2005. *The Terrestrial Natural Communities of Missouri.* Jefferson City: Missouri Natural Areas Committee.

Madson, John. 1982. *Where the Sky Began: Land of the Tallgrass Prairie.* Boston: Houghton Mifflin.

Niederhofer, Relda E., and Ronald L. Stuckey. 1998. *Edwin Lincoln Moseley (1865–1948): Naturalist, Scientist, Educator.* Columbus, Ohio: RLS Creations.

Panzer, Ron, D. Stillwaugh, R. Gnaedinger, and G. Derkovitz. 1995. "Prevalence of Remnant Dependence among Prairie and Savanna Inhabiting Insects of the Chicago Region." *Natural Areas Journal* 15:101–16.

Pielou, E. C. 1991. *After the Ice Age: The Return of Life to Glaciated North America.* Chicago: University of Chicago Press.

Platt, John R. 2015. "For the First Time U.S. Considers Declaring a Bee Endangered." *Take Part.* September 22.

http://www.takepart.com/article/2015/09/22/us-considers-giving-endangered-species-protection-rusty-patched-bumblebee.

Popelka, Bernice Benedict, 2011. *Saving Peacock Prairie.* Madison, Wisconsin: Caritas Communications.

Pringle, Heather. "The First Americans." *Scientific American,* November, 36–45.

Richman, G. M. and D. S. Fullerton. 1986. "Summation of Quaternary Glaciations of the United States of America." *Quaternary Science Reviews* 5:183–196.

Reichman, O. J. 1987. *Konza Prairie: A Tallgrass Natural History.* Lawrence: University Press of Kansas.

Robertson, Ken R. 2008. *The Tallgrass Prairie in Illinois.* http://www.inhs.uiuc.edu/~kenr/tallgrass.html.

Rothenberger, Steven J., and Susan George-Bloomfield, eds. 2000. *A Prairie Mosaic: An Atlas of Central Nebraska's Land, Culture, and Nature.* Kearney: University of Nebraska at Kearney.

Runkel, Sylvan T., and Dean M. Roosa. 1989. *Wildflowers of the Tallgrass Prairie: The Upper Midwest.* Ames: Iowa State University Press.

Savage, Candace. 2004. *Prairie: A Natural History.* Vancouver, British Columbia: Graystone Books.

Schwegman, John. 1983. "Illinois Prairie: Then and Now." *Outdoor Highlights.* January 17. 3–13.

Sears, Paul B. 1935. "Glacial and Post Glacial Vegetation." *Botanical Review* 1:37–51.

———. 1948. "Forest Sequence and Climate Change in Northeastern North America Since Early Wisconsin Time." *Ecology* 29 (3): 326–33.

———. 1967. "The Castalia Prairie." *Ohio Journal of Science* 67 (2): 78–88.

Shane, Linda. 1987. "Late-Glacial Vegetational and Climate History of the Allegheny Plateau and the Till Plains of Ohio and Indiana, U.S.A." *Boreas* 16:1–20.

Smith, Daryl, Dave Williams, G. Houseal, and K. Henderson. 2010. *The Tallgrass Prairie Center Guide to Prairie Restoration in the Upper Midwest.* Iowa City: University of Iowa Press.

Springer, Joseph T., ed. 1999. *Proceedings of the Sixteenth North American Prairie Conference: The Central Nebraska Loess Hills Prairie.* Kearney: University of Nebraska at Kearney.

Steyermark, Julian A. 1996. *Flora of Missouri.* 7th printing. Ames: Iowa State University Press.

Stuckey, Ronald L. 1981. "The Origin and Development of the Concept of the Prairie Peninsula." In Stuckey and Reese 1981, 4–23.

———. 2001. *E. Lucy Braun (1889–1971): Ohio's Foremost Woman Botanist; Her* Studies of Prairies and Their Phytogeographical Relationships. Columbus, Ohio: RLC Creations.

Stuckey, Ronald L., and Guy L. Denny. 1981. "Prairie Fens and Bog Fens in Ohio: Floristic Similarities, Differences, and Geographic Affinities." In *Geobotany II: Proceedings of the Geobotany Conference.* Ed. Robert C. Romans, 1–34. New York: Plenum Press.

Stuckey, Ronald L. and Karen J. Reese, eds. 1981. *The Prairie Peninsula—In The "Shadow" of Transeau: Proceedings of the Sixth North American Prairie Conference.* Columbus: Ohio State University.

Swink, Floyd, and Gerould Wilhelm, 1994. *Plants of the Chicago Region.* 4th ed. Indianapolis: Indiana Academy of Science.

Theberger, John B, ed. 1989. *Legacy: The Natural History of Ontario.* Toronto: McClelland & Stewart.

Tilman, David, and Jason Hill. 2007. "Fuel for Thought: All Biofuels Are Not Created Equal." *Seattle Times.* April 15.

Tilman, David, Jason Hill, and C. Lehman. 2006. "Carbon-Negative Biofuels from Low-Input High-Diversity Grassland Biomass." *Science* 314:1598–1600.

Transeau, Edgar Nelson. 1935. "The Prairie Peninsula." *Ecology* 16(3): 423–37.

———. 1981. "The Vanishing Prairies of Ohio." In Stuckey and Reese 1981, 61–62.

U.S. Geological Survey. 1999. "Geology of the Loess Hills, Iowa." Pamphlet. http://pubs.usgs.gov/info-handout/loess/.

Vestal, A. G. 1918. "Local Inclusions of Prairie within Forests." *Transaction of The Illinois State Academy of Science* 11:122–26.

Voss, Edward G., and Anton A. Reznicek. 2012. *Field Manual of Michigan Flora.* Ann Arbor: University of Michigan Press.

Weaver, J. E. 1954. *North American Prairie.* Lincoln, Nebraska: Johnson Publishing.

———, 1968. *Prairie Plants and Their Environment.* Lincoln: University of Nebraska Press.

Wendt, Keith M. 1984. *A Guide to Minnesota Prairies.* St. Paul: Natural Heritage Program, Minnesota Department of Natural Resources.

Wright, Christopher K., and Michael C. Wimberly. 2013. *Recent Land Use Change in the Western Corn Belt Threatens Grasslands & Wetlands.* Brookings: Geographic Information Center of Excellence, South Dakota State University.

Wright, H. E., Jr. 1968. "History of the Prairie Peninsula." *Quaternary of Illinois.* University of Illinois College of Agriculture Special Publication 14.

Index

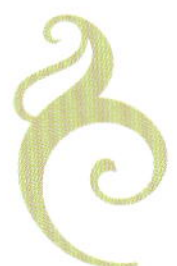